"Father Copleston has accomplished his purpose of giving 'an intelligible and coherent account of the development of medieval philosophy and of the phases through which it passed' in a way which combines penetrating scholarship, critical insight, and interesting presentation. . . . it is, perhaps, the most comprehensive English textbook on the subject from a scholastic point of view. College students, seminarians, teachers, and, in fact, anyone interested in the philosophic legacy of the Middle Ages will find this volume a stimulating, informative, and interesting contribution to an appreciation of the medieval world-view with all its philosophical complexity."

Catholic Library World

"To say that Father Copleston's work fills a definite need is to be guilty of an understatement. Certainly nothing comparable to it exists in English. . . . It is a scholarly, urbanely objective work, capably and professionally executed."

The Catholic World

"Here is a continuation of the same objective, progressive, critical scholarship that marked the first volume (*Greece and Rome*), producing a skillful, discerning analysis of the interplay of philosophical currents in Christian thought over eleven centuries."

America

"Philosophy in our day has become extremely restricted in scope, and the rise of existentialism is one side of how its restrictions irk. The wider horizons of medieval philosophy are capable of serving as a release; and Fr. Copleston's new volume is to be welcomed as an effective agent in the task of widening the scope of philosophy once more."

The (London) Times Literary Supplement

A History of Philosophy

VOLUME II

Mediaeval Philosophy

PART II

Albert the Great to Duns Scotus

by Frederick Copleston, S.J.

IMAGE BOOKS
A Division of Doubleday & Company, Inc.
Garden City, New York

Image Books edition 1962
by special arrangement with The Newman Press

Image Books edition published September, 1962

DE LICENTIA SUPERIORUM ORDINIS:
Martinus D'Arcy, S.J.
Praep. Prov. Angliae

NIHIL OBSTAT:
T. Corbishley, S.J.
Censor Deputatus

IMPRIMATUR:
✠ Joseph, Archiepiscopus Birmingamiensis
Die 24 Aprilis 1948

ISBN: 0-385-03235-8
Copyright 1950 by The Newman Press,
Westminster, Maryland
Printed in the United States of America
Cover by Ronald Clyne

CONTENTS

A HISTORY OF PHILOSOPHY
VOLUME II PART II

Chapter Thirty

ST. ALBERT THE GREAT

Life and intellectual activity—Philosophy and theology—God —Creation—The soul—Reputation and importance of St. Albert.

1. Albert the Great was born in 1206 at Lauingen in Swabia, but left Germany in order to study the arts at Padua, where he entered the Dominican Order in 1223. After having lectured in theology at Cologne and other places he received the doctorate at Paris in 1245, having Thomas Aquinas among his pupils from 1245 to 1248. In the latter year he returned to Cologne accompanied by Thomas, in order to establish the Dominican house of studies there. His purely intellectual work was interrupted, however, by administrative tasks which were laid upon him. Thus from 1254 until 1257 he was Provincial of the German Province and from 1260 until 1262 Bishop of Ratisbon. Visits to Rome and the preaching of a Crusade in Bohemia also occupied his time, but he seems to have adopted Cologne as his general place of residence. It was from Cologne that he set out for Paris in 1277, to defend the opinions of Thomas Aquinas (died 1274), and it was at Cologne that he died on November 15th, 1280.

It is clear enough from his writings and activities that Albert the Great was a man of wide intellectual interests and sympathies, and it is hardly to be expected that a man of his type would ignore the rise of Aristotelianism in the Parisian Faculty of Arts, especially as he was well aware of the stir and trouble caused by the new tendencies. As a man of open mind and ready intellectual sympathy he was not one to adopt an uncompromisingly hostile attitude to the new movement, though, on the other hand, he was not without strong sympathy for the neo-Platonist and Augustinian tradition. Therefore, while he adopted Aristotelian elements and incorporated them into his philosophy, he retained much of the Augustinian and non-Aristotelian tradition, and his philosophy bears the character of a transitional stage on the way to that fuller incorporation of Aristotelianism which was achieved by his great pupil, St. Thomas Aquinas. Moreover, being primarily a theologian, Albert could not but be sensible of the important points on which Aristotle's thought clashes with Christian doctrine, and that uncritical acceptance of Aristotle which became fashionable in a section of the Faculty of Arts was impossible for him. It is indeed no matter for surprise that though he composed paraphrases on many of the logical, physical (for example, on the *Physics* and *De Caelo et Mundo*), metaphysical and ethical works (*Nicomachean Ethics* and *Politics*) of Aristotle, he did not hesitate to point out errors committed by the Philosopher and published a *De unitate intellectus* against Averroes. His declared intention in composing the paraphrases was to make Aristotle intelligible to the Latins, and he professed to give simply an objective account of Aristotle's opinions; but in any case he could not criticise Aristotle without showing something of his own ideas, even if his commentaries are for the most part impersonal paraphrases and explanations of the Philosopher's works.

It has not been found possible to determine with any degree of accuracy the dates of Albert's writings or even the order in which he published them, but it seems that the publication of his Commentary on the *Sentences* of Peter Lombard and the *Summa de Creaturis* antedate the publication of his paraphrases of Aristotle's works. He also published Commentaries on the books of the Pseudo-Dionysius. The *De unitate intellectus* appears to have been composed after 1270, and the *Summa theologiae*, which may be a compilation due to other hands, remained unfinished.

One cannot pass over in silence a remarkable side of Albert's interest and activity, his interest in the physical sciences. In an enlightened manner he insisted on the necessity of observation and experiment in these matters, and in his *De vegetalibus* and *De animalibus* he gives the results of his own observations as well as ideas of earlier writers. Apropos of his description of trees and plants he remarks that what he has set down is the result of his own experience or has been borrowed from authors whom he knows to have confirmed their ideas by observation, for in such matters experience alone can give certainty.[1] His speculations are often very sensible, as when, in opposition to the idea that the earth south of the equator is uninhabitable, he affirms that the reverse is probably true, though the cold at the poles may be so excessive as to prevent habitation. If, however, there are animals living there, we must suppose that they have coats thick enough to protect them against the climate and these coats are probably white in colour. In any case it is unreasonable to suppose that people living on the lower part of the earth would fall off, since the term 'lower' is only relative to us.[2] Naturally Albert relies very much on the opinions, observations and guesses of his predecessors; but he frequently appeals to his own observation, to what he has personally noticed of the habits of migrating birds, or of the nature of plants, for example, and he shows a robust common sense, as when he makes it plain that *a priori* arguments for the uninhabitable character of the 'torrid zone' cannot outweigh the evident fact that parts of lands which we know to be inhabited lie in that zone. Again, when speaking of the lunar halo or 'rainbow',[3] he remarks that according to Aristotle this phenomenon occurs only twice in fifty years, whereas he and others have observed it twice in one year, so that Aristotle must have been speaking from hearsay and not from experience. In any case, whatever value the particular conclusions drawn by St. Albert have, it is the spirit of curiosity and the reliance on observation and experiment which is remarkable and helps to distinguish him from so many Scholastics of a later period. Incidentally this spirit of inquiry and wide interests brings him near, in this respect, to Aristotle, since the Philosopher himself was well aware of the value of empirical research in scientific matters, however much later disciples may have received all his dicta as unquestionable and lacked his inquiring spirit and many-sided interests.

2. St. Albert the Great is quite clear as to the distinction between theology and philosophy, and so between the theology which takes as its foundation the data of revelation and the theology which is the work of the unaided natural reason and belongs to metaphysical philosophy. Thus metaphysics or first theology treats of God as the first Being (*secundum*

quod substat proprietatibus entis primi), while theology treats of God as known by faith (*secundum quod substat attributis quae per fidem attribuuntur*). Again, the philosopher works under the influence of the general light of reason given to all men, by which light he sees the first principles, while the theologian works by the supernatural light of faith, through which he receives the revealed dogmas.[4] St. Albert has, therefore, little sympathy for those who deny or belittle philosophy, since not only does he make use of dialectic in theological reasoning, but he also recognises philosophy itself as an independent science. Against those who assert that it is wrong to introduce philosophic reasoning into theology, he admits that such reasoning cannot be primary, since a dogma is proved *tamquam ex priori*, that is, a dogma is shown by the theologian to have been revealed and is not a conclusion from philosophic argument; but he goes on to say that philosophic arguments can be of real utility in a secondary capacity, when dealing with objections brought by hostile philosophers, and speaks of the ignorant people who want to attack in every way the employment of philosophy and who are like 'brute animals blaspheming against that of which they are ignorant'.[5] Even in the Order of Preachers there was opposition to philosophy and the study of such 'profane' science, and one of the greatest services rendered by St. Albert was to promote the study and use of philosophy in his own Order.

3. The doctrine of St. Albert is not a homogeneous system, but rather a mixture of Aristotelian and neo-Platonic elements. For instance, he appeals to Aristotle when giving a proof for God's existence from motion,[6] and he argues that an infinite chain of *principia* is impossible and contradictory, since there would in reality be no *principium*. The *primum principium* or first principle must, by the very fact that it is the first principle, have its existence from itself and not from another: its existence (*esse*) must be its substance and essence.[7] It is the necessary Being, without any admixture of contingence or of potency, and Albert shows also that it is intelligent, living, omnipotent, free, and so on, in such a way that it is its own intelligence; that in God's knowledge of Himself there is no distinction between subject and object; that His will is not something distinct from His essence. Finally he carefully distinguishes God, the first Principle, from the world by observing that none of the names which

we ascribe to God can be predicated of Him in their primary sense. If, for example, He is called substance, this is not because He falls within the category of substance, but because He is above all substances and the whole category of substance. Similarly, the term 'being' primarily refers to the general abstract idea of being, which cannot be predicated of God.[8] In fine, it is truer to say of God that we know what He is not rather than what He is.[9] One may say, then, that in the philosophy of St. Albert God is depicted, in dependence on Aristotle, as first unmoved Mover, as pure Act and as the self-knowing Intellect, but emphasis is laid, in dependence on the writings of the Pseudo-Dionysius, on the fact that God transcends all our concepts and all the names we predicate of Him.

4. This combination of Aristotle and the Pseudo-Dionysius safeguards the divine transcendence and is the foundation for a doctrine of analogy; but when it comes to describing the creation of the world Albert interprets Aristotle according to the doctrine of the *Peripatetici*, that is to say, according to what are in reality neo-Platonic interpretations. Thus he uses the words *fluxus* and *emanatio* (*fluxus est emanatio formae a primo fonte, qui omnium formarum est fons et origo*)[10] and maintains that the first principle, *intellectus universaliter agens*, is the source whence flows the second intelligence, the latter the source whence flows the third intelligence, and so on. From each subordinate intelligence is derived its own proper sphere, until eventually the earth comes into being. This general scheme (Albert gives several particular schemes, culled from the 'ancients') might seem to impair the divine transcendence and immutability, as also the creative activity of God; but St. Albert does not, of course, think of God as becoming less through the process of emanation or as undergoing any change, while he also insists that a subordinate cause works only in dependence on, with the help of, the higher cause, so that the whole process must ultimately be referred to God. This process is variously represented as a graded diffusion of goodness or as a graded diffusion of light. However, it is clear that in this picture of creation St. Albert is inspired far more by the *Liber de causis*, the neo-Platonists and the neo-Platonising Aristotelians than by the historic Aristotle, while on the other hand he does not appear to have realised that the neo-Platonic notion of emanation, though not strictly pantheistic, since God remains

distinct from all other beings, is yet not fully in tune with the Christian doctrine of free creation out of nothing. I do not mean to suggest for a moment that St. Albert intended to substitute the neo-Platonic emanation process for the Christian doctrine: rather did he try to express the latter in terms of the former, without apparently realising the difficulties involved in such an attempt.

St. Albert departs from the Augustinian-Franciscan tradition by holding that reason cannot demonstrate with certainty the world's creation in time, that is, that the world was not created from eternity,[11] and also by denying that angels and the human soul are composed of matter and form, in this evidently thinking of matter as related to quantity; but on the other hand he accepts the doctrine of the *rationes seminales* and that of light as the *forma corporeitatis*. Moreover, besides adopting doctrines sometimes from Aristotelianism and sometimes from Augustinianism or neo-Platonism, St. Albert adopts phrases from the one tradition while interpreting them in the sense of the other, as when he speaks of seeing essences in the divine light, while meaning that the human reason and its operation is a reflection of the divine light, an effect thereof, but not that a special illuminating activity of God is required over and above the creation and conservation of the intellect. In general he follows the Aristotelian theory of abstraction. Again, Albert by no means always makes his meaning clear, so that it remains doubtful whether or not he considered that the distinction between essence and existence is real or conceptual. As he denied the presence of matter in the angels, while affirming that they are composed of 'essential parts', it would indeed seem reasonable to suppose that he maintained the theory of the real distinction, and he speaks in this sense on occasion; but at other times he speaks as if he held the Averroist theory of a conceptual distinction. We are left in difficulty as to the interpretation of his thought on this and other points owing to his habit of giving various different theories without any definite indication of which solution to the problem he himself adopted. It is not always clear how far he is simply reporting the opinions of others and how far he is committing himself to the affirmation of the opinions in question. It is impossible, then, to speak of a completed 'system' of Albert the Great: his thought is really a stage in the adoption of the Aristotelian philosophy as an intellectual instrument for the expression of the Christian outlook. The process of adopting and adapting the Aristotelian philosophy was carried much further by St. Albert's great pupil, Thomas Aquinas; but it would be a mistake to exaggerate the Aristotelianism even of the latter. Both men remained to a great extent in the tradition of Augustine, though both men, St. Albert in an incomplete, St. Thomas in a more complete fashion, interpreted Augustine according to the categories of Aristotle.

5. St. Albert was convinced that the immortality of the soul can be demonstrated by reason. Thus in his book on the nature and origin of the soul[12] he gives a number of proofs, arguing, for example, that the soul transcends matter in its intellectual operations, having the principle of such operations in itself, and so cannot depend on the body *secundum esse et essentiam*. But he will not allow that the arguments for the unicity of the active intellect in all men are valid, arguments which, if probative, would deny personal immortality. He treats of this matter not only in the *De Anima*, but also in his special work on the subject, the *Libellus de unitate intellectus contra Averroem*. After remarking that the question is very difficult and that only trained philosophers, accustomed to metaphysical thinking, should take part in the dispute,[13] he goes on to expose thirty arguments which the Averroists bring forward or can bring forward to support their contention and observes that they are very difficult to answer. However, he proceeds to give thirty-six arguments against the Averroists, outlines his opinion on the rational soul and then answers in turn[14] the thirty arguments of the Averroists. The rational soul is the form of man, so that it must be multiplied in individual men: but what is multiplied numerically must also be multiplied substantially. If it can be proved, then, as it can be proved, that the rational soul is immortal, it follows that the multiplicity of rational souls survive death. Again, *esse* is the act of the final form of each thing (*formae ultimae*), and the final or ultimate form of man is the rational soul. Now, either individual men have their own separate *esse* or they have not. If you say that they do not possess their own individual *esse*, you must be prepared to admit that they are not individual men, which is patently false, while if you admit that each man has his own individual *esse*, then he must also have his own individual rational soul.

6. St. Albert the Great enjoyed a high reputation, even

during his own lifetime, and Roger Bacon, who was far from being an enthusiastic admirer of his work, tells us that 'just as Aristotle, Avicenna and Averroes are quoted (*allegantur*) in the Schools, so is he'. Roger Bacon means that St. Albert was cited by name, which was contrary to the custom then in vogue of not mentioning living writers by name and which gives witness to the esteem he had won for himself. This reputation was doubtless due in large part to the Saint's erudition and to his many-sided interests, as theologian, philosopher, man of science and commentator. He had a wide knowledge of Jewish and Arabian philosophy and frequently quotes the opinions of other writers, so that, in spite of his frequent indefiniteness of thought and expression and his mistakes in historical matters, his writings give the impression of a man of extensive knowledge who had read very widely and was interested in many lines of thought. His disciple, Ulric of Strasbourg, a Dominican, who developed the neo-Platonic side of St. Albert's thought, called him 'the wonder and miracle of our time';[15] but, apart from his devotion to experimental science, St. Albert's thought is of interest to us primarily because of its influence on St. Thomas Aquinas, who, unlike Ulric of Strasbourg and John of Fribourg, developed the Aristotelian aspect of that thought. The master, who outlived his pupil, was devoted to the latter's memory, and we are told that when St. Albert, as an old man, used to think of Thomas at the commemoration of the dead in the Canon of the Mass, he would shed tears as he thought of the death of him who had been the flower and glory of the world.

St. Albert's reputation as a man of learning and wide-ranging interests was justly merited; but his chief merit, as several historians have noticed, was that he saw what a treasure for the Christian West was contained in the system of Aristotle and in the writings of the Arabian philosophers. Looking back on the thirteenth century from a much later date, one is inclined to contemplate the invasion and growing dominance of Aristotelianism in the light of the arid Scholastic Aristotelianism of a later period, which sacrificed the spirit to the letter and entirely misunderstood the inquiring mind of the great Greek philosopher, his interest in science and the tentative nature of many of his conclusions; but to regard the thirteenth century in this light is to be guilty of an anachronism, for the attitude of the decadent Aristotelians of a later period was not the attitude of St. Albert. The Christian West possessed nothing of its own in the way of pure philosophy or of natural science which could compare with the philosophy of Aristotle and the Arabians. St. Albert realised this fact clearly; he saw that a definite attitude must be adopted towards Aristotelianism, that it could not simply be disregarded, and he was rightly convinced that it would be wasteful and even disastrous to attempt to disregard it. He saw too, of course, that on some points Aristotle and the Arabians held doctrines which were incompatible with dogma; but at the same time he realised that this was no reason for rejecting in its entirety what one had to reject in part. He endeavoured to make Aristotelianism intelligible to the Latins and to show them its value, while pointing out its errors. That he accepted this or that point, rejected this or that theory, is not so important as the fact that he realised the general significance and value of Aristotelianism, and it is surely not necessary to be a rigid Aristotelian oneself in order to be able to appreciate his merits in this respect. It is a mistake so to stress St. Albert's independence, in regard to some of Aristotle's scientific observations, for example, that one loses sight of the great service he did in drawing attention to Aristotle and displaying something of the wealth of Aristotelianism. The passage of years certainly brought a certain unfortunate ossification in the Aristotelian tradition; but the blame for that cannot be laid at the door of St. Albert the Great. If one tries to imagine what mediaeval philosophy would have been without Aristotle, if one thinks away the Thomistic synthesis and the philosophy of Scotus, if one strips the philosophy of St. Bonaventure of all Aristotelian elements, one will hardly look on the invasion of Aristotelianism as an historical misfortune.

Chapter Thirty-one

ST. THOMAS AQUINAS–I

*Life–Works–Mode of exposing St. Thomas's philosophy–
The spirit of St. Thomas's philosophy.*

1. Thomas Aquinas was born in the castle of Roccasecca, not
far from Naples, at the end of 1224 or beginning of 1225,
his father being the Count of Aquino. At the age of five
years he was placed by his parents in the Benedictine Abbey
of Monte Cassino as an oblate, and it was there that the
future Saint and Doctor made his first studies, remaining in
the monastery from 1230 to 1239, when the Emperor Frederick II expelled the monks. The boy returned to his family
for a few months and then went to the University of Naples
in the autumn of the same year, being then fourteen years
old. In the city there was a convent of Dominican friars, and
Thomas, attracted by their life, entered the Order in the
course of the year 1244. This step was by no means acceptable to his family, who no doubt wished the boy to enter the
abbey of Monte Cassino, as a step to ecclesiastical prefer-
ment, and it may have partly been due to this family opposition that the Dominican General resolved to take Thomas
with him to Bologna, where he was himself going for a General Chapter, and then to send him on to the University of
Paris. However, Thomas was kidnapped by his brothers on
the way and was kept a prisoner at Aquino for about a year.
His determination to remain true to his Order was proof
against this trial, and he was able to make his way to Paris
in the autumn of 1245.

Thomas was probably at Paris from 1245 until the summer
of 1248, when he accompanied St. Albert the Great to

Cologne, where the latter was to found a house of studies (*studium generale*) for the Dominican Order, remaining there until 1252. During this period, first at Paris, then at Cologne, Thomas was in close contact with Albert the Great, who realised the potentialities of his pupil, and while it is obvious that his taste for learning and study must in any case have been greatly stimulated by intimate contact with a professor of such erudition and such intellectual curiosity, we can hardly suppose that St. Albert's attempt to utilise what was valuable in Aristotelianism was without direct influence on his pupil's mind. Even if St. Thomas did not at this early date in his career conceive the idea of completing what his master had begun, he must at least have been profoundly influenced by the latter's open-mindedness. Thomas did not possess the all-embracing curiosity of his master (or one might say, perhaps that he had a better sense of mental economy), but he certainly possessed greater powers of systematisation, and it was only to be expected that the meeting of the erudition and open-mindedness of the older man with the speculative power and synthesising ability of the younger would result in splendid fruit. It was St. Thomas who was to achieve the expression of the Christian ideology in Aristotelian terms, and who was to utilise Aristotelianism as an instrument of theological and philosophical analysis and synthesis; but his sojourn at Paris and Cologne in company with St. Albert was undoubtedly a factor of prime importance in his intellectual development. Whether or not we choose to regard St. Albert's system as incomplete Thomism is really irrelevant: the main fact is that St. Albert (*mutatis mutandis*) was Thomas's Socrates.

In 1252 St. Thomas returned from Cologne to Paris and continued his course of studies, lecturing on the Scriptures as *Baccalaureus Biblicus* (1252–4) and on the *Sentences* of Peter Lombard as *Baccalaureus Sententiarius* (1254–6), at the conclusion of which period he received his Licentiate, the licence or permission to teach in the faculty of theology. In the course of the same year he became *Magister* and lectured as Dominican professor until 1259. Of the controversy which arose concerning the Dominican and Franciscan chairs in the university mention has already been made. In 1259 he left Paris for Italy and taught theology at the *studium curiae* attached to the Papal court until 1268. Thus he was at Anagni with Alexander IV (1259–61), at Orvieto with Urban IV (1261–4), at Santa Sabina in Rome (1265–7), and at Viterbo with Clement IV (1267–8). It was at the court of Urban IV that he met the famous translator, William of Moerbeke, and it was Urban who commissioned Thomas to compose the Office for the feast of Corpus Christi.

In 1268 Thomas returned to Paris and taught there until 1272, engaging in controversy with the Averroists, as also with those who renewed the attack on the religious Orders. In 1272 he was sent to Naples in order to erect a Dominican *studium generale*, and he continued his professorial activity there until 1274, when Pope Gregory X summoned him to Lyons to take part in the Council. The journey was begun but never completed, as St. Thomas died on the way on March 7th, 1274, at the Cistercian monastery of Fossanuova, between Naples and Rome. He was forty-nine years of age at the time of his death, having behind him a life devoted to study and teaching. It had not been a life of much external activity or excitement, if we except the early incident of his imprisonment, the more or less frequent journeys and the controversies in which the Saint was involved; but it was a life devoted to the pursuit and defence of truth, a life also permeated and motivated by a deep spirituality. In some ways Thomas Aquinas was rather like the professor of legend (there are several stories concerning his fits of abstraction, or rather concentration, which made him oblivious to his surroundings), but he was a great deal more than a professor or theologian, for he was a Saint, and even if his devotion and love are not allowed to manifest themselves in the pages of his academic works, the ecstasies and mystical union with God of his later years bear witness to the fact that the truths of which he wrote were the realities by which he lived.

2. St. Thomas's Commentary on the *Sentences* of Peter Lombard dates probably from 1254 to 1256, the *De principiis naturae* from 1255, the *De ente et essentia* from 1256 and the *De Veritate* from between 1256 and 1259. It may be that the *Quaestiones quodlibetales* 7, 8, 9, 10 and 11 were also composed before 1259, i.e. before Thomas left Paris for Italy. The *In Boethium de Hebdomadibus* and the *In Boethium de Trinitate* are also to be assigned to this period. While in Italy St. Thomas wrote the *Summa contra Gentiles*, the *De Potentia*, the *Contra errores Graecorum*, the *De emptione et venditione* and the *De regimine principum*. To this period belong also a number of the Commentaries on Aris-

totle: for example, those on the *Physics* (probably), the *Metaphysics*, the *Nicomachean Ethics*, the *De Anima*, the *Politics* (probably). On his return to Paris, where he became engaged in controversy with the Averroists, St. Thomas wrote the *De aeternitate mundi contra murmurantes* and the *De unitate intellectus contra Averroistas*, the *De Malo* (probably), the *De spiritualibus creaturis*, the *De anima* (i.e. the *Quaestio disputata*), the *De unione Verbi incarnati*, as well as the *Quaestiones quodlibetales* 1 to 6 and the commentaries on the *De causis*, the *Meteorologica*[1] and the *Perihermeneias*, also belong to this period. While during his stay at Naples St. Thomas wrote the *De mixtione elementorum*, the *De motu cordis*, the *De virtutibus*, and the commentaries on Aristotle's *De Caelo* and *De generatione et corruptione*. As to the *Summa Theologica*, this was composed between 1265 (at the earliest) and 1273, the *Pars prima* being written in Paris, the *Prima secundae* and *Secunda secundae* in Italy, and the *Tertia pars* in Paris between 1272 and 1273. The *Supplementum*, made up from previous writings of St. Thomas, was added by Reginald of Piperno, St. Thomas's secretary from the year 1261. One must add that Peter of Auvergne completed the commentary on the *De Caelo* and that on the *Politics* (from Book 3, *lectio* 7), while Ptolemy of Lucca was responsible for part of the *De regimine principum*, St. Thomas having written only the first book and the first four chapters of the second book. The *Compendium theologiae*, an unfinished work, was a product of the later years of St. Thomas's life, but it is not certain if it was written before or after his return to Paris in 1268.

A number of works have been attributed to St. Thomas which were definitely not written by him, while the authenticity of certain other small works is doubtful, for example, the *De natura verbi intellectus*. The chronology which has been given above is not universally agreed upon, Mgr. Martin Grabmann and Père Mandonnet, for instance, ascribing certain works to different years. On this subject the relevent works mentioned in the Bibliography can be consulted.

3. To attempt to give a satisfactory outline of the 'philosophical system' of the greatest of the Schoolmen is to attempt a task of considerable magnitude. It does not indeed appear to me an acute question whether one should attempt a systematic or a genetic exposition, since the literary period of St. Thomas's life comprises but twenty years and though

there were modifications and some development of opinion in that period, there was no such considerable development as in the case of Plato and still less was there any such succession of phases or periods as in the case of Schelling.[2] To treat the thought of Plato genetically might well be considered desirable (though actually, for purposes of convenience and clarity, I adopted a predominantly systematic form of exposition in my first volume) and to treat the thought of Schelling genetically is essential; but there is no real reason against presenting the system of St. Thomas systematically: on the contrary, there is every reason why one should present it systematically.

The difficulty lies rather in answering the question, what precise form the systematic exposition should take and what emphasis and interpretation one should give to the component parts of its content. St. Thomas was a theologian and although he distinguished the sciences of revealed theology and philosophy, he did not himself elaborate a systematic exposition of philosophy by itself (there is theology even in the *Summa contra Gentiles*), so that the method of exposition is not already decided upon by the Saint himself.

Against this it may be objected that St. Thomas certainly did fix the starting-point for an exposition of his philosophy, and M. Gilson, in his outstanding work on St. Thomas,[3] argues that the right way of exposing the Thomistic philosophy is to expose it according to the order of the Thomistic theology. St. Thomas was a theologian and his philosophy must be regarded in the light of its relation to his theology. Not only is it true to say that the loss of a theological work like the *Summa Theologica* would be a major disaster in regard to our knowledge of St. Thomas's philosophy, whereas the loss of the Commentaries on Aristotle, though deplorable, would be of less importance; but also St. Thomas's conception of the content of philosophy or of the object which the philosopher (i.e. theologian-philosopher) considers, was that of *le révélable*, that which could have been revealed but has not been revealed and that which has been revealed but need not have been revealed, in the sense that it can be ascertained by the human reason, for example, the fact that God is wise. As M. Gilson rightly remarks, the problem for St. Thomas was not how to introduce philosophy into theology without corrupting the essence and nature of *philosophy*, but how to introduce philosophy without corrupting the essence and nature of *theology*. Theology treats of the revealed, and revelation must remain intact; but some truths are taught in theology which can be ascertained without revelation (God's existence, for example), while there are other truths which have not been revealed but which might have been revealed and which are of importance for a total view of God's creation. St. Thomas's philosophy should thus be regarded in the light of its relation to theology, and it is a mistake to collect the philosophical items from St. Thomas's works, including his theological works, and construct a system out of them according to one's own idea of what a philosophical system should be, even though St. Thomas would very likely have refused to recognise such a system as corresponding with his actual intentions. To reconstruct the Thomistic system in such a way is legitimate enough for a philosopher, but it is the part of the historian to stick to St. Thomas's own method.

M. Gilson argues his point with his customary lucidity and cogency, and it seems to me that his point must, in general, be admitted. To begin an historical exposition of St. Thomas's philosophy by a theory of knowledge, for example, especially if the theory of knowledge were separated from psychology or the doctrine of the soul, would scarcely represent St. Thomas's own procedure, though it would be legitimate in an exposition of 'Thomism' which did not pretend to be primarily historical. On the other hand, St. Thomas certainly wrote some philosophical works before he composed the *Summa Theologica*, and the proofs of the existence of God in the latter work obviously presuppose a good many philosophical ideas. Moreover, as those philosophical ideas are not mere ideas, but are, on the principles of St. Thomas's own philosophy, abstracted from experience of the concrete, there seems to me ample justification for starting with the concrete sensible world of experience and considering some of St. Thomas's theories about it before going on to consider his natural theology. And this is the procedure which I have actually adopted.

Another point. St. Thomas was an extremely clear writer; but none the less there have been and are divergences of interpretation in regard to certain of his doctrines. To discuss fully the *pros* and *cons* of different interpretations is, however, not possible in a general history of philosophy: one can do little more than give the interpretation which commends itself in one's own eyes. At the same time, as far as the present writer is concerned, he is not prepared to state that on points where a difference of interpretation has arisen, he can give what is the indubitably correct interpretation. After all, concerning which great philosopher's system is there complete and universal agreement of interpretation? Plato, Aristotle, Descartes, Leibniz, Kant, Hegel? In the case of some philosophers, especially in the case of those who have expressed their thought clearly and carefully, like St. Thomas, there is a pretty generally accepted interpretation as to the main body of the system; but it is doubtful if the consent ever is or ever will be absolute and universal. A philosopher may write clearly and yet not express his final thought on all problems which arise in connection with his system, especially as some of those problems may not have occurred to him: it would be absurd to expect of any philosopher that he should have answered all questions, settled all problems, even that he should have rounded off and sealed his system in such a way that there could be no possible ground for divergence of interpretation. The present writer has the greatest respect and reverence for the genius of St. Thomas Aquinas, but he does not see that anything is to be gained by confusing the finite mind of the Saint with Absolute Mind or by claiming for his system what its author himself would certainly never have dreamed of claiming.

4. The philosophy of St. Thomas is essentially realist and concrete. St. Thomas certainly adopts the Aristotelian statement that first philosophy or metaphysic studies being as being; but it is perfectly clear that the task he sets himself is the explanation of existent being, so far as this is attainable by the human mind. In other words, he does not presuppose a notion from which reality is to be deduced; but he starts from the existent world and inquires what its being is, how it exists, what is the condition of its existence. Moreover, his thought concentrates on the supreme Existence, on the Being which does not merely possess existence, but is Its own existence, which is the very plenitude of existence, *ipsum esse subsistens*: his thought remains ever in contact with the concrete, the existent, both with that which has existence as something derived, something received, and with that which does not receive existence but is existence. In this sense it is true to say that Thomism is an 'existential philosophy', though it is very misleading, in my opinion, to call St.

Thomas an 'existentialist', since the *Existenz* of the existentialists is not the same thing as St. Thomas's *esse*; nor is St. Thomas's method of approach to the problem of existence the same as that of the philosophers who are now called existentialists.

It has been maintained that St. Thomas, by bringing *esse* to the forefront of the philosophic stage, advanced beyond the philosophies of essence, particularly beyond Plato and the philosophies of Platonic inspiration. There is certainly truth in this contention: although Plato did not disregard the question of existence, the salient characteristic of his philosophy is the explanation of the world in terms of essence rather than of existence, while even for Aristotle, God, although pure Act, is primarily Thought, or Idea, the Platonic Good rendered 'personal'. Moreover, although Aristotle endeavoured to explain form and order in the world and the intelligible process of development, he did not explain the existence of the world; apparently he thought that no explanation was needed. In neo-Platonism again, though the derivation of the world is accounted for, the general scheme of emanation is primarily that of an emanation of essences, though existence is certainly not left out of account: God is primarily the One or the Good, not *ipsum esse subsistens*, not the *I am who am*. But one should remember that creation out of nothing was not an idea at which any Greek philosopher arrived without dependence on Judaism or Christianity and that without this idea the derivation of the world tends to be explained as a necessary derivation of essences. Those Christian philosophers who depended on and utilised neo-Platonic terminology spoke of the world as flowing from or emanating from God, and even St. Thomas used such phrases on occasion; but an orthodox Christian philosopher, whatever his terminology, regards the world as created freely by God, as receiving *esse* from *ipsum esse subsistens*. When St. Thomas insisted on the fact that God is subsistent existence, that His essence is not primarily goodness or thought but existence, he was but rendering explicit the implications of the Jewish and Christian view of the world's relation to God. I do not mean to imply that the idea of creation cannot be attained by reason; but the fact remains that it was not attained by the Greek philosophers and could hardly be attained by them, given their idea of God.

Of St. Thomas's general relation to Aristotle I shall speak

later; but it may be as well to point out now one great effect
which Aristotelianism had on St. Thomas's philosophical outlook and procedure. One might expect that St. Thomas, being
a Christian, a theologian, a friar, would emphasise the soul's
relation to God and would begin with what some modern
philosophers call 'subjectivity', that he would place the interior life in the foreground even of his philosophy, as St.
Bonaventure did. In point of fact, however, one of the chief
characteristics of St. Thomas's philosophy is its 'objectivity'
rather than its 'subjectivity'. The immediate object of the
human intellect is the essence of the material thing, and St.
Thomas builds up his philosophy by reflection on sense-experience. In the proofs which he gives of God's existence
the process of argument is always from the sensible world to
God. No doubt certain of the proofs could be applied to the
soul itself as a starting-point and be developed in a different
way; but in actual fact this was not the way of St. Thomas,
and the proof which he calls the *via manifestior* is the one
which is most dependent on Aristotle's own arguments. This
Aristotelian 'objectivity' of St. Thomas may appear discon-
certing to those for whom 'truth is subjectivity'; but at the
same time it is a great source of strength, since it means that
his arguments can be considered in themselves, apart from St.
Thomas's own life, on their own merits or demerits, and that
observations about 'wishful thinking' are largely irrelevant,
the relevant question being the objective cogency of the arguments themselves. Another result is that St. Thomas's philosophy appears 'modern' in a sense in which the philosophy of
St. Bonaventure can hardly do. The latter tends to appear as
essentially bound up with the general mediaeval outlook and
with the Christian spiritual life and tradition, so that it seems
to be on a different plane from the 'profane' philosophies of
modern times, whereas the Thomistic philosophy can be divorced from Christian spirituality and, to a large extent, from
the mediaeval outlook and background, and can enter into
direct competition with more recent systems. A Thomistic
revival has taken place, as everybody knows; but it is a little
difficult to imagine a Bonaventurian revival, unless one were
at the same time to change the conception of philosophy,
and in this case the modern philosopher and the Bonaventurian would scarcely speak the same language.

Nevertheless, St. Thomas was a Christian philosopher. As
already mentioned, St. Thomas follows Aristotle in speaking

of metaphysics as the science of being as being; but the fact that his thought centres round the concrete and the fact that he was a Christian theologian led him to emphasise also the view that 'first philosophy is wholly directed to the knowledge of God as the last end' and that 'the knowledge of God is the ultimate end of every human cognition and operation'.[4] But actually man was created for a profounder and more intimate knowledge of God than he can attain by the exercise of his natural reason in this life, and so revelation was morally necessary in order that his mind might be raised to something higher than his reason can attain to in this life and that he should desire and zealously strive towards something 'which exceeds the whole state of this life.'[5] Metaphysics has its own object, therefore, and a certain autonomy of its own, but it points upwards and needs to be crowned by theology: otherwise man will not realise the end for which he was created and will not desire and strive towards that end. Moreover, as the primary object of metaphysics, God, exceeds the apprehension of the metaphysician and of the natural reason in general, and as the full knowledge or vision of God is not attainable in this life, the conceptual knowledge of God is crowned in this life by mysticism. Mystical theology does not enter the province of philosophy, and St. Thomas's philosophy can be considered without reference to it; but one should not forget that for St. Thomas philosophical knowledge is neither sufficient nor final.

Chapter Thirty-two

ST. THOMAS AQUINAS–II:
PHILOSOPHY AND THEOLOGY

Distinction between philosophy and theology—Moral necessity of revelation—Incompatibility of faith and science in the same mind concerning the same object—Natural end and supernatural end—St. Thomas and St. Bonaventure—St. Thomas as 'innovator'.

1. That St. Thomas made a formal and explicit distinction between dogmatic theology and philosophy is an undoubted and an indubitable fact. Philosophy and the other human sciences rely simply and solely on the natural light of reason: the philosopher uses principles which are known by the human reason (with God's natural concurrence, of course, but without the supernatural light of faith), and he argues to conclusions which are the fruit of human reasoning. The theologian, on the other hand, although he certainly uses his reason, accepts his principles on authority, on faith; he receives them as revealed. The introduction of dialectic into theology, the practice of starting from a revealed premiss or from revealed premisses and arguing rationally to a conclusion, leads to the development of Scholastic theology, but it does not turn theology into philosophy, since the principles, the data, are accepted as revealed. For instance, the theologian may attempt with the aid of categories and forms of reasoning borrowed from philosophy to understand a little better the mystery of the Trinity; but he does not thereby cease to act as a theologian, since all the time he accepts the dogma of the Trinity of Persons in one Nature on the authority of God revealing: it is for him a datum or principle, a

revealed premiss accepted on faith, not the conclusion of a philosophical argument. Again, while the philosopher starts from the world of experience and argues by reason to God in so far as He can be known by means of creatures, the theologian starts with God as He has revealed Himself, and the natural method in theology is to pass from God in Himself to creatures rather than to ascend from creatures to God, as the philosopher does and must do.

It follows that the principal difference between theology and philosophy lies in the fact that the theologian receives his principles as revealed and considers the objects with which he deals as revealed or as deducible from what is revealed, whereas the philosopher apprehends his principles by reason alone and considers the objects with which he deals, not as revealed but as apprehensible and apprehended by the natural light of reason. In other words, the fundamental difference between theology and philosophy does not lie in a difference of objects concretely considered. Some truths are proper to theology, since they cannot be known by reason and are known only by revelation, the mystery of the Trinity, for example, while other truths are proper to philosophy alone in the sense that they have not been revealed; but there are some truths which are common to both theology and philosophy, since they have been revealed, though at the same time they can be established by reason. It is the existence of these common truths which makes it impossible to say that theology and philosophy differ primarily because each science considers different truths: in some instances they consider the same truths, though they consider them in a different manner, the theologian considering them as revealed, the philosopher as conclusions of a process of human reasoning. For example, the philosopher argues to God as Creator, while the theologian also treats of God as Creator; but for the philosopher the knowledge of God as Creator comes as the conclusion of a purely rational argument, while the theologian accepts the fact that God is Creator from revelation, so that it is for him a premiss rather than a conclusion, a premiss which is not hypothetically assumed but revealed. In technical language it is not *primarily* a difference of truths considered 'materially', or according to their content, which constitutes the difference between a truth of theology and a truth of philosophy, but rather a difference of truths considered 'formally'. That is to say, the same truth may be enunciated by both the theologian and the philosopher; but it is arrived at and considered by the theologian in a different way from that in which it is arrived at and considered by the philosopher. *Diversa ratio cognoscibilis diversitatem scientiarum inducit.* . . . 'There is, therefore, no reason why another science should not treat of the very same objects, as known by the light of divine revelation, which the philosophical sciences treat of according as they are knowable by the light of natural reason. Hence the theology which belongs to sacred doctrine differs generically from that theology which is a part of philosophy.'[1] Between dogmatic theology and natural theology there is a certain overlapping; but the sciences differ generically from one another.

2. According to St. Thomas, almost the whole of philosophy is directed to the knowledge of God, at least in the sense that a good deal of philosophical study is presupposed and required by natural theology, that part of metaphysics which treats of God. Natural theology, he says, is the last part of philosophy to be learnt.[2] Incidentally, this statement does not support the view that one should start the exposition of the Thomist philosophy with natural theology; but in any case the point I now want to make is that St. Thomas, seeing that natural theology, if it is to be properly grasped, requires much previous study and reflection, insists that revelation is morally necessary, given the fact that God is man's end. Moreover, not only does natural theology require more reflection and study and ability than most men are in the position to devote to it, but also, even when the truth is discovered, history shows that it is often contaminated by error. Pagan philosophers have certainly discovered God's existence; but error was often involved in their speculations, the philosopher either not realising properly the unity of God or denying divine providence or failing to see that God is Creator. If it were a question simply of astronomy or natural science, errors would not matter so much, since man can perfectly well attain his end even if he holds erroneous opinions concerning astronomical or scientific matters; but God is Himself man's end, and knowledge of God is essential in order that man should direct himself rightly towards that end, so that truth concerning God is of great importance and error concerning God is disastrous. Granted, then, that God is man's end, we can see that it is morally necessary that the discovery of truths so important for life should not be left simply to the unaided

powers of those men who have the ability, the zeal and the leisure to discover them, but that these truths should also be revealed.[3]

3. At once the question arises whether the same man can at the same time believe (accept on authority by faith) and know (as a result of rational demonstration) the same truth. If God's existence, for instance, has been demonstrated by a philosopher, can he at the same time believe it by faith? In the *De Veritate*[4] St. Thomas answers roundly that it is impossible for there to be faith and knowledge concerning the same object, that the same truths should be both known scientifically (philosophically) and at the same time believed (by faith) by the same man. On this supposition it would seem that a man who has proved the unity of God cannot believe that same truth by faith. In order, then, that it should not appear that this man is failing to give assent to articles of faith, St. Thomas finds himself compelled to say that such truths as the unity of God are not properly speaking articles of faith, but rather *praeambula ad articulos*.[5] He adds, however, that nothing prevents such truths being the object of belief to a man who cannot understand or has no time to consider the philosophical demonstration,[6] and he maintains his opinion that it was proper and fitting for such truths to be proposed for belief.[7] The question whether a man who understands the demonstration but who is not attending to it or considering it at the moment, can exercise faith in regard to the unity of God he does not explicitly answer. As to the opening phrase of the Creed (*Credo in unum Deum*, I believe in one God), which might seem to imply that faith in the unity of God is demanded of all, he would, on his premises, have to say that the unity of God is here not to be understood by itself but together with what follows, that is, as a unity of Nature in a Trinity of Persons.

To go into this question further and to discuss with what sort of faith the uneducated believe the truths which are known (demonstratively) by the philosopher, would be inappropriate here, not only because it is a theological question, but also because it is a question which St. Thomas does not explicitly discuss: the main point in mentioning the matter at all is to illustrate the fact that St. Thomas makes a real distinction between philosophy on the one hand and theology on the other. Incidentally, if we speak of a 'philosopher', it must not be understood as excluding the theologian: most of the Scholastics were both theologians and philosophers, and St. Thomas distinguishes the sciences rather than the men. That St. Thomas took this distinction seriously can also be seen from the position he adopted towards the question of the eternity of the world (to which I shall return later). He considered that it can be demonstrated that the world was created, but he did not think that reason can demonstrate that the world was not created from eternity, although it can refute the proofs adduced to show that it *was* created from eternity. On the other hand we know by revelation that the world was not created from eternity but had a beginning in time. In other words, the theologian knows through revelation that the world was not created from eternity, but the philosopher cannot prove this—or rather no argument which has been brought forward to prove it is conclusive. This distinction obviously presupposes or implies a real distinction between the two sciences of philosophy and theology.

4. It is sometimes said that St. Thomas differs from St. Augustine in that while the latter considers man simply in the concrete, as man called to a supernatural end, St. Thomas distinguishes two ends, a supernatural end, the consideration of which he assigns to the theologian, and a natural end, the consideration of which he assigns to the philosopher. Now, that St. Thomas distinguishes the two ends is quite true. In the *De Veritate*[8] he says that the final good as considered by the philosopher is different from the final good as considered by the theologian, since the philosopher considers the final good (*bonum ultimum*) which is proportionate to human powers, whereas the theologian considers as the final good that which transcends the power of nature, namely life eternal, by which he means, of course, not simply survival but the vision of God. This distinction is of great importance and it has its repercussion both in morals, where it is the foundation of the distinction between the natural and the supernatural virtues, and in politics, where it is the foundation of the distinction between the ends of the Church and the State and determines the relations which should exist between the two societies; but it is not a distinction between two ends which correspond to two mutually exclusive orders, the one supernatural, the other that of 'pure nature': it is a distinction between two orders of knowledge and activity in the same concrete human being. The concrete human being was created by God for a supernatural end, for perfect hap-

piness, which is attainable only in the next life through the
vision of God and which is, moreover, unattainable by man
by his own unaided natural power; but man can attain an
imperfect happiness in this life by the exercise of his natural
powers, through coming to a philosophic knowledge of God
through creatures and through the attainment and exercise
of the natural virtues.[9] Obviously these ends are not exclusive, since man can attain the imperfect felicity in which his
natural end consists without thereby putting himself outside
the way to his supernatural end; the natural end, imperfect
beatitude, is proportionate to human nature and human
powers, but inasmuch as man has been created for a supernatural final end, the natural end cannot satisfy him, as St.
Thomas argues in the *Contra Gentiles*[10]; it is imperfect and
points beyond itself.

How does this affect the question of the relation between
theology and philosophy? In this way. Man has one final end,
supernatural beatitude, but the existence of this end, which
transcends the powers of mere human nature, even though
man was created to attain it and given the power to do so by
grace, cannot be known by natural reason and so cannot be
divined by the philosopher: its consideration is restricted to
the theologian. On the other hand, man can attain through
the exercise of his natural powers to an imperfect and limited
natural happiness in this life, and the existence of this end
and the means to attain it are discoverable by the philosopher,
who can prove the existence of God from creatures, attain
some analogical knowledge of God, define the natural virtues
and the means of attaining them. Thus the philosopher may
be said to consider the end of man in so far as this end is
discoverable by human reason, i.e. only imperfectly and in-
completely. But both theologian and philosopher are considering man in the concrete: the difference is that the philosopher, while able to view and consider human nature as such,
cannot discover all there is in man, cannot discover his
supernatural vocation; he can only go part of the way in discovering man's destiny, precisely because man was created for
an end which transcends the powers of his nature. It is, therefore, not true to say that for St. Thomas the philosopher
considers man in a hypothetical state of pure nature, that is,
man as he would have been, had he never been called to a
supernatural end: he considers man in the concrete, but he
cannot know all there is to be known about that man in the

concrete. When St. Thomas raises the question whether God could have created man *in puris naturalibus*[11] he is asking simply if God could have created man (who even in this hypothesis was created for a supernatural end) without sanctifying grace, that is to say, if God could have first created man without the means of attaining his end and then afterwards have given it; he is not asking if God could have given man a purely natural ultimate end, as later writers interpreted him as saying. Whatever, then, the merit of the idea of the state of pure nature considered in itself may be (this is a point I do not propose to discuss), it does not play a part in St. Thomas's conception of philosophy. Consequently he does not differ from St. Augustine so much as has been sometimes asserted, though he defined the spheres of the two sciences of philosophy and theology more clearly than Augustine had defined them: what he did was to express Augustinianism in terms of the Aristotelian philosophy, a fact which compelled him to utilise the notion of natural end, though he interpreted it in such a way that he cannot be said to have adopted a starting-point in philosophy totally different from that of Augustine.

Actually the idea of the state of pure nature seems to have been introduced into Thomism by Cajetan. Suarez, who himself adopted the idea, remarks that 'Cajetan and the more modern theologians have considered a third state, which they have called purely natural, a state which can be thought of as possible, although it has not in fact existed'.[12] Dominicus Soto[13] says that it is a perversion of the mind of St. Thomas, while Toletus[14] observes that there exist in us a natural desire and a natural appetite for the vision of God, though this opinion, which is that of Scotus and seems to be that of St. Thomas, is contrary to that of Cajetan.

5. St. Thomas certainly believed that it is *theoretically* possible for the philosopher to work out a true metaphysical system without recourse to revelation. Such a system would be necessarily imperfect, inadequate and incomplete, because the metaphysician is primarily concerned with the Truth itself, with God who is the principle of all truth, and he is unable by purely human rational investigation to discover all that knowledge of Truth itself, of God, which is necessary for man if he is to attain his final end. The mere philosopher can say nothing about the supernatural end of man or the supernatural means of attaining that end, and as the knowl-

edge of these things is required for man's salvation, the insufficiency of philosophical knowledge is apparent. On the other hand, incompleteness and inadequacy do not necessarily mean falsity. The truth that God is one is not vitiated by the very fact that nothing is said or known of the Trinity of Persons; the further truth completes the first, but the first truth is not false, even taken by itself. If the philosopher states that God is one and simply says nothing about the Trinity, because the idea of the Trinity has never entered his head; or if he knows of the doctrine of the Trinity and does not himself believe it, but simply contents himself with saying that God is one; or even if he expresses the view that the Trinity, which he understands wrongly, is incompatible with the divine unity; it still remains true that the statement that God is one in Nature is a correct statement. Of course, if the philosopher states positively that God is one Person, he is stating what is false; but if he simply says that God is one and that God is personal, without going on to state that God is one Person, he is stating the truth. It may be unlikely that a philosopher would stop short at saying that God is personal, but it is at least theoretically possible. Unless one is prepared to condemn the human intellect as such or at any rate to debar it from the discovery of a true metaphysic, one must admit that the establishment of a satisfactory metaphysic is abstractly possible, even for the pagan philosopher. St. Thomas was very far from following St. Bonaventure in excluding Aristotle from the ranks of the metaphysicians: on the contrary, the latter was in Thomas's eyes the philosopher *par excellence*, the very embodiment of the intellectual power of the human mind acting without divine faith, and he attempted, wherever possible, to interpret Aristotle in the most 'charitable' sense, that is, in the sense which was most compatible with Christian revelation.

If one emphasises simply this aspect of St. Thomas's attitude towards philosophy, it would seem that a Thomist could not legitimately adopt a consistently hostile and polemical attitude towards modern philosophy. If one adopts the Bonaventurian position and maintains that a metaphysician cannot attain truth unless he philosophises in the light of faith (though without, of course, basing his philosophical proofs on theological premisses), one would only expect that a philosopher who rejected the supernatural or who confined religion within the bounds of reason alone, should go sadly astray; but if one is prepared to admit the possibility of even a pagan philosopher elaborating a more or less satisfactory metaphysic, it is unreasonable to suppose that in several centuries of intensive human thought, no truth has come to light. It would seem that a Thomist should expect to find fresh intellectual illumination in the pages of the modern philosophers and that he should approach them with an initial sympathy and expectancy rather than with an *a priori* suspicion, reserve and even hostility.

On the other hand, though St. Thomas's attitude towards the pagan philosophers, and towards Aristotle in particular, differed from that of St. Bonaventure, it is not right to exaggerate their difference of outlook. As has already been mentioned, St. Thomas gives reasons why it is fitting that even those truths about God which can be discovered by reason should be proposed for men's belief. Some of the reasons he gives are not indeed relevant to the particular point I am discussing. For example, it is perfectly true that many people are so occupied with earning their daily bread that they have not the time to give to metaphysical reflection, even when they have the capacity for such reflection, so that it is desirable that those metaphysical truths which are of importance for them in their lives should be proposed for their belief: otherwise they will never know them at all,[15] just as most of us would have neither the time nor the energy to discover America for ourselves, did we not already accept the fact that it exists on the testimony of others; but it does not necessarily follow that those who have the time and ability for metaphysical reflection will probably draw wrong conclusions, except in so far as metaphysical thinking is difficult and requires prolonged attention and concentration, whereas 'certain people', as St. Thomas remarks, are lazy. However, there is this further point to be borne in mind,[16] that on account of the weakness of our intellect in judging and on account of the intrusion of the imagination falsity is generally (*plerumque*) mixed with truth in the human mind's conclusions. Among the conclusions which are truly demonstrated there is sometimes (*aliquando*) included a false conclusion which has not been demonstrated but is asserted on the strength of a probable or sophistical reasoning passing under the name of demonstration. The practical result will be that even certain and sure conclusions will not be whole-heartedly accepted by many people, particularly when they see philosophers teaching different doctrines while they themselves are unable to distinguish a doctrine which has been truly demonstrated from one which rests on a merely probable or sophistical argument. Similarly, in the *Summa Theologica*, St. Thomas observes that the truth about God is arrived at by the human reason only by a few men and after a long time and 'with the admixture of many errors'.[17] When the Saint says that it is desirable that even those truths about God which are rationally demonstrable should be proposed as objects of belief, to be accepted on authority, he emphasises indeed the practical requirements of the many rather than the speculative insufficiency of metaphysics as such, but he does admit that error is frequently mixed with the truth, either because of over-hastiness in jumping to conclusions or because of the influence of passion and emotion or of imagination. Possibly he did not himself apply this idea with perfect consistency in regard to Aristotle and was too ready to interpret Aristotle in the sense which was most compatible with Christian doctrine, but the fact remains that he acknowledges theoretically the weakness of the human intellect in its present condition, though not its radical perversion. Accordingly, though he differs from St. Bonaventure in that he admits the abstract possibility, and indeed, in Aristotle's case, the concrete fact, of a 'satisfactory' metaphysic being elaborated by a pagan philosopher and also refuses to allow that its incompleteness vitiates a metaphysical system, he also admits it is likely that any independent metaphysical system will contain errors.

Perhaps it is not fanciful to suggest that the two men's abstract opinions were largely settled by their attitude towards Aristotle. It might, of course, be retorted that this is to put the cart before the horse, but it will appear more reasonable if one considers the actual circumstances in which they lived and wrote. For the first time Latin Christendom was becoming acquainted with a great philosophical system which owed nothing to Christianity and which was represented by its fervent adherents, such as Averroes, as being the last word in human wisdom. The greatness of Aristotle, the depth and comprehensiveness of his system, was a factor which could not be ignored by any Christian philosopher of the thirteenth century; but it could be met and treated in more than one way. On the one hand, as expounded by Averroes, Aristotelianism conflicted on several very important points with Christian doctrine, and it was possible to adopt a hostile and unreceptive attitude towards the Aristotelian metaphysic on this count. If, however, one adopted this course, as St. Bonaventure did, one had to say either that Aristotle's system affirmed philosophical truth but that what was true in philosophy might not be true in theology, since God could override the demands of natural logic, or else that Aristotle went wrong in his metaphysics. St. Bonaventure adopted the second course. But why, in Bonaventure's view, did Aristotle go wrong, the greatest systematiser of the ancient world? Obviously because any independent philosophy is bound to go wrong on important points simply because it is independent: it is only in the light of the Christian faith that one can elaborate anything like a complete and satisfactory philosophical system, since it is only in the light of the Christian faith that the philosopher will be enabled to leave his philosophy open to revelation: if he has not that light, he will round it off and complete it, and if he rounds it off and completes it, it will be thereby vitiated in part at least, especially in regard to those parts, the most important parts, which deal with God and the end of man. On the other hand, if one saw in the Aristotelian system a magnificent instrument for the expression of truth and for the welding together of the divine truths of theology and philosophy, one would have to admit the power of the pagan philosopher to attain metaphysical truth, though in view of the interpretation of Aristotle given by Averroes and others one would have also to allow for and explain the possibility of error even on the part of the Philosopher. This was the course adopted by St. Thomas.

6. When one looks back on the thirteenth century from a much later date, one does not always recognise the fact that St. Thomas was an innovator, that his adoption of Aristotelianism was bold and 'modern'. St. Thomas was faced with a system of growing influence and importance, which seemed in many respects to be incompatible with Christian tradition, but which naturally captivated the minds of many students and masters, particularly in the faculty of arts at Paris, precisely because of its majesty, apparent coherence and comprehensiveness. That Aquinas boldly grasped the bull by the horns and utilised Aristotelianism in the building up of his own system was very far from being an obscurantist action: it was, on the contrary, extremely 'modern' and was of the greatest importance for the future of Scholastic philosophy

and indeed for the history of philosophy in general. That some Scholastics in the later Middle Ages and at the time of the Renaissance brought Aristotelianism into discredit by their obscurantist adherence to all the Philosopher's *dicta*, even on scientific matters, does not concern St. Thomas: the plain fact is that they were not faithful to the spirit of St. Thomas. The Saint rendered, on any count, an incomparable service to Christian thought by utilising the instrument which presented itself, and he naturally interpreted Aristotle in the most favourable sense from the Christian standpoint, since it was essential to show, if he was to succeed in his undertaking, that Aristotle and Averroes did not stand or fall together. Moreover, it is not true to say that St. Thomas had no sense of accurate interpretation: one may not agree with all his interpretations of Aristotle, but there can be no doubt that, given the circumstances of the time and the paucity of relevant historical information at his disposal, he was one of the most conscientious and the finest commentators of Aristotle who have ever existed.

In conclusion, however, it must be emphasised that though St. Thomas adopted Aristotelianism as an instrument for the expression of his system, he was no blind worshipper of the Philosopher, who discarded Augustine in favour of the pagan thinker. In theology he naturally treads in the footsteps of Augustine, though his adoption of the Aristotelian philosophy as an instrument enabled him to systematise, define and argue logically from theological doctrines in a manner which was foreign to the attitude of Augustine: in philosophy, while there is a great deal which comes straight from Aristotle, he often interprets Aristotle in a manner consonant with Augustine or expresses Augustine in Aristotelian categories, though it might be truer to say that he does both at once. For instance, when treating of divine knowledge and providence, he interprets the Aristotelian doctrine of God in a sense which at least does not exclude God's knowledge of the world, and in treating of the divine ideas he observes that Aristotle censured Plato for making the ideas independent both of concrete things and of an intellect, with the tacit implication that Aristotle would not have censured Plato, had the latter placed the ideas in the mind of God. This is, of course, to interpret Aristotle *in meliorem partem* from the theological standpoint, and although the interpretation tends to bring Aristotle and Augustine closer together, it most probably does not represent Aristotle's actual theory of the divine knowledge. However, of St. Thomas's relation to Aristotle I shall speak later.

Chapter Thirty-three

ST. THOMAS AQUINAS—III:
PRINCIPLES OF CREATED BEING

Reasons for starting with corporeal being—Hylomorphism—Rejection of rationes seminales—*Rejection of plurality of substantial forms—Restriction of hylomorphic composition to corporeal substances—Potentiality and act—Essence and existence.*

1. In the *Summa Theologica*, which, as its name indicates, is a theological synopsis, the first philosophical problem of which St. Thomas treats is that of the existence of God, after which he proceeds to consider the Nature of God and then the divine Persons, passing subsequently to creation. Similarly, in the *Summa contra Gentiles*, which more nearly resembles a philosophical treatise (though it cannot be called simply a philosophical treatise, since it also treats of such purely dogmatic themes as the Trinity and the Incarnation), St. Thomas also starts with the existence of God. It might seem, then, that it would be natural to begin the exposition of St. Thomas's philosophy with his proofs of God's existence; but apart from the fact (mentioned in an earlier chapter) that St. Thomas himself says that the part of philosophy which treats of God comes after the other branches of philosophy, the proofs themselves presuppose some fundamental concepts and principles, and St. Thomas had composed the *De ente et essentia*, for example, before he wrote either of the *Summae*. It would not in any case be natural, then, to start immediately with the proofs of God's existence, and M. Gilson himself, who insists that the natural way of expounding St. Thomas's philosophy is to expound it according

to the order adopted by the Saint in the *Summae,* actually begins by considering certain basic ideas and principles. On the other hand, one can scarcely discuss the whole general metaphysic of St. Thomas and all those ideas which are explicitly or implicitly presupposed by his natural theology: it is necessary to restrict the basis of one's discussion.

To a modern reader, familiar with the course and problems of modern philosophy, it might seem natural to begin with a discussion of St. Thomas's theory of knowledge and to raise the question whether or not the Saint provides an epistemological justification of the possibility of metaphysical knowledge. But although St. Thomas certainly had a 'theory of knowledge' he did not live after Kant, and the problem of knowledge did not occupy that position in his philosophy which it has come to occupy in later times. It seems to me that the natural starting-point for an exposition of the Thomist philosophy is the consideration of corporeal substances. After all, St. Thomas expressly teaches that the immediate and proper object of the human intellect in this life is the essence of material things. The fundamental notions and principles which are presupposed by St. Thomas's natural theology are not, according to him, innate, but are apprehended through reflection on and abstraction from our experience of concrete objects, and it seems, therefore, only reasonable to develop those fundamental notions and principles first of all through a consideration of material substances. St. Thomas's proofs of God's existence are *a posteriori;* they proceed from creatures to God, and it is the creature's nature, the lack of self-sufficiency on the part of the immediate objects of experience, which reveals the existence of God. Moreover, we can, by the natural light of reason, attain only that knowledge of God which can be attained by reflection on creatures and their relation to Him. On this count too it would seem only 'natural' to begin the exposition of the Thomist philosophy with a consideration of those concrete objects of experience by reflection on which we arrive at those fundamental principles which lead us on to develop the proofs of God's existence.

2. In regard to corporeal substances St. Thomas adopts from the very outset the common-sense standpoint, according to which there are a multiplicity of substances. The human mind comes to know in dependence on sense-experience, and

the first concrete objects the mind knows are material objects into relation with which it enters through the senses. Reflection on these objects, however, at once leads the mind to form a distinction, or rather to discover a distinction, in the objects themselves. If I look out of my window in the spring I see the beech-tree with its young and tender green leaves, while in the autumn I see that the leaves have changed colour, though the same beech-tree stands out there in the park. The beech is substantially the same, a beech-tree, in spring and autumn, but the colour of its leaves is not the same: the colour changes without the beech-tree changing substantially. Similarly, if I go to the plantation, one year I see the larches as small trees, newly planted; later on I see them as bigger trees: their size has changed but they are still larches. The cows in the field I see now in this place, now in that, now in one posture, now in another, standing up or lying down, now doing one thing, now another, eating the grass or chewing the cud or sleeping, now undergoing one thing, now another, being milked or being rained on or being driven along, but all the time they are the same cows. Reflection thus leads the mind to distinguish between substance and accident, and between the different kinds of accident, and St. Thomas accepts from Aristotle the doctrine of the ten categories, substance and the nine categories of accident.

So far reflection has led us only to the idea of accidental change and the notion of the categories: but further reflection will introduce the mind to a profounder level of the constitution of material being. When the cow eats grass, the grass no longer remains what it was in the field, but becomes something else through assimilation, while on the other hand it does not simply cease to be, but something remains in the process of change. The change is substantial, since the grass itself is changed, not merely its colour or size, and the analysis of substantial change leads the mind to discern two elements, one element which is common to the grass and to the flesh which the grass becomes, another element which confers on that something its determination, its substantial character, making it to be first grass, then cow-flesh. Moreover, ultimately we can conceive any material substance changing into any other, not necessarily directly or immediately, of course, but at least indirectly and mediately, after a series of changes. We come thus to the conception on the one hand of an underlying substrate of change which, *when considered in itself,*

cannot be called by the name of any definite substance, and
on the other hand of a determining or characterising element.
The first element is 'prime matter', the indeterminate substrate of substantial change, the second element is the substantial form, which makes the substance what it is, places
it in its specific class and so determines it as grass, cow, oxy-
gen, hydrogen, or whatever it may be. Every material substance is composed in this way of matter and form.

St. Thomas thus accepts the Aristotelian doctrine of the
hylomorphic composition of material substances, defining
prime matter as pure potentiality and substantial form as the
first act of a physical body, 'first act' meaning the principle
which places the body in its specific class and determines its
essence. Prime matter is in potentiality to all forms which
can be the forms of bodies, but considered in itself it is
without any form, pure potentiality: it is, as Aristotle said,
*nec quid nec quantum nec quale nec aliud quidquam eorum
quibus determinatur ens.*[1] For this reason, however, it cannot
exist by itself, for to speak of a being actually existing without act or form would be contradictory: it did not, then,
precede form temporally, but was created together with
form.[2] St. Thomas is thus quite clear on the fact that only
concrete substances, individual compositions of matter and
form, actually exist in the material world. But though he is
at one with Aristotle in denying the separate existence of
universals (though we shall see presently that a reservation
must be made in regard to this statement), he also follows
Aristotle in asserting that the form needs to be individuated.
The form is the universal element, being that which places
an object in its class, in its species, making it to be horse or
elm or iron: it needs, then, to be individuated, in order that
it should become the form of this particular substance. What
is the principle of individuation? It can only be matter. But
matter is of itself pure potentiality: it has not those determinations which are necessary in order that it should individ-
uate form. The accidental characteristics of quantity and so
on are logically posterior to the hylomorphic composition of
the substance. St. Thomas was, therefore, compelled to say
that the principle of individuation is *materia signata quan-
titate*, in the sense of matter having an exigency for the
quantitative determination which it receives from union with
form. This is a difficult notion to understand, since although
matter, and not form, is the foundation of quantitative mul-

tiplication, matter considered in itself is without quantitative determination: the notion is in fact a relic of the Platonic element in Aristotle's thought. Aristotle rejected and attacked the Platonic theory of forms, but his Platonic training influenced him to the extent of his being led to say that form, being of itself universal, requires individuation, and St. Thomas followed him in this. Of course, St. Thomas did not think of forms first existing separately and then being individuated, for the forms of sensible objects do not exist in a state of temporal priority to the composite substances; but the idea of individuation is certainly due originally to the Platonic way of thinking and speaking of forms: Aristotle substituted the notion of the immanent substantial form for that of the 'transcendent' exemplar form, but it would not become an historian to turn a blind eye to the Platonic legacy in Aristotle's thought and consequently in that of St. Thomas.

3. As a logical consequence of the doctrine that prime matter as such is pure potentiality, St. Thomas rejected the Augustinian theory of *rationes seminales:*[3] to admit this theory would be to attribute act in some way to what is in itself without act.[4] Nonspiritual forms are educed out of the potentiality of matter under the action of the efficient agent, but they are not previously in prime matter as inchoate forms. The agent does not, of course, work on prime matter as such, since this latter cannot exist by itself; but he or it so modifies or changes the dispositions of a given corporeal substance that it develops an exigency for a new form, which is educed out of the potentiality of matter. Change thus presupposes, for Aquinas as for Aristotle, a 'privation' or an exigency for a new form which the substance has not yet got but 'demands' to have in virtue of the modifications produced in it by the agent. Water, for example, is in a state of potentiality to becoming steam, but it will not become steam until it has been heated to a certain point by an external agent, at which point it develops an exigency for the form of steam, which does not come from outside, but is educed out of the potentiality of matter.

4. Just as St. Thomas rejected the older theory of *rationes seminales,* so he rejected the theory of the plurality of substantial forms in the composite substance, affirming the unicity of the substantial form in each substance. In his Commentary on the *Sentences* St. Thomas seems indeed to accept the *forma corporeitatis* as the first substantial form in the

corporeal substance;[5] but even if he accepted it at first, he certainly rejected it afterwards. In the *Contra Gentiles*[6] he argues that if the first form constituted the substance as substance, the subsequent forms would arise in something which was already *hoc aliquid in actu*, something actually subsisting, and so could be no more than accidental forms. Similarly he argues against the theory of Avicebron[7] by pointing out that only the first form can be the substantial form, since it would confer the character of substance, with the result that other subsequent forms, arising in an already constituted substance, would be accidental. (The necessary implication is, of course, that the substantial form directly informs prime matter.) This view aroused much opposition, being stigmatised as a dangerous innovation, as we shall see later when dealing with the controversies in which St. Thomas's Aristotelianism involved him.

5. The hylomorphic composition which obtains in material substances was restricted by St. Thomas to the corporeal world: he would not extend it, as St. Bonaventure did, to the incorporeal creation, to angels. That angels exist, St. Thomas considered to be rationally provable, quite apart from revelation, for their existence is demanded by the hierarchic character of the scale of being. We can discern the ascending orders or ranks of forms from the forms of inorganic substances, through vegetative forms, the irrational sensitive forms of animals, the rational soul of man, to the infinite and pure Act, God; but there is a gap in the hierarchy. The rational soul of man is created, finite and embodied, while God is uncreated, infinite and pure spirit: it is only reasonable, then, to suppose that between the human soul and God there are finite and created spiritual forms which are without body. At the summit of the scale is the absolute simplicity of God: at the summit of the corporeal world is the human being, partly spiritual and partly corporeal: there must, therefore, exist between God and man beings which are wholly spiritual and yet which do not possess the absolute simplicity of the Godhead.[8]

This line of argument was not new: it had been employed in Greek philosophy, by Poseidonius, for example. St. Thomas was also influenced by the Aristotelian doctrine of separate Intelligences connected with the motion of the spheres, this astronomical view reappearing in the philosophy of Avicenna, with which St. Thomas was familiar; but the argument which weighed most with him was that drawn from the exigencies of the hierarchy of being. As he distinguished the different grades of forms in general, so he distinguished the different 'choirs' of angels, according to the object of their knowledge. Those who apprehend most clearly the goodness of God in itself and are inflamed with love thereat are the Seraphim, the highest 'choir', while those who are concerned with the providence of God in regard to particular creatures, for example, in regard to particular men, are the angels in the narrower sense of the word, the lowest choir. The choir which is concerned with, *inter alia*, the movement of the heavenly bodies (which are universal causes affecting this world) is that of the Virtues. Thus St. Thomas did not postulate the existence of angels primarily in order to account for the movement of the spheres.

Angels exist therefore; but it remains to be asked if they are hylomorphically composed. St. Thomas affirmed that they are not so composed. He argued that the angels must be purely immaterial, since they are intelligences which have as their correlative object immaterial objects, and also that their very place in the hierarchy of being demands their complete immateriality.[9] Moreover, as St. Thomas places in matter an exigency for quantity (which possibly does not altogether square with its character of pure potentiality), he could not in any case attribute hylomorphic composition to the angels. St. Bonaventure, for example, had argued that angels must be hylomorphically composed, since otherwise they would be pure act and God alone is pure act; but St. Thomas countered this argument by affirming that the distinction between essence and existence in the angels is sufficient to safeguard their contingency and their radical distinction from God.[10] To this distinction I shall return shortly.

A consequence of the denial of the hylomorphic composition of the angels is the denial of the multiplicity of angels within one species, since matter is the principle of individuation and there is no matter in the angels. Each angel is pure form: each angel, then, must exhaust the capacity of its species and be its own species. The choirs of angels are not, then, so many species of angels; they consist of angelic hierarchies distinguished not specifically but according to function. There are as many species as there are angels. It is of interest to remember that Aristotle, when asserting in the *Metaphysics* a plurality of movers, of separated intelligences, raised the question how this could be possible if matter is the principle of individuation, though he did not answer the question. While St. Bonaventure, admitting the hylomorphic composition of angels, could and did admit their multiplicity within the species, St. Thomas, holding on the one hand that matter is the principle of individuation and denying its presence in the angels on the other hand, was forced to deny their multiplicity within the species. For St. Thomas, then, the intelligences really became separate universals, though not, of course, in the sense of hypostatised concepts. It was one of the discoveries of Aristotle that a separate form must be intelligent, though he failed to see the historic connection between his theory of separate intelligences and the Platonic theory of separate forms.

6. The establishment of the hylomorphic composition of material substances reveals at once the essential mutability of those substances. Change is not, of course, a haphazard affair, but proceeds according to a certain rhythm (one cannot assume that a given substance can become immediately any other substance one likes, while change is also guided and influenced by the general causes, such as the heavenly bodies); yet substantial change cannot take place except in bodies, and it is only matter, the substrate of change, which makes it possible. On the principle which St. Thomas adopted from Aristotle that what is changed or moved is changed or moved 'by another', *ab alio*, one might argue at once from the changes in the corporeal world to the existence of an unmoved mover, with the aid of the principle that an infinite regress in the order of dependence is impossible; but before going on to prove the existence of God from nature, one must first penetrate more deeply into the constitution of finite being.

Hylomorphic composition is confined by St. Thomas to the corporeal world; but there is a more fundamental distinction, of which the distinction between form and matter is but one example. Prime matter, as we have seen, is pure potentiality, while form is act, so that the distinction between matter and form is a distinction between potency and act, but this latter distinction is of wider application than the former. In the angels there is no matter, but there is none the less potentiality. (St. Bonaventure argued that because matter is potentiality, therefore it can be in angels. He was thus forced to admit the *forma corporeitatis*, in order to distinguish corporeal matter from matter in the general sense. St. Thomas, on the other hand, as he made matter pure potentiality and yet denied its presence in the angels, was forced to attribute to matter an exigency for quantity, which comes to it through form. Obviously there are difficulties in both views.) The angels can change by performing acts of intellect and will, even though they cannot change substantially: there is, therefore, some potentiality in the angels. The distinction between potentiality and act runs, therefore, through the whole of creation, whereas the distinction between form and matter is found only in the corporeal creation. Thus, on the principle that the reduction of potentiality to act requires a principle which is itself act, we should be in a position to argue from the fundamental distinction which obtains in all creation to the existence of pure Act, God; but first of all we must consider the basis of potentiality in the angels. In passing, one can notice that the distinction of potency and act is discussed by Aristotle in the *Metaphysics*.

7. We have seen that hylomorphic composition was restricted by St. Thomas to corporeal substance; but there is a profounder composition which affects every finite being. Finite being is being because it exists, because it has existence: the substance is that which is or has being, and 'existence is that in virtue of which a substance is called a being'.[11] The essence of a corporeal being is the substance composed of matter and form, while the essence of an immaterial finite being is form alone; but that by which a material substance or an immaterial substance is a real being (*ens*) is existence (*esse*), existence standing to the essence as act to potentiality. Composition of act and potentiality is found, therefore, in every finite being and not simply in corporeal being. No finite being exists necessarily; it has or possesses existence which is distinct from essence as act is distinct from potentiality. The form determines or completes in the sphere of essence, but that which actualises the essence is existence. 'In intellectual substances which are not composed of matter and form (in them the form is a subsistent substance), the form is that which is; but existence is the act by which the form is; and on that account there is in them only one composition of act and potentiality, namely composition of substance and existence. . . . In substances composed of matter and form, however, there is a double composition of act and potentiality, the first a composition in the substance itself, which is

composed of matter and form, the second a composition of the substance itself, which is already composite, with existence. This second composition can also be called a composition of the *quod est* and *esse*, or of the *quod est* and the *quo est*.'[12] Existence, then, is neither matter nor form; it is neither an essence nor part of an essence; it is the act by which the essence is or has being. '*Esse* denotes a certain act; for a thing is not said to be (*esse*) by the fact that it is in potentiality, but by the fact that it is in act.'[13] As neither matter nor form, it can be neither a substantial nor an accidental form; it does not belong to the sphere of essence, but is that by which forms are.

Controversy has raged in the Schools round the question whether St. Thomas considered the distinction between essence and existence to be a real distinction or a conceptual distinction. Obviously the answer to this question depends largely on the meaning attached to the phrase 'real distinction'. If by real distinction were meant a distinction between two things which could be separated from one another, then certainly St. Thomas did not hold that there is a real distinction between essence and existence, which are not two separable physical objects. Giles of Rome practically held this view, making the distinction a physical distinction; but for St. Thomas the distinction was metaphysical, essence and existence being the two constitutive metaphysical principles of every finite being. If, however, by real distinction is meant a distinction which is independent of the mind, which is objective, it seems to me not only that St. Thomas maintained such a distinction as obtaining between essence and existence, but that it is essential to his system and that he attached great importance to it. St. Thomas speaks of *esse* as *adveniens extra*, in the sense that it comes from God, the cause of existence; it is act, distinct from the potentiality which it actualises. In God alone, insists St. Thomas, are essence and existence identical: God exists necessarily because His essence is existence: all other things receive or 'participate in' existence, and that which receives must be distinct from that which is received.[14] The fact that St. Thomas argues that that whose existence is other than its essence must have received its existence from another, and that it is true of God alone that His existence is not different from or other than His essence, seems to me to make it perfectly clear that he regarded the distinction between essence and existence as objective and independent of the mind. The 'third way' of proving the existence of God appears to presuppose the real distinction between essence and existence in finite things.

Existence determines essence in the sense that it is act and through it the essence has being; but on the other hand existence, as act, is determined by essence, as potentiality, to be the existence of this or that kind of essence.[15] Yet we must not imagine that essence existed before receiving existence (which would be a contradiction in terms) or that there is a kind of neutral existence which is not the existence of any thing in particular until it is united with essence: the two principles are not two physical things united together, but they are two constitutive principles which are concreated as principles of a particular being. There is no essence without existence and no existence without essence; the two are created together, and if its existence ceases, the concrete essence ceases to be. Existence, then, is not something accidental to the finite being: it is that by which the finite being is a being. If we rely on the imagination, we shall think of essence and existence as two things, two beings; but a great deal of the difficulty in understanding St. Thomas's doctrine on the subject comes from employing the imagination and supposing that if he maintained the real distinction, he must have understood it in the exaggerated and misleading fashion of Giles of Rome.

The Moslem philosophers had already discussed the relation of existence to essence. Alfarabi, for example, had observed that analysis of the essence of a finite object will not reveal its existence. If it did, then it would be sufficient to know what human nature is, in order to know that man exists, which is not the case. Essence and existence are, therefore, distinct, and Alfarabi drew the somewhat unfortunate conclusion that existence is an accident of the essence. Avicenna followed Alfarabi in this matter. Although St. Thomas certainly did not regard existence as an 'accident', in the *De ente et essentia*[16] he follows Alfarabi and Avicenna in their way of approaching the distinction. Every thing which does not belong to the concept of the essence comes to it from without (*adveniens extra*) and forms a composition with it. No essence can be conceived without that which forms part of the essence; but every finite essence can be conceived without existence being included in the essence. I can conceive 'man' or 'phoenix' and yet not know if they exist in nature.

It would, however, be a mistake to interpret St. Thomas as though he maintained that the essence, prior to the reception of existence, was something on its own, so to speak, with a diminutive existence proper to itself: it exists only through existence, and created existence is always the existence of this or that kind of essence. Created existence and essence arise together, and although the two constitutive principles are objectively distinct, existence is the more fundamental. Since created existence is the act of a potentiality, the latter has no actuality apart from existence, which is 'among all things the most perfect' and 'the perfection of all perfections'.[17]

St. Thomas thus discovers in the heart of all finite being a certain instability, a contingency or non-necessity, which immediately points to the existence of a Being which is the source of finite existence, the author of the composition between essence and existence, and which cannot be itself composed of essence and existence but must have existence as its very essence, existing necessarily. It would indeed be absurd and most unjust to accuse Francis Suarez (1548–1617) and other Scholastics who denied the 'real distinction' of denying the contingent character of finite being (Suarez denied a real distinction between essence and existence and maintained that the finite object is limited because *ab alio*); but I do not personally feel any doubt that St. Thomas himself maintained the doctrine of the real distinction, provided that the real distinction is not interpreted as Giles of Rome interpreted it. For St. Thomas, existence is not a state of the essence, but rather that which places the essence in a state of actuality.

It may be objected that I have evaded the real point at issue, namely the precise way in which the distinction between essence and existence is objective and independent of the mind. But St. Thomas did not state his doctrine in such a manner that no controversy about its meaning is possible. Nevertheless it seems clear to me that St. Thomas held that the distinction between essence and existence is an objective distinction between two metaphysical principles which constitute the whole being of the created finite thing, one of these principles, namely existence, standing to the other, namely essence, as act to potency. And I do not see how St. Thomas could have attributed that importance to the distinction which he did attribute to it, unless he thought that it was a 'real' distinction.

Chapter Thirty-four

ST. THOMAS AQUINAS–IV:
PROOFS OF GOD'S EXISTENCE

Need of proof—St. Anselm's argument—Possibility of proof—The first three proofs—The fourth proof—The proof from finality—The 'third way' fundamental.

1. Before actually developing his proofs of God's existence St. Thomas tried to show that the provision of such proofs is not a useless superfluity, since the idea of God's existence is not, properly speaking, an innate idea nor is 'God exists' a proposition the opposite of which is inconceivable and cannot be thought. To us indeed, living in a world where atheism is common, where powerful and influential philosophies eliminate or explain away the notion of God, where multitudes of men and women are educated without any belief in God, it seems only natural to think that God's existence requires proof. Kierkegaard and those philosophers and theologians who follow him may have rejected natural theology in the ordinary sense; but normally speaking we should not dream of asserting that God's existence is what St. Thomas calls a *per se notum*. St. Thomas, however, did not live in a world where theoretic atheism was common, and he felt himself compelled to deal not only with statements of certain early Christian writers which seemed to imply that knowledge of God is innate in man, but also with the famous argument of St. Anselm which purports to show that the non-existence of God is inconceivable. Thus in the *Summa Theologica*[1] he devotes an article to answering the question *utrum Deum esse sit per se notum*, and two chapters in the *Summa contra Gentiles*[2] to the consideration *de opinione dicentium quod*

Deum esse demonstrari non potest, quum sit per se notum.

St. John Damascene[3] asserts that the knowledge of God's existence is naturally innate in man; but St. Thomas explains that this natural knowledge of God is confused and vague and needs elucidation to be made explicit. Man has a natural desire of happiness (*beatitudo*), and a natural desire supposes a natural knowledge; but although true happiness is to be found only in God, it does not follow that every man has a natural knowledge of God as such: he has a vague idea of happiness since he desires it, but he may think that happiness consists in sensual pleasure or in the possession of wealth, and further reflection is required before he can realise that happiness is to be found only in God. In other words, even if the natural desire for happiness may form the basis for a proof of God's existence, a proof is none the less required. Again, in a sense it is *per se notum* that there is truth, since a man who asserts that there is no truth inevitably asserts that it is true that there is no truth, but it does not follow that the man knows that there is a primal or first Truth, a Source of truth, God: further reflection is necessary if he is to realise this. Once again, although it is true that without God we can know nothing, it does not follow that in knowing anything we have an actual knowledge of God, since God's influence, which enables us to know anything, is not the object of direct intuition but is known only by reflection.[4]

In general, says St. Thomas, we must make a distinction between what is *per se notum secundum se* and what is *per se notum quoad nos*. A proposition is said to be *per se nota secundum se* when the predicate is included in the subject, as in the proposition that man is an animal, since man is precisely a rational animal. The proposition that God exists is thus a proposition *per se nota secundum se*, since God's essence is His existence and one cannot know God's nature, what God is, without knowing God's existence, that He is; but a man has no *a priori* knowledge of God's nature and only arrives at knowledge of the fact that God's essence is His existence after he has come to know God's existence, so that even though the proposition that God exists is *per se nota secundum se*, it is not *per se nota quoad nos*.

2. In regard to the 'ontological' or *a priori* proof of God's existence given by St. Anselm, St. Thomas answers first of all that not everyone understands by God 'that than which no greater can be thought'. Possibly this observation, though

doubtless true, is not altogether relevant, except in so far as St. Anselm considered that everyone understands by 'God' that Being whose existence he intended to prove, namely the supremely perfect Being. It must not be forgotten that Anselm reckoned his argument to be an argument or proof, not the statement of an immediate intuition of God. He then argues, both in the *Summa contra Gentiles* and in the *Summa Theologica*, that the argument of St. Anselm involves an illicit process or transition from the ideal to the real order. Granted that God is conceived as the Being than which no greater can be thought, it does not follow necessarily that such a Being exists, apart from its being conceived, that is, outside the mind. This, however, is not an adequate argument, when taken by itself at least, to disprove the Anselmian reasoning, since it neglects the peculiar character of God, of the Being than which no greater can be thought. Such a Being is its own existence and if it is possible for such a Being to exist, it must exist. The Being than which no greater can be thought is the Being which exists necessarily, it is the necessary Being, and it would be absurd to speak of a merely possible necessary Being. But St. Thomas adds, as we have seen, that the intellect has no *a priori* knowledge of God's nature. In other words, owing to the weakness of the human intellect we cannot discern *a priori* the positive possibility of the supremely perfect Being, the Being the essence of which is existence, and we come to a knowledge of the fact that such a Being exists not through an analysis or consideration of the idea of such a Being, but through arguments from its effects, *a posteriori*.

3. If God's existence cannot be proved *a priori*, through the idea of God, through His essence, it remains that it must be proved *a posteriori*, through an examination of God's effects. It may be objected that this is impossible since the effects of God are finite while God is infinite, so that there is no proportion between the effects and the Cause and the conclusion of the reasoning process will contain infinitely more than the premisses. The reasoning starts with sensible objects and should, therefore, end with a sensible object, whereas in the proofs of God's existence it proceeds to an Object infinitely transcending all sensible objects.

St. Thomas does not deal with this objection at any length, and it would be an absurd anachronism to expect him to discuss and answer the Kantian Critique of metaphysics in advance; but he points out that though from a consideration of effects which are disproportionate to the cause we cannot obtain a perfect knowledge of the cause, we can come to know that the cause exists. We can argue from an effect to the existence of a cause, and if the effect is of such a kind that it can proceed only from a certain kind of cause, we can legitimately argue to the existence of a cause of that kind. (The use of the word 'effect' must not be taken as begging the question, as a *petitio principii*: St. Thomas argues from certain facts concerning the world and argues that these facts require a sufficient ontological explanation. It is true, of course, that he presupposes that the principle of causality is not purely subjective or applicable only within the sphere of 'phenomena' in the Kantian sense; but he is perfectly well aware that it has to be shown that sensible objects are effects, in the sense that they do not contain in themselves their own sufficient ontological explanation.)

A modern Thomist, wishing to expound and defend the natural theology of the Saint in the light of post-mediaeval philosophic thought, would rightly be expected to say something in justification of the speculative reason, of metaphysics. Even if he considered that the onus of proof falls primarily on the opponent of metaphysics, he could not neglect the fact that the legitimacy and even the significance of metaphysical arguments and conclusions have been challenged, and he would be bound to meet this challenge. I cannot see, however, how an historian of mediaeval philosophy in general can justly be expected to treat St. Thomas as though he were a contemporary and fully aware not only of the Kantian criticism of the speculative reason, but also of the attitude towards metaphysics adopted by the logical positivists. Nevertheless, it is true that the Thomist theory of knowledge itself provides, apparently at least, a strong objection against natural theology. According to St. Thomas the proper object of the human intellect is the *quidditas* or essence of the material object: the intellect starts from the sensible objects, knows in dependence on the phantasm and is proportioned, in virtue of its embodied state, to sensible objects. St. Thomas did not admit innate ideas nor did he have recourse to any intuitive knowledge of God, and if one applies strictly the Aristotelian principle that there is nothing in the intellect which was not before in the senses (*Nihil in intellectu quod non prius fuerit in sensu*), it might well appear that the human intellect is confined to knowledge of corporeal objects and cannot, owing to its nature or at least its present state, transcend them. As this objection arises out of the doctrine of Thomas himself, it is relevant to inquire if the Saint attempted to meet it and, if so, how he met it. With the Thomist theory of human knowledge I shall deal later;[5] but I shall give immediately a brief statement of what appears to be St. Thomas's position on this point without development or references.

Objects, whether spiritual or corporeal, are knowable only in so far as they partake of being, are in act, and the intellect as such is the faculty of apprehending being. Considered simply in itself, therefore, the intellect has as its object all being; the primary object of intellect is being. The fact, however, that a particular kind of intellect, the human intellect, is embodied and is dependent on sense for its operation, means that it must start from the things of sense and that, naturally speaking, it can come to know an object which transcends the things of sense (consideration of self-knowledge is here omitted) only in so far as sensible objects bear a relation to that object and manifest it. Owing to the fact that the human intellect is embodied its natural and proper object, proportionate to its present state, is the corporeal object; but this does not destroy the primary orientation of the intellect to being in general, and if corporeal objects bear a discernible relation to an object which transcends them, the intellect can know that such an object exists. Moreover, in so far as material objects reveal the character of the Transcendent, the intellect can attain some knowledge of its nature; but such a knowledge cannot be adequate or perfect, since sense-objects cannot reveal adequately or perfectly the nature of the Transcendent. Of our natural knowledge of God's nature I shall speak later:[6] let it suffice to point out here that when St. Thomas says that the corporeal object is the natural object of the human intellect, he means that the human intellect in its present state is orientated towards the essence of the corporeal object, but that just as the embodied condition of the human intellect does not destroy its primary character as intellect, so its orientation, in virtue of its embodied state, towards the corporeal object does not destroy its primary orientation towards being in general. It can therefore attain to some natural knowledge of God, in so far as corporeal objects are related to Him and reveal Him; but this knowledge is necessarily imperfect and inadequate and cannot be intuitive in character.

4. The first of the five proofs of God's existence given by St. Thomas is that from motion, which is found in Aristotle[7] and was utilised by Maimonides and St. Albert. We know through sense-perception that some things in the world are moved, that motion is a fact. Motion is here understood in the wide Aristotelian sense of reduction of potency to act, and St. Thomas, following Aristotle, argues that a thing cannot be reduced from potency to act except by something which is already in act. In this sense 'every thing which is moved is moved by another'. If that other is itself moved, it must be moved by yet another agent. As an infinite series is impossible, we come in the end to an unmoved mover, a first mover, 'and all understand that this is God'.[8] This argument St. Thomas calls the *manifestior via*.[9] In the *Summa contra Gentiles*[10] he develops it at considerable length.

The second proof, which is suggested by the second book of Aristotle's *Metaphysics*[11] and which was used by Avicenna, Alan of Lille and St. Albert, also starts from the sensible world, but this time from the order or series of efficient causes. Nothing can be the cause of itself, for in order to be this, it would have to exist before itself. On the other hand, it is impossible to proceed to infinity in the series of efficient causes: therefore there must be a first efficient cause, 'which all men call God'.

The third proof, which Maimonides took over from Avicenna and developed, starts from the fact that some beings come into existence and perish, which shows that they can not be and can be, that they are contingent and not necessary, since if they were necessary they would always have existed and would neither come into being nor pass away. St. Thomas then argues that there must exist a necessary being, which is the reason why contingent beings come into existence. If there were no necessary being, nothing at all would exist.

There are several remarks which must be made, though very briefly, concerning these three proofs. First of all, when St. Thomas says that an infinite series is impossible (and this principle is utilised in all three proofs), he is not thinking of a series stretching back in time, of a 'horizontal' series, so to speak. He is not saying, for example that because the child owes its life to its parents and its parents owe their lives to their parents and so on, there must have been an original pair, who had no parents but were directly created by God. St. Thomas did not believe that it can be proved philosophically that the world was not created from eternity: he admits the abstract possibility of the world's creation from eternity and this cannot be admitted without the possibility of a beginningless series being admitted at the same time. What he denies is the possibility of an infinite series in the order of actually depending causes, of an infinite 'vertical' series. Suppose that the world had actually been created from eternity. There would be an infinite horizontal or historic series, but the whole series would consist of contingent beings, for the fact of its being without beginning does not make it necessary. The whole series, therefore, must depend on something outside the series. But if you ascend upwards, without ever coming to a stop, you have no explanation of the existence of the series: one must conclude with the existence of a being which is not itself dependent.

Secondly, consideration of the foregoing remarks will show that the so-called mathematical infinite series has nothing to do with the Thomist proofs. It is not the possibility of an infinite series as such which St. Thomas denies, but the possibility of an infinite series in the ontological order of dependence. In other words, he denies that the movement and contingency of the experienced world can be without any ultimate and adequate ontological explanation.

Thirdly, it might seem to be rather cavalier behaviour on St. Thomas's part to assume that the unmoved mover or the first cause or the necessary being is what we call God. Obviously if anything exists at all, there must be a necessary Being: thought must arrive at this conclusion, unless metaphysics is rejected altogether; but it is not so obvious that the necessary being must be the personal Being whom we call God. That a purely philosophical argument does not bring us to the full revealed notion of God needs no elaboration; but, even apart from the full notion of God as revealed by Christ and preached by the Church, does a purely philosophical argument give us a personal Being at all? Did St. Thomas's belief in God lead him perhaps to find more in the conclusion of the argument than was actually there? Because he was looking for arguments to prove the existence of the God in whom he believed, was he not perhaps over-hasty in identifying the first mover, the first cause and the necessary being

with the God of Christianity and religious experience, the
personal Being to whom man can pray? I think that we must
admit that the actual phrases which St. Thomas appends to
the proofs given in the *Summa Theologica* (*et hoc omnes
intelligunt Deum, causam efficientem primam quam omnes
Deum nominant, quod omnes dicunt Deum*) constitute, if
considered in isolation, an over-hasty conclusion; but, apart
from the fact that the *Summa Theologica* is a summary (and
mainly) theological text-book, these phrases should not be
taken in isolation. For example, the actual summary proof
of the existence of a necessary being contains no explicit argument to show whether that being is material or immaterial,
so that the observation at the end of the proof that this being
is called by everyone God might seem to be without sufficient
warrant; but in the first article of the next question St.
Thomas asks if God is material, a body, and argues that He
is not. The phrases in the question should, therefore, be
understood as expressions of the fact that God is recognised
by all who believe in Him to be the first Cause and necessary
Being, not as an unjustifiable suppression of further argument. In any case the proofs are given by St. Thomas simply
in outline: it is not as though he had in mind the composition
of a treatise against professed atheists. If he had to deal with
Marxists, he would doubtless treat the proofs in a different,
or at least in a more elaborate and developed manner: as it
is, his main interest is to give a proof of the *praeambula
fidei*. Even in the *Summa contra Gentiles* the Saint was not
dealing primarily with atheists, but rather with the Moham-
medans, who had a firm belief in God.

5. The fourth proof is suggested by some observations in
Aristotle's *Metaphysics*[12] and is found substantially in St.
Augustine and St. Anselm. It starts from the degrees of perfection, of goodness, truth, etc., in the things of this world,
which permit of one making such comparative judgements as
'this is more beautiful than that', 'this is better than that'.
Assuming that such judgements have an objective foundation, St. Thomas argues that the degrees of perfection necessarily imply the existence of a best, a most true, etc., which
will be also the supreme being (*maxime ens*).

So far the argument leads only to a relatively best. If one
can establish that there actually are degrees of truth, goodness and being, a hierarchy of being, then there must be one
being or several beings which are comparatively or relatively

supreme. But this is not enough to prove the existence of God, and St. Thomas proceeds to argue that what is supreme in goodness, for example, must be the cause of goodness in all things. Further, inasmuch as goodness, truth and being are convertible, there must be a supreme Being which is the cause of being, goodness, truth, and so of all perfection in every other being; *et hoc dicimus Deum.*

As the term of the argument is a Being which transcends all sensible objects, the perfections in question can obviously be only those perfections which are capable of subsisting by themselves, pure perfections, which do not involve any necessary relation to extension or quantity. The argument is Platonic in origin and presupposes the idea of participation. Contingent beings do not possess their being of themselves, nor their goodness or ontological truth; they receive their perfections, share them. The ultimate cause of perfection must itself be perfect: it cannot receive its perfection from another, but must be its own perfection: it is self-existing being and perfection. The argument consists, then, in the application of principles already used in the foregoing proofs to pure perfections: it is not really a departure from the general spirit of the other proofs, in spite of its Platonic descent. One of the main difficulties about it, however, is, as already indicated, to show that there actually are objective degrees of being and perfection before one has shown that there actually exists a Being which is absolute and self-existing Perfection.

6. The fifth way is the teleological proof, for which Kant had a considerable respect on account of its antiquity, clarity and persuasiveness, though, in accordance with the principles of the *Kritik der reinen Vernunft*, he refused to recognise its demonstrative character.

St. Thomas argues that we behold inorganic objects operating for an end, and as this happens always or very frequently, it cannot proceed from chance, but must be the result of intention. But inorganic objects are without knowledge: they cannot, then, tend towards an end unless they are directed by someone who is intelligent and possessed of knowledge, as 'the arrow is directed by the archer'. Therefore there exists an intelligent Being, by whom all natural things are directed to an end; *et hoc dicimus Deum.* In the *Summa contra Gentiles* the Saint states the argument in a slightly different manner, arguing that when many things with differ-

ent and even contrary qualities co-operate towards the realisation of one order, this must proceed from an intelligent
Cause or Providence; *et hoc dicimus Deum*. If the proof as
given in the *Summa Theologica* emphasises the internal finality of the inorganic object, that given in the *Summa contra
Gentiles* emphasises rather the co-operation of many objects
in the realisation of the one world order or harmony. By itself
the proof leads to a Designer or Governor or Architect of the
universe, as Kant observed; further reasoning is required in
order to show that this Architect is not only a 'Demiurge', but
also Creator.

7. The proofs have been stated in more or less the same
bold and succinct way in which St. Thomas states them.
With the exception of the first proof, which is elaborated at
some length in the *Summa contra Gentiles*, the proofs are
given only in very bare outline, both in the *Summa Theologica* and in the *Summa contra Gentiles*. No mention has
been made, however, of Aquinas's (to our view) somewhat
unfortunate physical illustrations, as when he says that fire is
the cause of all hot things, since these illustrations are really
irrelevant to the validity or invalidity of the proofs as such.
The modern disciple of St. Thomas naturally has not only
to develop the proofs in far greater detail and to consider
difficulties and objections which could hardly have occurred
to St. Thomas, but also to justify the very principles on which
the general line of proof rests. Thus, in regard to the fifth
proof given by St. Thomas, the modern Thomist must take
some account of recent theories which profess to render intelligible the genesis of the order and finality in the universe
without recourse to the hypothesis of any spiritual agent distinct from the universe, while in regard to all the proofs he
has not only, in face of the Kantian Critique, to justify the
line of argument on which they rest, but he has to show, as
against the logical positivists, that the word 'God' has some
significance. It is not, however, the task of the historian to
develop the proofs as they would have to be developed to-day,
nor is it his task to justify those proofs. The way in which St.
Thomas states the proofs may perhaps cause some dissatis-
faction in the reader; but it must be remembered that the
Saint was primarily a theologian and that, as already mentioned, he was concerned not so much to give an exhaustive
treatment of the proofs as to prove in a summary fashion the
praeambula fidei. He, therefore, makes use of traditional

proofs, which either had or seemed to have some support in Aristotle and which had been employed by some of his predecessors.

St. Thomas gives five proofs, and among these five proofs he gives a certain preference to the first, to the extent at least of calling it the *via manifestior*. However, whatever we may think of this assertion, the fundamental proof is really the third proof or 'way', that from contingency. In the first proof the argument from contingency is applied to the special fact of motion or change, in the second proof to the order of causality or causal production, in the fourth proof to degrees of perfection and in the fifth proof to finality, to the co-operation of inorganic objects in the attainment of cosmic order. The argument from contingency itself is based on the fact that everything must have its sufficient reason, the reason why it exists. Change or motion must have its sufficient reason in an unmoved mover, the series of secondary causes and effects in an uncaused cause, limited perfection in absolute perfection, and finality and order in nature in an Intelligence or Designer. The 'interiority' of the proofs of God's existence as given by St. Augustine or St. Bonaventure is absent from the five ways of St. Thomas; but one could, of course, apply the general principles to the self, if one so wished. As they stand, the five proofs of St. Thomas may be said to be an explicitation of the words of the *Book of Wisdom*[13] and of St. Paul in *Romans*[14] that God can be known from His works, as transcending His works.

Chapter Thirty-five

ST. THOMAS AQUINAS—V:
GOD'S NATURE

The negative way—The affirmative way—Analogy—Types of analogy—A difficulty—The divine ideas—No real distinction between the divine attributes—God as existence itself.

1. Once it has been established that the necessary Being exists, it would seem only natural to proceed to the investigation of God's nature. It is very unsatisfactory simply to know that a necessary Being exists, unless at the same time we can know what sort of a Being the necessary Being is. But a difficulty at once arises. We have in this life no intuition of the divine essence; we are dependent for our knowledge on sense-perception, and the ideas which we form are derived from our experience of creatures. Language too is formed to express these ideas and so refers primarily to our experience and would seem to have objective reference only within the sphere of our experience. How, then, can we come to know a Being which transcends sense-experience? How can we form ideas which express in any way the nature of a Being which transcends the range of our experience, the world of creatures? How can the words of any human language be at all applicable to the Divine Being?

St. Thomas was well aware of this difficulty, and indeed the whole tradition of Christian philosophy, which had undergone the influence of the writings of the Pseudo-Dionysius, himself dependent on neo-Platonism, would have helped, if help had been needed, to prevent him indulging in any over-confidence in the power of the human reason to penetrate the divine essence. Rationalism of the Hegelian type was quite foreign to his mind, and we find him saying that we cannot come to know of God *quid sit*, what He is (His essence), but only *an sit* or *quod sit*, that He is (His existence). This statement, if taken alone, would seem to involve complete agnosticism as regards the divine nature, but this is not St. Thomas's meaning, and the statement must be interpreted according to his general doctrine and his explanation of it. Thus in the *Summa contra Gentiles*[1] he says that 'the divine substance exceeds by its immensity every form which our intellect attains; and so we cannot apprehend it by knowing what it is, but we have some notion of it by coming to know what it is not.' For example, we come to know something of God by recognising that He is not, and cannot be, a corporeal substance: by denying of Him corporeality we form some notion of His nature, since we know that He is not body, though this does not give us of itself a positive idea of what the divine substance is in itself, and the more predicates we can deny of God in this way, the more we approximate to a knowledge of Him.

This is the famous *via remotionis* or *via negativa*, so dear to the Pseudo-Dionysius and other Christian writers who had been strongly influenced by neo-Platonism; but St. Thomas adds a very useful observation concerning the negative way.[2] In the case of a created substance, he says, which we can define, we first of all assign it to its genus by which we know in general what it is, and then we add the difference by which it is distinguished from other things; but in the case of God we cannot assign Him to a genus, since He transcends all genera, and so we cannot distinguish Him from other beings by positive differences (*per affirmativas differentias*). Nevertheless, though we cannot approach to a clear idea of God's nature in the same way in which we can attain a clear idea of human nature, that is, by a succession of positive or affirmative differentiations, such as living, sensitive or animal, rational, we can attain some notion of His nature by the negative way, by a succession of negative differentiations. For example, if we say that God is not an accident, we distinguish Him from all accidents; if we say that He is not corporeal, we distinguish Him from some substances; and thus we can proceed until we obtain an idea of God which belongs to Him alone (*propria consideratio*) and which suffices to distinguish Him from all other beings.

It must, however, be borne in mind that when predicates

are denied of God, they are not denied of Him because He lacks any perfection expressed in that predicate, but because He infinitely exceeds that limited perfection in richness. Our natural knowledge has its beginning in sense and extends as far as it can be led by the help of sensible objects.[3] As sensible objects are creatures of God, we can come to know that God exists, but we cannot attain by means of them any adequate knowledge of God, since they are effects which are not fully proportionate to the divine power. But we can come to know about Him what is necessarily true of Him precisely as cause of all sensible objects. As their cause, He transcends them and is not and cannot be a sensible object Himself: we can, then, deny of Him any predicates which are bound up with corporeality or which are inconsistent with His being the first Cause and necessary Being. But *haec non removentur ab eo propter ejus defectum, sed quia superexcedit.*[4] If we say, therefore, that God is not corporeal, we do not mean that God is less than body, that He *lacks* the perfection involved in being body, but rather that He is *more than* body, that He possesses none of the imperfections necessarily involved in being a corporeal substance.

Arguing by means of the negative way St. Thomas shows that God cannot be corporeal, for example, since the unmoved Mover and the necessary Being must be pure Act, whereas every corporeal substance is in potentiality. Again, there cannot be any composition in God, either of matter and form or of substance and accident or of essence and existence. If there were composition of essence and existence, for instance, God would owe His existence to another being, which is impossible, since God is the first Cause. There cannot in fine be any composition in God, as this would be incompatible with His being as first Cause, necessary Being, pure Act. We express this absence of composition by the positive word 'simplicity', but the idea of the divine simplicity is attained by removing from God all the forms of composition which are found in creatures, so that 'simplicity' here means absence of composition. We cannot form an adequate idea of the divine simplicity as it is in itself, since it transcends our experience: we know, however, that it is at the opposite pole, so to speak, from simplicity or comparative simplicity in creatures. In creatures we experience the more complex substance is the higher, as a man is higher than an oyster; but God's simplicity means that He possesses the fullness of His being and perfection in one undivided and eternal act.

Similarly, God is infinite and perfect, since His *esse* is not something received and limited, but is self-existent; He is immutable, since the necessary Being is necessarily all that it is and cannot be changed; He is eternal, since time requires motion and in the immutable Being there can be no motion. He is one, since He is simple and infinite. Strictly speaking, however, says St. Thomas, God is not eternal, but is eternity, since He is His own subsistent *esse* in one undivided act. To go through all the various attributes of God which can be known by the negative way is unnecessary: it is sufficient to have given some examples to show how, after proving that God exists as unmoved Mover, first Cause, and necessary Being, St. Thomas then proceeds to remove from God, to deny of God, all those predicates of creatures which are incompatible with God's character as unmoved Mover, first Cause and necessary Being. There cannot be in God corporeality, composition, limitation, imperfection, temporality, etc.

2. Predicates or names such as 'immutable' and 'infinite' suggest by their very form their association with the negative way, immutable being equivalent to not-mutable and infinite to not-finite; but there are other predicates applied to God which suggest no such association, such as good, wise, etc. Moreover, while a negative predicate, says St. Thomas,[5] refers directly not to the divine substance, but to the 'removal' of something from the divine substance, that is, the denial of some predicate's applicability to God, there are positive predicates or names which are predicated of the divine substance affirmatively. For example, the predicate 'non-corporeal' denies corporeality of God, removes it from Him, whereas the predicate good or wise is predicated affirmatively and directly of the divine substance. There is, then, an affirmative or positive way, in addition to the negative way. But what is its justification if these perfections, goodness, wisdom, etc., are experienced by us as they are in creatures, and if the words we use to express these perfections express the ideas we derive from creatures? Are we not applying to God ideas and words which have no application save within the realm of experience? Are we not faced with the following dilemma? Either we are predicating of God predicates which apply only to creatures, in which case our statements about

God are false, or we have emptied the predicates of their reference to creatures, in which case they are without content, since they are derived from our experience of creatures and express that experience?

First of all, St. Thomas insists that when affirmative predicates are predicated of God, they are predicated positively of the divine nature or substance. He will not allow the opinion of those who, like Maimonides, make all predicates of God equivalent to negative predicates, nor the opinion of those who say that 'God is good' or 'God is living' means simply 'God is the cause of all goodness' or 'God is the cause of life'. When we say that God is living or God is life, we do not mean merely that God is not non-living: the statement that God is living has a degree of affirmation about it that is wanting to the statement that God is not a body. Nor does the man who states that God is living mean only that God is the cause of life, of all living things: he means to say something positive about God Himself. Again, if the statement that God is living meant no more than that God is the cause of all living things, we might just as well say that God is body, since He is the cause of all bodies. Yet we do not say that God is body, whereas we do say that God is living, and this shows that the statement that God is living means more than that God is the cause of life, and that a positive affirmation is being made concerning the divine substance.

On the other hand, none of the positive ideas by means of which we conceive the nature of God represent God perfectly. Our ideas of God represent God only in so far as our intellects can know Him; but we know Him by means of sensible objects in so far as these objects represent or mirror God, so that inasmuch as creatures represent God or mirror Him only imperfectly, our ideas, derived from our experience of the natural world, can themselves represent God only imperfectly. When we say that God is good or living, we mean that He contains, or rather is the perfection of, goodness or life, but in a manner which exceeds and excludes all the imperfections and limitations of creatures. As regards *what is predicated* (goodness, for example), the affirmative predicate which we predicate of God signifies a perfection without any defect; but as regards the *manner of predicating it* every such predicate involves a defect, for by the word (*nomen*) we express something in the way it is conceived by the intellect. It follows, then, that predicates of this kind may, as the Pseudo-

Dionysius observed, be both affirmed and denied of God; affirmed *propter nominis rationem*, denied *propter significandi modum*. For example, if we make the statement that God is wisdom, this affirmative statement is true in regard to the perfection as such; but if we meant that God is wisdom in precisely that sense in which we experience wisdom, it would be false. God is wise, but He is wisdom in a sense transcending our experience; He does not possess wisdom as an inhering quality or form. In other words, we affirm of God the essence of wisdom or goodness or life in a 'supereminent' way, and we deny of God the imperfections attendant on human wisdom, wisdom as we experience it.[6] When, therefore, we say that God is good, the meaning is not that God is the cause of goodness or that God is not evil, but that what we call goodness in creatures pre-exists in God *secundum modum altiorem*. From this it does not follow that goodness belongs to God inasmuch as He causes goodness, but rather that because He is good, He diffuses goodness into things, according to the saying of Augustine, 'because He is good, we exist'.[7]

3. The upshot of the foregoing considerations is, therefore, that we cannot in this life know the divine essence as it is in itself, but only as it is represented in creatures, so that the names we apply to God signify the perfections manifested in creatures. From this fact several important conclusions must be drawn, the first being this, that the names we apply to God and to creatures are not to be understood in an univocal sense. For example, when we say that a man is wise and that God is wise, the predicate 'wise' is not to be understood in an univocal sense, that is, in precisely the same sense. Our concept of wisdom is drawn from creatures, and if we applied precisely this concept to God, we should be saying something false about God, since God is not, and cannot be, wise in precisely the same sense in which a man is wise. On the other hand, the names we apply to God are not purely equivocal, that is to say, they are not entirely and completely different in meaning from the meaning they bear when applied to creatures. If they were purely equivocal, we should have to conclude that we can gain no knowledge of God from creatures. If wisdom as predicated of man and wisdom as predicated of God signified something completely different, the term 'wise' as applied to God would have no content, no significance, since our knowledge of wisdom is drawn from

creatures and is not based on direct experience of the divine wisdom. Of course, it might be objected that, though it is true that if the terms predicated of God were used in an equivocal sense, we should know nothing of God from creatures, it does not follow that we can know anything about God from creatures; but St. Thomas's insistence that we can know something of God from creatures is based on the fact that creatures, as effects of God, must manifest God, though they can do this only imperfectly.

Yet if the concepts derived from our experience of creatures and then applied to God are used neither in an univocal nor in an equivocal sense, in what sense are they used? Is there any halfway house? St. Thomas replies that they are used in an analogical sense. When an attribute is predicated analogically of two different beings, this means that it is predicated according to the relation they have to some third thing or according to the relation the one has to the other. As an example of the first type of analogical predication St. Thomas gives his favourite example, health.[8] An animal is said to be healthy because it is the subject of health, possesses health, while medicine is said to be healthy as being the cause of health, and a complexion is said to be healthy as being the sign of health. The word 'healthy' is predicated in different senses of the animal in general, the medicine and the complexion, according to the different relations they bear to health; but it is not predicated in a purely equivocal sense, for all three bear some real relation to health. Medicine is not healthy in the same sense that animal is healthy, for the term 'healthy' is not employed univocally, but the senses in which it is used are not equivocal or purely metaphorical, as when we speak of a smiling meadow. But this, says St. Thomas, is not the way in which we predicate attributes of God and creatures, for God and creatures have no relation to any third object: we predicate attributes of God and creatures, in so far as the creature has a real relation to God. When, for example, we predicate being of God and creatures, we attribute being first and foremost to God, as self-existing being, secondarily to creatures, as dependent on God. We cannot predicate being univocally of God and creatures, since they do not possess being in the same way, nor do we predicate being in a purely equivocal sense, since creatures have being, though their being is not like the divine being but is dependent, participated being.

As regards what is meant by the words we apply to God and creatures, it is attributed primarily to God and only secondarily to creatures. Being, as we have seen, belongs essentially to God, whereas it does not belong essentially to creatures but only in dependence on God: it is being, but it is a different kind of being from the divine being, since it is received, derived, dependent, finite. Nevertheless, though the thing signified is attributed primarily to God, the name is predicated primarily of creatures. The reason is that we know creatures before we know God, so that since our knowledge of wisdom, for example, is derived from creatures and the word primarily denotes the concept derived from our experience of creatures, the idea of wisdom and the word are predicated primarily of creatures and analogically of God, even though in actual fact wisdom itself, the thing signified, belongs primarily to God.

4. Analogical predication is founded on resemblance. In the *De Veritate*[9] St. Thomas distinguishes resemblance of proportion (*convenientia proportionis*) and resemblance of proportionality (*convenientia proportionalitatis*). Between the number 8 and the number 4 there is a resemblance of proportion, while between the proportions of 6 to 3 and of 4 to 2 there is a resemblance of proportionality, that is, a resemblance or similarity of two proportions to one another. Now, analogical predication in a general sense may be made according to both types of resemblance. The predication of being in regard to created substance and accident, each of which has a relation to the other, is an example of analogical predication according to proportion, while the predication of vision in regard to both ocular and intellectual vision is an example of analogical predication according to proportionality. What corporeal vision is to the eye, that intellectual apprehension or vision is to the mind. There is a certain similarity between the relation of the eye to its vision and the relation of mind to its intellectual apprehension, a similarity which enables us to speak of 'vision' in both cases. We apply the word 'vision' in the two cases neither univocally nor purely equivocally, but analogically.

Now, it is impossible to predicate anything analogically of God and creatures in the same way that it is possible to predicate being of substance and accident, for God and creatures have no mutual real relationship: creatures have a real relation to God, but God has no real relation to creatures.

Nor is God included in the definition of any creature in the way that substance is included in the definition of accident. It does not follow, however, that there can be no analogy of proportion between God and creatures. Though God is not related to creatures by a real relation, creatures have a real relation to God, and we are able to apply the same term to God and creatures in virtue of that relation. There are perfections which are not bound up with matter and which do not necessarily imply any defect or imperfection in the being of which they are predicated. Being, wisdom and goodness are examples of such perfections. Obviously we gain knowledge of being or goodness or wisdom from creatures; but it does not follow that these perfections exist primarily in creatures and only secondarily in God, or that they are predicated primarily of creatures and only secondarily of God. On the contrary, goodness, for instance, exists primarily in God, who is the infinite goodness and the cause of all creaturely goodness, and it is predicated primarily of God and only secondarily of creatures, even though creaturely goodness is what we first come to know. Analogy of proportion is possible, then, in virtue of the creature's relation and likeness to God. To this point I shall return shortly.

It has been argued that St. Thomas came to abandon analogy of proportionality in favour of the analogy of proportion (in the acceptable sense); but this does not seem to me likely. In the Commentary on the *Sentences*[10] he gives both types of analogy, and even if in later works, like the *De Potentia*, the *Summa contra Gentiles* and the *Summa Theologica*, he seems to emphasise analogy of proportion, that does not seem to me to indicate that he ever abandoned analogy of proportionality. This type of analogical prediction may be used in two ways, symbolically or properly. We can speak of God as 'the Sun', meaning that what the sun is to the bodily eye, that God is to the soul; but we are then speaking symbolically, since the word 'sun' refers to a material thing and can be predicated of a spiritual being only in a symbolic sense. We can say, however, that there is a certain similarity between God's relation to His intellectual activity and man's relation to his intellectual activity, and in this case we are not speaking merely symbolically, since intellectual activity as such is a pure perfection.

The foundation of all analogy, then, that which makes analogical predication possible, is the likeness of creatures to

God. We do not predicate wisdom of God merely because God is the cause of all wise things, for in that case we might just as well call God a stone, as being the cause of all stones; but we call Him wise because creatures, God's effects, manifest God, are like to Him, and because a pure perfection like wisdom can be formally predicated of Him. But what is this likeness? In the first place it is only a one-way likeness, that is, the creature is like to God, but we cannot properly say that God is like the creature. God is the absolute standard, as it were. In the second place creatures are only imperfectly like God; they cannot bear a perfect resemblance to Him. This means that the creature is *at the same time* both like and unlike God. It is like God in so far as it is an imitation of Him; it is unlike God in so far as its resemblance to Him is imperfect and deficient. Analogical predication, therefore, lies between univocal and equivocal predication. In analogical predication the predicate is applied to God and creatures neither in precisely the same sense nor in totally different senses; it is applied at the same time in similar and dissimilar senses.[11] This notion of simultaneous similarity and difference is fundamental in analogy. The notion may, it is true, occasion considerable difficulties from the logical standpoint; but it would be inappropriate to discuss here the objections of modern positivists to analogy.

St. Thomas distinguishes, then, *analogy of proportion* (*analogia secundum convenientiam proportionis*) and *analogy of proportionality* (*analogia secundum convenientiam proportionalitatis*). As we have seen, he does not admit in regard to God and creatures that analogy of proportion which is applicable to substance and accident in respect of being; by analogy of proportion in natural theology he means that analogy in which a predicate is applied primarily to one analogue, namely God, and secondarily and imperfectly to the other analogue, namely the creature, in virtue of the creature's real relation and likeness to God. The perfection attributed to the analogues is really present in both of them, but it is not present in the same way, and the one predicate is used at the same time in senses which are neither completely different nor completely similar. Terminology has changed since the time of St. Thomas, and this kind of analogy is now called analogy of attribution. Analogy of proportionality, the resemblance of proportions, is sometimes called analogy of proportion, in distinction from the analogy of attribution; but not all Scholastics and commentators on St. Thomas employ the terms in precisely the same way.

Some Scholastics have maintained that being, for example, is predicable of God and creatures only by analogy of proportionality and not by analogy of attribution. Without, however, wishing to enter on a discussion of the value of analogy of proportionality as such, I do not see how we could know that God has any perfection save by way of the analogy of attribution. All analogical predication rests on the real relation and likeness of creatures to God, and it seems to me that the analogy of proportionality presupposes analogy of proportion or attribution and that the latter is the more fundamental of the two kinds of analogy.

5. If one reads what St. Thomas has to say of analogy, it may appear that he is simply examining the way in which we speak about God, the verbal and conceptual implications of our statements, and that he is not actually establishing anything about our real knowledge of God. But it is a fundamental principle with St. Thomas that the perfections of creatures must be found in the Creator in a super-eminent manner, in a manner compatible with the infinity and spirituality of God. For example, if God has created intellectual beings, God must be possessed of intellect; we cannot suppose that He is less than intellectual. Moreover, a spiritual being must be an intellectual form, as Aristotle says, and the infinite spiritual being must be possessed of infinite intelligence. On the other hand, God's intelligence cannot be a faculty distinct from His essence or nature, since God is pure Act and not a composite being, nor can God know things successively, since He is changeless and incapable of accidental determination. He knows future events in virtue of His eternity, by which all things are present to Him.[12] God must possess the perfection of intellectuality, but we cannot form any adequate concept of what the divine intelligence is, since we have no experience of it: our knowledge of the divine intelligence is imperfect and inadequate, but it is not false; it is analogical knowledge. It would be false only if we were unaware of its imperfection and actually meant to ascribe to God finite intelligence as such: we cannot help thinking and speaking of the divine intelligence in terms of human concepts and language, since there are no others available to us, but at the same time we are aware that our concepts and language are imperfect. We cannot, for instance, help speak-

ing as though God 'foresaw' future events, but we are aware that for God there is not past or future. Similarly we must ascribe to God the perfection of free will in respect of other objects than Himself, but God's free will cannot involve changeableness: He willed freely to create the world in time, but He willed it freely from all eternity, in virtue of the one act of will which is identical with His essence. Of the divine free will we can, therefore, form no adequate conception; but the relation of creatures to God shows us that God must possess free will and we can realise some of the things which the divine free will cannot mean; yet the positive reality of the divine free will exceeds our comprehension, precisely because we are creatures and not God. Only God can comprehend Himself.

It can scarcely be denied, however, that a grave difficulty arises in connection with the doctrine of analogy. If our idea of intelligence, for example, is derived from human intelligence, it obviously cannot, as such, be applied to God, and St. Thomas insists that no predicate which is applied to God and creatures is applied univocally. On the other hand, unless we were willing to acquiesce in agnosticism, we could not allow that such predicates are used in a purely equivocal sense. What, then, is the positive content of our concept of the divine intelligence? If St. Thomas adhered simply to the *via negativa* the difficulty would not arise: he would be saying simply that God is not not-intelligent or that He is superintelligent, admitting that we have no positive idea of what the divine intelligence is. But St. Thomas does not stick simply to the *via negativa*: he admits the *via affirmativa*. Our idea of divine intelligence has, therefore, a positive content; but what can that positive content be? Is the reply that a positive content is obtained by denying the limitations of human intelligence, its finiteness, discursive character, potentiality and so on? In this case, however, we either attain a positive concept of the divine intelligence as such or we attain a concept of the 'essence' of intelligence, apart from finitude or infinity, which would seem to be univocal in respect of God and creatures. It might even appear that the negations either cancel out the content altogether or make it into an idea of the essence of intelligence which would be univocal in respect of divine and human intelligence. It was for this reason that Duns Scotus later insisted that we can form univocal concepts applicable to both God and creatures, though there is no univocity in the real order in respect of God and creatures. It is sometimes said that analogical concepts are partly the same as and partly different from univocal concepts; but the same difficulty recurs. The element of 'sameness' will be an univocal element, while the element of 'difference' will either be negative or it will have no content, since we have no immediate experience of God from which the idea can be derived. But further consideration of this point is best reserved for our treatment of St. Thomas's doctrine of knowledge.[13]

6. Mention of the divine intelligence naturally leads one on to raise the question what St. Thomas thought of the doctrine of the divine ideas. In the first place he establishes that there must be ideas in the divine mind, *necesse est ponere in mente divina ideas*,[14] since God has created things not by chance, but intelligently, according to the exemplary idea He conceived in His mind. He remarks that Plato erred in asserting the existence of ideas which were not in any intellect, and he observes that Aristotle blamed Plato on this account. As a matter of fact, Aristotle, who did not believe in any free creation by God, did not blame Plato for making the ideas independent of the divine mind, but for maintaining their subsistence apart from the human mind, if one is considering their subjective reality, and apart from things, if one is considering their objective reality as forms. In asserting the existence of ideas in the divine mind St. Thomas is therefore following in the wake of the tradition which began with Plato, was developed in Middle Platonism and neo-Platonism and lived on, in a Christian setting, in the philosophy of Augustine and those who followed him.

One of the reasons why the neo-Platonists placed the ideas in the *Nous*, the second hypostasis or first emanating divine being, and not in the One or supreme Godhead was that the presence of a multiplicity of ideas in God would, they thought, impair the divine unity. How did St. Thomas meet this difficulty, when the only real distinction he could admit in God was the distinction between the three divine Persons in the Trinity (and with this distinction he was not, of course, concerned as philosopher)? His answer is that from one point of view we must say that there is a plurality of ideas in God, as Augustine said, since God knows each individual thing to be created, but that from another point of view there cannot be a plurality of ideas in God, since this would contradict the divine simplicity. What he means is this. If by idea one refers to the content of the idea, then one must admit a plurality of ideas in God, since God knows many objects; but if by idea one means the subjective mental determination, the species, then one cannot admit a plurality of ideas in God, since God's intellect is identical with His undivided essence and cannot receive determinations or any sort of composition. God knows His divine essence not only as it is in itself, but also as imitable outside itself in a plurality of creatures. This act of knowledge, as it exists in God, is one and undivided and is identical with His essence; but since God not only knows His essence as imitable in a multiplicity of creatures, but also knows that in knowing His essence He knows a multiplicity of creatures, we can and must speak of a plurality of ideas in God, for 'idea' signifies, not the divine essence as it is in itself, but the divine essence as the exemplar of this or that object. And it is the exemplar of many objects. In other words, the truth or falsity of our statements in regard to God must be estimated in terms of human language. To deny a plurality of ideas in God without qualification would be to deny that God knows a plurality of objects; but the truth that God knows His essence as imitable by a plurality of creatures must not be stated in such a way as to imply that there is a multiplicity of real species or really distinct modifications in the divine intellect.[15]

This discussion of the divine ideas is of some interest because it shows that St. Thomas is by no means simply an Aristotelian, but that in this respect at least he adheres to the Platonic-Augustinian tradition. Indeed, although he sees clearly that he has to provide against any impairing of the divine simplicity, he is not content with saying that God by one act of His intellect, one 'idea', knows His essence as imitable in a plurality of creatures, but he asserts that there is a plurality of ideas in God. He certainly gives his reasons for doing so, but one has the impression that one unstated reason was his reverence for Augustine and Augustine's mode of speaking. However, it is true that a distinction must be made. When we to-day use the term 'idea' we naturally refer to the subjective idea or mental modification, and in this sense St. Thomas does not admit in God a plurality of ideas really distinct from one another; but St. Thomas was primarily thinking of 'idea' in the sense of exemplary form, and since the divine essence as known by the divine intellect is known as imitable in a plurality of creatures, as the exemplar of many objects, he felt himself entitled to speak of a plurality of *rationes* in God, though he had to insist that this plurality consists simply in God's knowledge of His essence in respect of the multiplicity of creatures and not in a real distinction in God.

7. We have spoken of the divine intelligence and the divine will, the divine goodness, unity, simplicity and so on. Are these attributes of God really distinct from one another? And if they are not distinct from one another, what is our justification for speaking of them as though they were distinct? The attributes of God are not really distinct from one another, since God is simple: they are identical with the divine essence. The divine intelligence is not really distinct from the divine essence, nor is the divine will: the divine justice and the divine mercy are identical as they exist in God. Nevertheless, apart from the fact that the structure of our language compels us to speak in terms of subject and predicate, we apprehend the divine perfection piecemeal, as it were. We attain our natural knowledge of God only by considerations of creatures, God's effects, and since the perfections of creatures, the manifestations or reflections of God in creatures are different, we use different names to signify those different perfections. But if we could comprehend the divine essence as it is in itself and if we could give it its proper name, we should use one alone.[16] We cannot, however, comprehend the divine essence, and we know it only by means of diverse concepts: we have, therefore, to employ diverse words to express the divine essence, though we know at the same time that the actual reality corresponding to all those names is one simple reality. If it is objected that to conceive an object otherwise than it is is to conceive it falsely, the answer is that we do not conceive the object to exist otherwise than it actually exists, for we know that God is actually a simple Being, but we conceive in a composite manner the object which we know to be non-composite. This means simply that our intelligences are finite and discursive and that they cannot apprehend God save by means of His different reflections in creatures. Our knowledge of God is thus inadequate and imperfect, but it is not false.[17] There is indeed a certain foundation in God for our composite and distinct concepts, this foundation, however, not being any real distinction in God between the divine attributes but simply His

infinite pefection which, precisely because of its infinite richness, cannot be apprehended by the human mind in one concept.

8. According to St. Thomas[18] the most appropriate name of God is the name He gave to Moses at the burning bush,[19] *Qui est*, He who is. In God there is no distinction between essence and existence; He does not receive His existence, but is His existence; His essence is to exist. In no creature, however, is the distinction between essence and existence absent. Every creature is good and every creature is true; but no creature is its own existence: it is not the essence of any creature to exist. Existence itself *ipsum esse*, is the essence of God, and the name which is derived from that essence is most appropriate to God. God is goodness, for example, and His goodness is identical with His essence, but goodness, in our human experience, follows on and accompanies *esse*; though not really distinct, it is conceived as secondary; but to say that God is *ipsum esse* is to give, as it were, His inner nature. Every other name is in some way inadequate. If we say, for example, that God is infinite Justice, we say what is true, but as our intelligences necessarily distinguish Justice and Mercy, even though we know that they are identical in God, the statement that God is infinite Justice is an inadequate expression of the divine essence. The names we employ in speaking of God are derived from our experience of determinate forms and express primarily those forms; but the name *He who is* signifies not a determinate form, but 'the infinite ocean of substance'.

Chapter Thirty-six

ST. THOMAS AQUINAS—VI:
CREATION

Creation out of nothing—God alone can create—God created freely—The motive of creation—Impossibility of creation from eternity has not been demonstrated—Could God create an actually infinite multitude?—Divine omnipotence—The problem of evil.

1. Since God is the first Cause of the world, since finite beings are contingent beings owing their existence to the necessary Being, finite beings must proceed from God through creation. Moreover, this creation must be creation out of nothing. If creatures were made out of a pre-existent material, this material would be either God Himself or something other than God. But God cannot be the material of creation, since He is simple, spiritual, unchangeable; nor can there be any thing independent of the first Cause: there can be but one necessary Being. God, therefore, is absolutely prior, and if He cannot change, cannot exteriorise Himself in creation, He must have created the world out of nothing, *ex nihilo*. This phrase must not be taken to imply that nothing, *nihil*, is a material out of which God made the world: when it is said that God created the world out of nothing, it is meant either that first there was nothing and then there was something or the phrase *ex nihilo* must be understood as equivalent to *non ex aliquo*, not out of something. The objection that out of nothing comes nothing is, therefore, irrelevant, since nothing is looked on neither as efficient cause nor as material cause; in creation God is the efficient Cause and there is no material cause whatsoever.[1] Creation is thus not a movement or

change in the proper sense, and since it is not a movement, there is no succession in the act of creation.

Creation, considered in the term of the act of creation, that is, in the creature, is a real relation to God as the principle of the creature's being. Every creature, by the very fact that it is created, has a real relation to God as Creator. But one cannot argue the other way round, that God has a real relation to the creature. Such a relation in God would either be identical with the divine substance or it would be an accident in God; but the divine substance cannot be necessarily related to creatures, since in that case God would depend in some way on creatures for His very existence, while on the other hand God, as absolutely simple, cannot receive or possess accidents.[2] The statement that God as Creator has no real relation to creatures certainly sounds rather strange at first hearing, as it might seem to follow that God has no care for His creatures; but it is a strictly logical conclusion from St. Thomas's metaphysic and doctrine of the divine Nature. That God is related to creatures by His very substance St. Thomas could not possibly admit, since in that case not only would creation necessarily be eternal, and we know from revelation that it is not eternal, but God could not exist apart from creatures: God and creatures would form a Totality and it would be impossible to explain the generation and perishing of individual creatures. On the other hand, if one is speaking of relation as falling within one of the nine categories of accidents, such a relation also is inadmissible in God. The acquisition of such an accident would allow of creation in time, it is true; but such an acquisition on the part of God is impossible if God is pure act, without potentiality. It was, therefore, impossible for St. Thomas to admit that God as Creator has a real relation to creatures; he had to say that the relation is a mental relation of reason alone (*relatio rationis*), attributed to God by the human intellect. The attribution is, however, legitimate, since God is Creator and we cannot express this fact in human language without speaking as though God were related to creatures: the important point is that, when we speak of creatures as related to God and of God as related to creatures, we should remember that it is creatures which depend on God and not God on creatures, and that consequently the real relation between them, which is a relation of dependence, is found in creatures alone.

2. The power of creation is a prerogative of God alone and

cannot be communicated to any creature.[3] The reason why
some philosophers, Avicenna, for example, introduced intermediary beings was because they thought of God as creating
by a necessity of nature, so that there must be intermediary
stages between the absolute simplicity of the supreme Godhead and the multiplicity of creatures; but God does not
create by a necessity of nature and there is no reason why
He should not create directly a multiplicity of creatures. Peter
Lombard thought that the power of creation is communicable
by God to a creature in such a way that the latter could act
as an instrument, not by its own power; but this is impossible,
since if the creature is to contribute in any way to creation,
its own power and activity will be involved, and this power,
being finite like the creature itself, cannot accomplish an act
which demands infinite power, the act of bridging the infinite
gulf between not-being and being.

3. But if God does not create by a necessity of nature, how
does He create? An intellectual being, in whom there is, so
to speak, no element of unconsciousness, but who is perfectly
self-luminous and 'self-possessed', cannot act in any other way
than according to wisdom, with full knowledge. To put the
matter crudely, God must act for a motive, in view of a purpose, a good. But God's nature is not only infinite intelligence, but also infinite will, and that will is free. God loves
Himself necessarily, since He is Himself the infinite good,
but objects distinct from Himself are not necessary to Him,
since, as infinite perfection, He is self-sufficient: His will is
free in their regard. Therefore, although we know that God's
intellect and will are not really distinct from His essence, we
are bound to say that God chose freely an object or end conceived by Him as good. The language employed is certainly
anthropomorphic, but we have only human language at our
disposal, and we cannot express the truth that God created
the world freely without making it clear that the act of will
by which God created was neither a blind act nor a necessary
act, but an act which followed, to speak in human fashion,
the apprehension of a good, apprehended as a good though
not as a good necessary to God.

4. What was the motive for which God acted in creation?
As infinite perfection God cannot have created in order to
acquire anything for Himself: He created, not in order to
obtain, but to give, to diffuse His goodness (*intendit solum
communicare suam perfectionem quae est ejus bonitas*).[4]

When it is said, then, that God created the world for His own glory the statement must not be taken to mean that God needed something which He had not already got; still less that He wanted to obtain, if one may so speak without irreverence, a chorus of admirers; but rather that God's will cannot depend on anything apart from God, that He Himself as the infinite good must be the end of His infinite act of will, and that in the case of the act of creation the end is His own goodness as communicable to beings outside Himself. The divine goodness is represented in all creatures, though rational creatures have God as their end in a manner peculiar to themselves, since they are able to know and to love God: all creatures glorify God by representing and participating in His goodness, while rational creatures are capable of consciously appreciating and loving the divine goodness. God's glory, the manifestation of His goodness, is thus not something separate from the good of creatures, for creatures attain their end, do the best for themselves, by manifesting the divine goodness.[5]

5. That God created the world freely, does not of itself show that He created it in time, that time had a beginning. As God is eternal, He might have created the world from eternity. That this had been shown to be an impossible supposition St. Thomas refused to allow. He believed that it can be philosophically proved that the world was created out of nothing, but he maintained that none of the philosophical proofs adduced to prove that this creation took place in time, that there is, ideally, a first assignable moment of time, were conclusive, differing on this point from St. Albert. On the other hand, St. Thomas maintained, against the Averroists, that it cannot be shown philosophically that the world cannot have begun in time, that creation in time is an impossibility. In other words, though well aware that the world was actually created in time and not from eternity, St. Thomas was convinced that this fact is known only through revelation, and that the philosopher cannot settle the question whether the world was created in time or from eternity. Thus he maintained, against the *murmurantes*, the possibility (as far as we can see) of creation from eternity. In practice this meant that he showed, or at least was satisfied that he could show, that the type of argument brought forward by St. Bonaventure to prove the impossibility of creation from eternity was inconclusive. It is, however, unnecessary to mention St. Thomas's replies again, since these, or some of them at least,

have already been given when we were considering the philosophy of St. Bonaventure.[6] Let it suffice to recall the fact that St. Thomas saw no contradiction in the notion of a series without a beginning. In his eyes the question whether it would be possible for the world to have passed through infinite time does not arise, since there is strictly no passing through an infinite series if there is no first term in the series. Moreover, for St. Thomas a series can be infinite *ex parte ante* and finite *ex parte post*, and it can be added to at the end at which it is finite. In general, there is no contradiction between being brought into existence and existing from eternity: if God is eternal, God could have created from eternity.

On the other hand, St. Thomas rejects the arguments adduced to show that the world must have been created from eternity. 'We must hold firmly, as the Catholic faith teaches, that the world has not always existed. And this position cannot be overcome by any physical demonstration.'[7] It may be argued, for example, that as God is the Cause of the world and as God is eternal, the world, God's effect, must also be eternal. As God cannot change, as He contains no element of potentiality and cannot receive new determinations or modifications, the creative act, God's free act of creation, must be eternal. The effect of this act must, therefore, also be eternal. St. Thomas has to agree, of course, that the creative act as such, that is, God's act of will, is eternal, since it is identical with God's essence; but he argues that what follows from this is simply that God willed freely from eternity to create the world, not that the world came into existence from eternity. If we consider the matter merely as philosophers, if, that is, we prescind from our knowledge, gained from revelation, that God actually created the world in time, all we can say is that God may have willed freely from eternity that the world should come into existence in time or that God may have willed freely from eternity that the world should come into existence from eternity: we are not entitled to conclude that God *must* have willed from eternity that the world should exist from eternity. In other words, God's creative act is certainly eternal, but the external effect of that act will follow in the way willed by God, and if God willed that the external effect should have *esse post non-esse* it will not have *esse ab aeterno*, even though the creative act, considered precisely as an act in God, is eternal.[8]

6. One of the reasons adduced by St. Bonaventure to show

that the world must have been created in time and could not have been created from eternity was that, if it had been created from eternity, there would be in existence now an infinite number of immortal human souls and that an infinite actual multitude is an impossibility. What did St. Thomas maintain concerning God's power to create an infinite multitude? The question arises in connection with a multitude *extra genus quantitatis*, since St. Thomas followed Aristotle in rejecting the possibility of an infinite quantity. In the *De Veritate*[9] the Saint remarks that the only valid reason for saying that God could not create an actual infinite multitude would be an essential repugnance or contradiction in the notion of such an infinity, but he defers any decision on the matter. In the *Summa Theologica*[10] he affirms categorically that there cannot be an actual infinite multitude, since every created multitude must be of a certain number, whereas an infinite multitude would not be of a certain number. But in the *De aeternitate mundi contra Murmurantes*, when dealing with the objection against the possibility of the world's creation from eternity that there would then be in existence an infinite number of immortal human souls, he replies that God might have made the world without men, or that He could have made the world from eternity but have made man only when He did make him, while on the other hand 'it has not yet been demonstrated that God cannot make an infinity in act'. It may be that the last remark indicates a change of mind on St. Thomas's part or a hesitancy concerning the validity of his own previous demonstration; but he does not explicitly recall what he said in the *Summa Theologica*, and the remark might be no more than an *argumentum ad hominem*, 'you have not yet demonstrated that an existing infinite multitude is impossible'. In any case, in view of the statement in the *Summa Theologica* and in view of the proximity in time of the *De aeternitate mundi* to the first part of the *Summa Theologica*, it would seem rash to conclude to more than a possible hesitancy on St. Thomas's part as to the impossibility of an infinite multitude in act.

7. The mention of God being able or unable to create an actually infinite multitude naturally raises the wider question of the sense in which the divine omnipotence is to be understood. If omnipotence means the ability to do all things, how can God be omnipotent if He cannot make it come about that a man should be a horse or that what has happened

should not have happened? In answer St. Thomas observes first of all that the divine attribute of omnipotence means that God can do all that is possible. But 'all that is possible' must not be understood, he goes on to say, as equivalent to 'all that is possible to God', for in this case when we say that God is omnipotent we should mean that God is able to do all that He is able to do, a statement which would tell us nothing. How, then, are we to understand the phrase 'all that is possible'? That possible which has no intrinsic repugnance to being, in other words, that the existence of which would not involve a contradiction. That which involves a contradiction in its very notion is neither actual nor possible, but not-being. For example, that a man, while remaining a man, should also be a horse, involves a contradiction: man is rational, a horse irrational, and rational and irrational are contradictories. We can certainly speak of a human horse or an equine man, but the phrases do not indicate a thing, whether actual or possible; they are mere verbiage, signifying nothing conceivable. To say, therefore, that God's omnipotence means that God can do all that is possible does not indicate a limit to God's power, for power has meaning only in regard to the possible. Whatever has or can have being is the object of divine omnipotence, but that which is intrinsically contradictory is not an object at all. 'So it is better to say that what involves contradiction cannot be done rather than that God cannot do it.'[11]

It must not, however, be imagined that there is a principle of contradiction which stands behind God and to which God is subject as the Greek gods were subject to *Moira* or Destiny. God is supreme Being, *ipsum esse subsistens*, and His will to create is a will to create His own similitude, something, that is, which can participate in being. That which involves a contradiction is at the utmost remove from Being; it neither has nor ever can have any likeness to God, any being. If God could will what is self-contradictory He could depart from His own nature, could love that which bears no resemblance whatsoever to Himself, that which is nothing at all, that which is utterly unthinkable. But if God could act in this way, He would not be God. It is not that God is subject to the principle of contradiction, but rather that the principle of contradiction is founded on the nature of God. To suppose, then, with St. Peter Damian (or with Leo Chestov) that God is superior to the principle of contradiction, in the sense that God can do what is self-contradictory, is to suppose that God can act in a manner inconsistent with and contrary to His own nature, and this is an absurd supposition.[12]

But this does not mean that God can do only what He actually does. It is certainly true that since God actually wills the order of things which He has created and which actually exists, He cannot will another order, since the divine will cannot change, as our finite wills can change; but the question is not concerning the divine power *ex suppositione*, on the supposition that God has already chosen, but concerning the absolute divine power, i.e. whether God was restricted to willing the actual order He has willed or whether He could have willed another order. The answer is that God did not will this present order of things necessarily, and the reason is that the end of creation is the divine goodness which so exceeds any created order that there is not and cannot be any link of necessity between a given order and the end of creation. The divine goodness and the created order are incommensurable, and there cannot be any one created order, any one universe, which is necessary to a divine goodness that is infinite and incapable of any addition. If any created order were proportionate to the divine goodness, to the end, then the divine wisdom would be determined to choose that particular order; but since the divine goodness is infinite and creation necessarily finite, no created order can be proportionate in the full sense to the divine goodness.[13]

From the above is made apparent the answer to the questions whether God could make better things than He has made or could make the things which He has made better than they are.[14] In one sense God must always act in the best possible manner, since God's act is identical with His essence and with infinite goodness; but we cannot conclude from this that the extrinsic object of God's act, creatures, must be the best possible and that God is bound, on account of His goodness, to produce the best possible universe if He produces one at all. As God's power is infinite, there can always be a better universe than the one God actually produces, and why He has chosen to produce a particular order of creation is His secret. St. Thomas says, therefore, that absolutely speaking God could make something better than any given thing. But if the question is raised in regard to the existent universe, a distinction must be drawn. God could not make a given thing better than it actually is in regard to its substance or essence, since that would be to make another thing. For example, rational life is in itself a higher perfection than merely sensitive life; but if God were to make a horse rational it would no longer be a horse and in that case God could not be said to make the horse better. Similarly, if God changed the order of the universe, it would not be the same universe. On the other hand, God could make a thing accidentally better; He could, for example, increase a man's bodily health or, in the supernatural order, his grace.

It is plain, then, that St. Thomas would not agree with the Leibnizian 'optimism' or maintain that this is the best of all possible worlds. In view of the divine omnipotence the phrase 'the best of all possible worlds' does not seem to have much meaning: it has meaning only if one supposes from the start that God creates from a necessity of His nature, from which it would follow, since God is goodness itself, that the world which proceeds from Him necessarily must be the best possible. But if God creates not from a necessity of nature, but according to His nature, according to intelligence and will, that is, freely, and if God is omnipotent, it must always be possible for God to create a better world. Why, then, did He create this particular world? That is a question to which we cannot give any adequate answer, though we can certainly attempt to answer the question why God created a world in which suffering and evil are present: that is to say, we can attempt to answer the problem of evil, provided that we remember that we cannot expect to attain any comprehensive solution of the problem in this life, owing to the finitude and imperfection of our intelligences and the fact that we cannot fathom the divine counsel and plans.

8. In willing this universe God did not will the evils contained in it. God necessarily loves His own essence, which is infinite goodness, and He freely wills creation as a communication of His goodness; He cannot love what is opposed to goodness, namely evil. But did not God, to speak in human language, foresee the evils in the world; and if He foresaw the evils in the world and yet willed the world, did He not will the evils in the world? If evil were a positive entity, something created, then it would have to be ascribed to God as Creator, since there is no ultimate principle of evil, as the Manichaeans thought; but evil is not a positive entity; it is, as St. Augustine taught, following Plotinus, a *privation*. It is not *aliquid*, a positive thing, and God cannot have created

it, since it is not creatable, but it only exists as a privation in what itself, as being, is good. Moreover, evil as such cannot be willed even by a human will, for the object of the will is necessarily the good or what appears as such. The adulterer, says St. Thomas, does not will the evil, the sin, precisely as such; he wills the sensible pleasure of an act which involves evil. It might be objected that some people have indulged in diabolic wickedness, have committed acts precisely because they were an offence against God; but even in this case it is some apparent good, complete independence, for example, which is the object of the will: the evil defiance of God appears as a good and is willed *sub specie boni*. No will, therefore, can desire evil precisely as such, and God, in creating a world the evils of which He 'foresaw', must be said, not to have willed the evils but to have willed the world which, as such, is good and to have willed to permit the evils which He foresaw.

It must not, however, be imagined that by maintaining the doctrine that evil as such is a privation St. Thomas means to imply that evil is unreal, in the sense of being an illusion. This would be to misunderstand his position completely. Evil is not a being, *entitas*, in the sense that it falls under any of the ten categories of being, but in reply to the question whether evil exists or not, the answer must be in the affirmative. This certainly sounds paradoxical, but St. Thomas means that evil exists as a privation in the good, not in its own right as a positive entity. For example, lack of ability to see is not a privation in a stone, for it does not pertain to a stone to see, and 'blindness' in a stone is the mere absence of a power which would be incompatible with the nature of the stone; but blindness in a man is a privation, the absence of something which belongs to the fullness of man's nature. This blindness is not, however, a positive entity, it is a privation of sight; yet the privation exists, is real, it is by no means an unreal illusion. It has no meaning or existence apart from the being in which it exists, but as existing in that being the privation is real enough. Similarly, evil cannot of and by itself cause anything, but it exists and can be a cause through the good being in which it exists. For example, the difformity in the will of a fallen angel cannot by itself be a cause, but it is a real privation and can be a cause by means of the positive being in which it exists. Indeed, the more powerful the being in which it exists, the greater are its effects.[15]

God did not, then, create evil as a positive entity, but must He not be said to have willed evil in some sense, since He created a world in which He foresaw that evil would exist? It is necessary to consider separately physical evil and moral evil (*malum culpae*). Physical evil was certainly permitted by God and it can in a sense be even said to have been willed by God. God did not will it for its own sake, of course, *per se*, but He willed a universe, a natural order, which involved at least the possibility of physical defect and suffering. By willing the creation of sensitive nature God willed that capacity for feeling pain as well as pleasure which is, naturally speaking, inseparable from human nature. He did not will suffering as such, but He willed that nature (a good) which is accompanied by the capacity for suffering. Moreover, the perfection of the universe requires, says St. Thomas, that there should be, besides incorruptible beings, corruptible beings, and if there are corruptible beings, corruption, death, will take place according to the natural order. God, then, did not will corruption (needless to say, the word is not being used in the moral sense) for its own sake, but He can be said to have caused it *per accidens*, in that He willed to create and created a universe the order of which demanded the capacity for defect and corruption on the part of some beings. Again, the preservation of the order of justice demands that moral evil should meet with punishment (*malum poenae*), and God may be said to will and cause that punishment not for its own sake, but so that the order of justice may be preserved.

In treating of physical evil, therefore, St. Thomas tends to treat God as an artist and the universe as a work of art. The perfection of that work of art requires a variety of beings, among which will be found beings which are mortal and capable of suffering, so that God may be said to have willed physical evil not *per se* but *per accidens*, for the sake of a good, the good of the whole universe. But when it is a question of the moral order, the order of freedom, and of considering human beings precisely as free agents, his attitude is different. Freedom is a good and without it human beings could not give God that love of which He is worthy, could not merit and so on: freedom makes man more like to God than he would be, were he not free. On the other hand, man's liberty, when he has not got the vision of God, involves the power of choosing against God and the moral law, of sinning. God did not will moral disorder or sin in any sense, but He permitted it. Why? For the sake of a greater good, that man might be free and that he might love and serve God of his own free choice. The physical perfection of the universe required the presence of some beings who could and would die, so that God, as we have seen, can be said to have willed death *per accidens;* but though the perfection of the universe required that man should be free, it did not require that he should misuse his freedom, should sin, and God can not be said to have willed moral evil either *per se* or *per accidens.* Nevertheless, it was impossible for there to be a human being in the natural order who should be free and at the same time incapable of sinning, so that it is true to say that God permitted a moral evil, though He permitted it only for the sake of a greater good.

There would, of course, be a great deal more to say on this subject, were one to introduce considerations drawn from theology, and any purely philosophical consideration of the problem is necessarily far less satisfactory than a treatment in which both theological and philosophical truths are utilised. The doctrines of the Fall and the Redemption, for instance, throw a light on the problem of evil which cannot be shed by purely philosophical reasoning. However, arguments based on revelation and dogmatic theology must be omitted here. St. Thomas's philosophical answer to the problem of evil in its relation to God can be summed up in the two statements, first that God did not will moral evil in any sense whatever but only permitted it for a greater good than could be attained by preventing it, that is, by not making man free, and secondly that though God did not will physical evil for its own sake, He may be said to have willed certain physical evils *per accidens,* for the perfection of the universe. I say 'certain *physical evils*', since St. Thomas does not mean to imply that God can be said to have willed all physical evils, even *per accidens.* Corruptibility or death pertains to a certain kind of being, but many physical evils and sufferings are not bound up with the perfection or good of the universe at all, but are the result of moral evil on man's part: they are not 'inevitable'. Such physical evils God only permitted.[16]

Chapter Thirty-seven

ST. THOMAS AQUINAS—VII: PSYCHOLOGY

One substantial form in man—The powers of the soul—The interior senses—Free will—The noblest faculty—Immortality—The active and passive intellects are not numerically the same in all men.

1. We have already seen[1] that St. Thomas maintained the Aristotelian doctrine of hylomorphism and that, departing from the views of his predecessors, he defended the unicity of the substantial form in the substance. It may be that at first St. Thomas accepted the existence of a *forma corporeitatis* as the first substantial form in a material substance;[2] but in any case he soon opposed this opinion and held that the specific substantial form informs prime matter immediately and not by the medium of any other substantial form. This doctrine he applied to man, maintaining that there is but one substantial form in the human *compositum*. This one substantial form is the rational soul, which informs matter directly: there is no *forma corporeitatis*, still less are there vegetative and sensitive substantial forms. The human being is a unity, and this unity would be impaired, were we to suppose a plurality of substantial forms. The name 'man' applies neither to the soul alone nor to the body alone, but to soul and body together, to the composite substance.

St. Thomas, then, follows Aristotle in stressing the unity of the human substance. It is the one soul in man which confers on him all his determinations as man, his corporeity (by informing prime matter), his vegetative, sensitive and intellectual operations. In a plant there is present only the vegetative principle or soul, conferring life and the powers of growth and reproduction; in the brute there is present only the sensitive soul which acts as the principle not only of vegetative life, but also of sensitive life; in man there is present only the rational principle or soul, which is not only the principle of the operations peculiar to itself, but also of the vegetative and sensitive functions. When death comes and the soul is separated from the body, the body disintegrates: it is not merely that rational functions cease, for the sensitive and vegetative functions also cease: the one principle of all these operations no longer informs the matter which it previously informed and instead of the unified human substance there results a multiplicity of substances, the new substantial forms being educed from the potentiality of matter.

Clearly, therefore, the Platonic idea of the relation of soul to body was unacceptable to St. Thomas. It is the one individual man who perceives not only that he reasons and understands, but also that he feels, and exercises sensation. But one cannot have sensation without a body, so that the body, and not the soul only, must belong to man.[3] A man is generated when the rational soul is infused and a man dies when the rational soul departs from the body: there is no other substantial form in man than the rational soul and this soul exercises the functions of inferior forms, itself performing in the case of man what the vegetative soul does in the case of plants and the sensitive soul in the case of irrational animals.[4] It follows from this that the union of soul with body cannot be something unnatural: it cannot be a punishment to the soul for sin in a preceding state, as Origen thought. The human soul has the power of sensation, for example, but it cannot exercise this function without a body; it has the power of intellection, but it has no innate ideas and has to form its ideas in dependence on sense-experience, for which it needs a body; the soul, then, is united to a body because it needs it, because it is naturally the form of a body. The union of soul and body is not to the detriment, but to the good of the soul, *propter animam*. Matter exists for the form and not the other way about, and the soul is united to the body in order that it (the soul) may act according to its nature.[5]

2. But though St. Thomas emphasised the unity of man, the close union between soul and body, he held that there is a real distinction between the soul and its faculties, and be-

tween the faculties themselves. In God alone are the power of acting and the act itself identical with the substance, since in God alone is there no potentiality: in the human soul there are faculties or powers of acting which are in potentiality to their acts and which are to be distinguished according to their respective acts and objects.[6] Some of these powers or faculties belong to the soul as such and are not intrinsically dependent on a bodily organ, while others belong to the *compositum* and cannot be exercised without the body: the former, therefore, remain in the soul even when it is separated from the body, whereas the latter remain in the separated soul only potentially or virtually (*virtute*), in the sense that the soul still has the remote power to exercise the faculties, but only if it were reunited with the body: in its separated state it cannot use them. For instance, the rational or intellectual faculty is not intrinsically dependent on the body, though in the state of union with the body there is a certain dependence in regard to the material of knowledge (in a sense to be explained later); but the power of sensation can obviously not be exercised without the body. On the other hand it cannot be exercised by the body without the soul. Its 'subject', therefore, is neither soul alone nor body alone but the human *compositum*. Sensation cannot be attributed simply to the soul using a body (as St. Augustine thought); body and soul play their respective parts in producing the act of sensation, and the power of sensation belongs to both in union rather than to either of them separately.

In the powers or faculties there is a certain hierarchy. The vegetative faculty, comprising the powers of nutrition, growth and reproduction, has as its object simply the body united to the soul or living by means of the soul. The sensitive faculty (comprising the exterior senses, of sight, hearing, smell, taste, touch, and the interior senses of *sensus communis*, *phantasia* or imagination, *vis aestimativa* and *vis memorativa* or memory) has as its object, not simply the body of the sentient subject but rather every sensible body. The rational faculty (comprising the active and passive intellects) has as its object, not only sensible bodies but being in general. The higher the power, therefore, the wider and more comprehensive its object. The first general faculty is concerned with the subject's own body; but the other two faculties, the sensitive and intellectual, are also concerned with objects extrinsic to the subject itself, and a consideration of this fact shows us that there are other powers in addition to those already mentioned. If we consider the aptitude of the external object to be received in the subject through cognition, we find there are two kinds of faculty, sensitive and intellective, the former of which is more restricted in scope than the latter; but if we consider the inclination and tendency of the soul towards the external object, we find that there are two other powers, that of locomotion, by which the subject attains the object through its own motion, and that of appetition, by which the object is desired as an end or *finis*. The power of locomotion belongs to the level of sensitive life; but the power of appetition is twofold, comprising desire on the sensitive level, the sensitive appetite, and desire on the intellectual level, volition. On the vegetative level of life, therefore, we find the three powers of nutrition, growth and reproduction, on the sensitive level the five exterior senses, the four interior senses, the power of locomotion and the sensitive appetite, on the rational level of life the active intellect, the passive intellect and the will. In man they are all present.

These powers and faculties proceed from the essence of the soul as from their principle, but they are really distinguished from one another. They have different formal objects (sight, for example, has colour as its object), their activities are different, and so they are really distinct powers (*operatio sequitur esse*). But real distinctions must not be multiplied without a sufficient reason. For instance, one of the interior senses is the *vis memorativa* or sensitive memory, by means of which the animal remembers friend or foe, what has given it pleasure and what has injured it, and according to St. Thomas the memory of the past as past belongs to the sensitive memory, since the past as past refers to particulars and it is the sensitive memory which is concerned with particulars. If, however, we mean by memory the conservation of ideas or concepts, it is necessary to refer this to the intellect, and we can speak of the intellectual memory; but the intellectual memory is not a power really distinct from the intellect itself, more precisely the passive intellect: it is the intellect itself regarded under one of its aspects or functions. Again, the act of apprehending a truth, of resting in the apprehension of the truth, does not proceed from a power or faculty different from the faculty by which we reason discursively: *intellectus* and *ratio* are not distinct faculties, for it is the same mind which apprehends truth and reasons from that truth to another truth. Nor is the 'higher reason' (*ratio superior*) concerned with eternal things, a faculty different from the *ratio inferior*, by which we attain rational knowledge of temporal things. The two are one and the same faculty, though the faculty receives different names according to the objects of its different acts, as Augustine said. The same applies to the speculative and practical intellects, which are but one faculty.

3. It may be as well to say a few more words on the subject of the 'interior senses', which are common to animal as well as human beings. St. Thomas observes[7] that Avicenna in his book *On the Soul* postulated five interior senses, but that in reality there are only four. What does St. Thomas mean by 'senses' in this connection? Obviously not senses in our use of the term, since when we use the word senses, we refer to the five exterior senses. Why, then, does he call them senses? To indicate that they are operations belonging to the level of sensitive life and that they do not involve reason. There must, for example, be an instinctive operation by which the bird 'judges' that the twigs it sees will be useful for building a nest: it cannot see the utility simply by vision, which is directed to colour, while on the other hand it does not reason or judge in the proper sense: it has, therefore, an 'interior sense' by which it apprehends the utility of the twigs.

First of all, there must be an interior sense by which the data of the special exterior senses are distinguished and collated. The eye sees colour, the ear hears sounds, but though the sense of sight distinguishes one colour from another, it cannot distinguish colour from sound, since it cannot hear; and for the same reason it cannot refer the sound to the coloured object seen, for example, when a man is talking to his dog. This function of distinction and collation is performed by the general sense or *sensus communis*. Secondly, the animal is able to conserve the forms apprehended by sense, and this function is performed by the imagination (*phantasia* or *imaginatio*), which is 'a certain treasury of the forms received through the senses'. Thirdly, the animal is able to apprehend things which it cannot perceive through the senses, for example, that something is useful to it, that someone or something is friendly or unfriendly, and this task is performed by the *vis aestimativa*, while, lastly, the *vis memorativa* conserves such apprehensions. As regards sensible forms, there is, says St. Thomas, no difference between men and animals, since they are affected by exterior sensible objects in the same way; but in regard to apprehensions of things which are not directly perceived by the exterior senses, there is a difference between men and animals. The latter perceive such things as utility and inutility, friendliness and hostility by a natural instinct, whereas man compares particular things. What in animals, therefore, he calls the *vis aestimativa naturalis*, St. Thomas calls *vis cogitativa* in the case of human beings. Something more than mere instinct is involved.

4. Besides the five exterior senses, the four interior senses, the power of locomotion, the sensitive appetite and the rational cognitive faculties (to which I shall return in the next chapter, when treating of St. Thomas's theory of knowledge), man has also will (*voluntas*). The will differs from the sensitive appetite, since it desires the good as such or the good in general (*bonum sub communi ratione boni*), whereas the sensitive appetite does not desire good in general, but the particular objects of desire presented by the senses. Moreover, the will is of its very nature orientated towards good in general, and it necessarily desires the good in general. This necessity is not, however, a necessity of coercion, a necessity which bears upon the will with violence; it proceeds from the will itself, which of its very nature desires the last end or happiness (*beatitudo*). The will, since it is an appetitive faculty, cannot be understood apart from its natural object of desire, its natural *finis*, and this object, says St. Thomas, following Aristotle, is beatitude, happiness, the good in general. We necessarily desire to be happy, we cannot help desiring it; but the necessity in question is not a necessity imposed from without by violence (*necessitas coactionis*) but a necessity of nature (*necessitas naturalis*) proceeding from the nature of the will.

Yet although man necessarily desires happiness, this does not mean that he is not free in regard to his particular choices. There are some particular goods which are not necessary to happiness, and a man is free to will them or not. Moreover, even though true happiness is to be found only in the possession of God, only in the attainment of the infinite Good, that does not mean that every man must have a conscious desire of God or that he must necessarily will those means which will bring him to God. In this life the intellect has not got that clear vision of God as the infinite good and only source of happiness which would be needed to determine the will: man necessarily desires happiness, but the connection between happiness and God is not so steadfastly clear to him that he is unable to will something other than God. In a sense, of course, he is always willing God, because he necessarily wills happiness and, *de facto*, happiness is to be found only in the attainment of God, the infinite Good; but owing to his lack of clear vision of God as the infinite Good, objects may appear to him as necessarily related to his happiness which are not so related, and he can place his happiness in something other than God. Whatever he wills, he wills as a good, real or apparent (he necessarily wills *sub ratione boni*), but he does not necessarily will the actual infinite Good. In an interpretative sense he may be said to be always willing God; but as far as conscious choice is concerned, he may will something other than God, even to the exclusion of God. If he shuts his eyes to the truth and turns his attention to sensual pleasures, for example, placing his happiness in them, he is morally guilty; but that does not alter the fact that the incompatibility beween indulgence in inordinate sensual pleasure and the attainment of true happiness is not so compellingly self-evident to him that he cannot take indulgence in inordinate pleasure of sense as his end. One can take a parallel example from the activity of the intellect. If a man knows what the terms mean, it is impossible for him not to assent to the first principles in the intellectual order, for example, the principle of identity, but when a chain of reasoning is involved, as in a metaphysical proof of God's existence, he may refuse his assent, not because the argument is insufficient, but because he does not wish to assent and turns away his intellect from perceiving or dwelling on the necessary connection of the conclusion with the premisses. Similarly, a man necessarily wills *sub ratione boni*, he necessarily desires happiness; but he can turn his attention away from the necessary connection between happiness and God and allow something other than God to appear to him as the source of true happiness.

Free will (*liberum arbitrium*) is not a power or faculty different from the will; but there is a mental distinction between them, since the term 'will' signifies the faculty as principle of all our volition, whether necessary (in regard to the end, happiness) or free (in regard to the choice of means to the end), whereas 'free will' signifies the same faculty as principle of our free choice of means to the end. As already mentioned, St. Thomas maintained that though man necessarily wills the end, happiness, he has no compelling vision of the connection between particular means and this end, and therefore he is free in regard to the choice of these means, being necessitated neither from without nor from within. That man is free follows from the fact that he is rational. A sheep 'judges' by a natural instinct that the wolf is to be avoided, but man judges that some good is to be attained or some evil to be avoided by a free act of his intelligence.[8] The reason, unlike instinct, is not determined in its judgement concerning particular choices. Choice concerns the means to the final end (happiness), and it is possible for a man to consider any particular object from more than one point of view: he may consider it under its aspect as a good and judge that it should be chosen or he may consider it under its aspect as evil, that is, as lacking some good, and judge that it should be avoided.[9] *Liberum arbitrium* is thus the power by which a man is able to judge freely.[10] It might seem, then, that freedom belongs to the intellect and not to will; but St. Thomas observes[11] that when it is said that *liberum arbitrium* is the power by which a man is able to judge freely, the reference is not to any kind of judgement but to the decisive judgement of choice which puts an end to the deliberation which arises from the fact that a man can consider a possible object of choice from different points of view. For example, if there is a question of my going for a walk or not going for a walk, I can regard the walk as a good, as healthy exercise, or as evil, as taking up time which should be given to writing a letter for the afternoon post. The decisive judgement which says that I will go for a walk (or not, as the case may be) is made under the influence of the will. *Liberum arbitrium*, therefore, is the will, but it designates the will not absolutely, but in its relation to the reason. Judgement as such belongs to the reason, but freedom of judgement belongs immediately to the will. Still, it is true that St. Thomas's account of freedom is intellectualist in character.

5. This intellectualism is apparent in his answer to the question whether the intellect or the will is the nobler faculty. St. Thomas answers that, absolutely speaking, the intellect is the nobler faculty, since the intellect through cognition possesses the object, contains it in itself through mental

assimilation, whereas the will tends towards the object as external, and it is more perfect to possess the perfection of the object in oneself than to tend towards it as existing outside oneself. In regard to corporeal objects, therefore, knowledge of them is more perfect and nobler than volition in respect to them, since by knowledge we possess the forms of these objects in ourselves, and these forms exist in a nobler way in the rational soul than they do in the corporeal objects. Similarly, the essence of the beatific vision consists in the act of knowledge by which we possess God. On the other hand, although possession of the object by the intellect is in itself more perfect than tending towards the object by volition, the will may be nobler than the intellect in certain respects, *secundum quid*, because of accidental reasons. For example, in this life our knowledge of God is imperfect and analogical, we know God only indirectly, whereas the will tends to God directly: love of God is, therefore, more perfect than knowledge of God. In the case of objects which are less noble than the soul, corporeal objects, we can have immediate knowledge, and such knowledge is more perfect than volition; but in the case of God, an object which transcends the human soul, we have only mediate knowledge in this life, and our love of God is more perfect than our knowledge of God. In the beatific vision in heaven, however, when the soul sees the essence of God immediately, the intrinsic superiority of intellect to will reasserts itself, as it were. In this way St. Thomas, while adopting the intellectualist attitude of Aristotle, interprets it in a Christian setting.[12]

6. We have seen that St. Thomas rejected the Platonic-Augustinian view of the relation of soul to body and adopted the Aristotelian view of the soul as form of the body, emphasising the closeness of the union between the two. There is no *forma corporeitatis*, there is but one substantial form in man, the rational soul, which directly informs prime matter and is the cause of all human activities on the vegetative, sensitive and intellectual levels: sensation is an act not of the soul using a body, but of the *compositum*; we have no innate ideas, but the mind is dependent on sense-experience for its knowledge. The question arises, therefore, whether the closeness of the union between soul and body has not been so emphasised that the possible subsistence of the human soul apart from the body must be ruled out. In other words, is not the Aristotelian doctrine of the relation of soul to body in-

compatible with personal immortality? If one starts with the Platonic theory of the soul, immortality is assured, but the union of soul and body is rendered difficult to understand; whereas if one starts with the Aristotelian theory of the soul, it might seem that one has to sacrifice immortality, that the soul is so closely bound to the body that it cannot subsist apart from the body.

The soul is indeed the form of the body and, according to St. Thomas, it always retains its aptitude to inform a body, precisely because it is naturally the form of the body; but it is none the less a rational soul and its powers are not exhausted in informing the body. When actually dealing with the immortality of the soul St. Thomas argues that the soul is incorruptible because it is a subsistent form. A thing which corrupts is corrupted either by itself (*per se*) or accidentally (*per accidens*), that is, through the corruption of something else on which it depends for existence. The soul of the brute is dependent on the body for all its operations and corrupts when the body corrupts (*corruptio per accidens*): the rational soul, however, being a subsistent form, cannot be affected by the corruption of the body on which it does not intrinsically depend.[13] If this were all St. Thomas had to say by way of proving immortality, he would obviously be guilty of a gross *petitio principii*, since it is presupposed that the human soul is a *forma subsistens*, and this is precisely the point which has to be proved. St. Thomas argues, however, that the rational soul must be spiritual and a subsistent form, because it is capable of knowing the natures of all bodies. If it were material, it would be determined to a specified object, as the organ of vision is determined to the perception of colour. Again, if it depended intrinsically on a bodily organ, it would be confined to the knowledge of some particular kind of bodily object, which is not the case,[14] while if it were itself a body, material, it could not reflect on itself.[15] For these and other reasons the human soul, which is a rational soul, must be immaterial, i.e. spiritual, from which it follows that it is incorruptible or naturally immortal. Physically speaking, it could, of course, be annihilated by the God who created it; but its immortality follows from its nature and is not simply gratuitous, save in the sense that its very existence, like the existence of any other creature, is gratuitous.

St. Thomas argues also from the desire of persistence in being. There is a natural desire for immortality and a natural desire, as implanted by God, cannot be in vain.[16] 'It is impossible for a natural appetite to be in vain. But man has a natural appetite for perpetual persistence in being. This is clear from the fact that existence (*esse*) is desired by all things, but a man has an intellectual apprehension of *esse* as such, and not only of *esse* here and now as the brutes have. Man therefore attains immortality as regards his soul, by which he apprehends *esse* as such and without temporal limit.'[17] Man, as distinct from the irrational animal, can conceive perpetual existence, divorced from the present moment, and to this apprehension there corresponds a natural desire for immortality. As this desire must have been implanted by the Author of Nature, it cannot be in vain (*frustra* or *inane*). Against this Duns Scotus later argued that, as far as a natural desire (*desiderium naturale*) is concerned, man and brute are on a level in that both naturally shun death, while in regard to an elicited or conscious desire we have first to show that its fulfilment is possible before we can argue that it must be fulfilled.[18] One might reply that the possibility of the fulfilment of the desire is shown by proving that the soul is not intrinsically dependent on the body but is spiritual. This would be to admit that the argument from the spirituality of the soul is fundamental.

In view of St. Thomas's epistemology, of his insistence on the origin of human ideas in sense-experience and on the rôle of the phantasm in the formation of such ideas, it might appear that he contradicts himself when he says that the human mind is not intrinsically dependent on the body, and it might also appear that the soul in a state of separation would be incapable of intellectual activity. In regard to the first point, however, he maintains that the mind needs the body for its activity not as an organ of mental activity, for this is an activity of the mind alone, but because of the natural object of the human mind in this life, when conjoined to a body. In other words, the mind is not intrinsically dependent on the body for its subsistence. Can it, then, exercise its activity in a state of separation from the body? Yes, for its mode of cognition follows the state in which it is. When united to the body, the rational soul does not come to know things save *convertendo se ad phantasmata*; but when it is in a state of separation it is no longer unable to know itself and other souls perfectly and directly, the angels imperfectly. It might seem indeed that in this case it is better for the soul to be in a state of separation from the body than united to it, since spirits are nobler objects of knowledge than corporeal things; but St. Thomas cannot admit this, since he has insisted that it is natural for the soul to be united to the body and that their union is for the good of the soul. He does not hesitate, then, to draw the conclusion that the state of separation is *praeter naturam* and that the soul's mode of cognition in the state of separation is also *praeter naturam*.[19]

7. When St. Thomas proves the immortality of the soul, he is naturally referring to personal immortality. Against the Averroists he argues that the intellect is not a substance distinct from the human soul and common to all men, but that it is multiplied 'according to the multiplication of bodies'.[20] It is impossible to explain the diversity of ideas and intellectual operations in different men on the supposition that all men have but one intellect. It is not only sensations and phantasms which differ from man to man but their intellectual lives and activities as well. It is as absurd to suppose that they have one intellect as it would be to suppose that they have one vision.

It is important to realise that it is not the opinion of Avicenna concerning the unicity and separate character of the *active* intellect which necessarily does away with personal immortality (some mediaeval philosophers who certainly maintained personal immortality identified the active intellect with God or God's activity in the soul), but rather the opinion of Averroes concerning the unicity and separate character of the *passive* as well as of the active intellect. That Averroes was the chief enemy on this point St. Thomas makes quite clear at the beginning of his *De unitate intellectus contra Averroistas*. If the Averroistic theory is accepted 'it follows that after death nothing remains of men's souls but one intellect; and in this way the bestowal of rewards and punishments is done away with.' This is not to say, of course, that St. Thomas accepted the theory of the unicity of the active intellect: he argues against it in the *Summa contra Gentiles*, for example,[21] as also in the *Summa Theologica*.[22] One of his arguments is to the effect that if the active intellect were one in all men, then its functioning would be independent of the individual's control and would be constant, whereas in point of fact we can pursue intellectual activity at will and abandon it at will. Incidentally, St. Thomas interprets the notoriously obscure passage in Aristotle's *De Anima*[23] as teaching the individual character of the active intellect in individual men. It is impossible to say with certainty that the Thomist interpretation of Aristotle is wrong though I incline to this opinion; but the rightness or wrongness of his interpretation of Aristotle obviously does not affect the question of the truth or falsity of his own idea of the active intellect.[24]

Against the unicity of the passive intellect St. Thomas argues in the *De unitate intellectus contra Averroistas* and in the *Summa contra Gentiles*.[25] His arguments presuppose for the most part the Aristotelian psychology and epistemology; but the presupposition is only to be expected, not only because St. Thomas accepted the Aristotelian doctrine as he understood and interpreted it, but also because the Averroists were Aristotelians. To say, then, that St. Thomas presupposed the Aristotelian psychology and epistemology is simply to say that he tried to show the Averroists that their notion of the unitary and separate character of the passive intellect was inconsistent with their own principles. If the soul is the form of the body, how could the passive intellect be one in all men? One principle could not be the form of a plurality of substances. Again, if the passive intellect were a separate principle, it would be eternal; it should, then, contain all the *species intelligibiles* which have ever been received, and every man should be able to understand all those things which have ever been understood by men, which is manifestly not the case. Furthermore, if the active intellect were separate and eternal, it would be functioning from eternity and the passive intellect, also supposed to be separate and eternal, would be receiving from eternity; but this would render the senses and imagination unnecessary for intellectual operations, whereas experience shows that they are indispensable. And how could one explain the different intellectual capacities of different men? Men's differences in this respect certainly depend to some extent on their different infra-intellectual capacities.

It may be somewhat difficult for us to-day to understand the excitement produced by the Averroistic theory and the interest it aroused; but it was obviously incompatible with the Christian doctrines of immortality and of sanctions in the next life, and even if St. Thomas shows a desire to dissociate Aristotle from Averroes, the moral and religious consequences of the Averroistic doctrine were more important to him than Averroes's attempt to father his doctrine on the Greek philosopher. Against the Averroists Augustinians and Aristotelians made common cause. One might compare the reaction provoked by modern metaphysical and psychological systems which appear to endanger the human personality. On this point absolute idealism, for instance, aroused opposition on the part of philosophers who were otherwise sharply divided among themselves.

Chapter Thirty-eight

ST. THOMAS AQUINAS—VIII:
KNOWLEDGE

'Theory of knowledge' in St. Thomas—The process of knowledge; knowledge of the universal and of the particular—The soul's knowledge of itself—The possibility of metaphysics.

1. To look for an epistemology in St. Thomas, in the sense of a justification of knowledge, a proof or attempted proof of the objectivity of knowledge in face of subjective idealism of one kind or another, would be to look in vain. That everyone, even the self-styled sceptic, is convinced that knowledge of some sort is attainable was as clear to St. Thomas as it was to St. Augustine, and so far as there is a problem of knowledge for St. Thomas it is rather how to safeguard and justify metaphysics in face of the Aristotelian psychology than to justify the objectivity of our knowledge of the extramental world in face of a subjective idealism which had not yet arisen or to show the legitimacy of metaphysics in face of a Kantian criticism which still lay far in the future. This is not to say, of course, that the Thomist principles cannot be developed in such a way as to afford answers to subjective idealism and Kantianism; but one should not be guilty of the anachronism of making the historic Thomas answer questions with which he was not actually faced. Indeed, to treat St. Thomas's theory of knowledge separately from his psychological doctrine is itself something of an anachronism, yet I think it is capable of being justified, since it is out of the psychology that a problem of knowledge arises, and one can, for the sake of convenience at least, treat this problem separately. For the purpose of making this problem clear it is necessary first of all

to give a brief sketch of the way in which we attain our natural ideas and knowledge, according to Aquinas.

2. Corporeal objects act upon the organs of sense, and sensation is an act of the *compositum*, of soul and body, not of the soul alone using a body, as Augustine thought. The senses are naturally determined to the apprehension of particulars, they cannot apprehend universals. Brutes have sensation, but they have no grasp of general ideas. The phantasm or image, which arises in the imagination and which represents the particular material object perceived by the senses, is itself particular, the phantasm of a particular object or objects. Human intellectual cognition, however, is of the universal: the human being in his intellectual operations apprehends the form of the material object in abstraction; he apprehends a universal. Through sensation we can apprehend only particular men or trees, for example, and the interior images or phantasms of men or trees are always particular. Even if we have a composite image of man, not representing any one actual man distinctly but representing many confusedly, it is still particular, since the images or parts of the images of particular actual men coalesce to form an image which may be 'generic' in respect of actual particular men but which is itself none the less particular, the image of a particular imagined man. The mind, however, can and does conceive the general idea of man as such, which includes all men in its extension. An image of man certainly will not apply to all men, but the intellectual idea of man, even though conceived in dependence on the sensitive apprehension of particular men, applies to all men. The image of a man must be either of a man who has or of a man who has not some hair on his head. If the former, it does not in that respect represent bald men; if the latter, it does not in that respect represent men who are not bald; but if we form the concept of man as a rational animal, this idea covers all men, whether they are bald or not, white or black, tall or short, because it is the idea of the essence of man.

How, then, is the transition from sensitive and particular knowledge to intellectual cognition effected? Although sensation is an activity of soul and body together, the rational and spiritual soul cannot be affected directly by a material thing or by the phantasm: there is need, therefore, of an activity on the part of the soul, since the concept cannot be formed simply passively. This activity is the activity of the active

intellect which 'illumines' the phantasm and abstracts from
it the universal or 'intelligible species'. St. Thomas thus
speaks of illumination, but he does not use the word in the
full Augustinian sense (not at least according to what is probably the true interpretation of Augustine's meaning); he
means that the active intellect by its natural power and without any special illumination from God renders visible the
intelligible aspect of the phantasm, reveals the formal and
potentially universal element contained implicitly in the
phantasm. The active intellect then abstracts the universal
element by itself, producing in the passive intellect the *species impressa*. The reaction of the passive intellect to this
determination by the active intellect is the *verbum mentis*
(*species expressa*), the universal concept in the full sense.
The function of the active intellect is purely active, to abstract the universal element from the particular elements of
the phantasm, to cause in the passive intellect the *species
impressa*. The intellect of man contains no innate ideas but
is in potentiality to the reception of concepts: it has, therefore, to be reduced to act, and this reduction to act must be
effected by a principle itself in act. As this active principle
has no ready-made ideas of itself to supply, it must draw its
materials from what is provided by the senses, and this means
that it must abstract the intelligible element from the phantasm. To abstract means to isolate intellectually the universal
apart from the particularising notes. Thus the active intellect
abstracts the universal essence of man from a particular phantasm by leaving out all particular notes which confine it to
a particular man or particular men. As the active intellect is
purely active, it cannot impress the universal on itself; it impresses it on the potential element of the human intellect,
on the passive intellect, and the reaction to this impression
is the concept in the full sense, the *verbum mentis*.

It is important to realise, however, that the abstract concept is not the object of cognition, but the means of cognition.
If the concept, the modification of the intellect, were itself
the object of knowledge, then our knowledge would be a
knowledge of ideas, not of things existing extramentally, and
the judgements of science would concern not things outside
the mind but concepts within the mind. In actual fact, however, the concept is the likeness of the object produced in
the mind and is thus the means by which the mind knows
the object: in St. Thomas's language it is *id quo intelligitur*,

not *id quod intelligitur*.[1] Of course, the mind has the power of reflecting on its own modifications and so can turn the concept into an object; but it is only secondarily an object of knowledge, primarily it is the instrument of knowledge. By saying this St. Thomas avoids putting himself in a position which would be that of subjective idealism and which would land him in the difficulties attending that form of idealism. The theory he actually contrasts with his own is the theory of Plato; but that does not alter the fact that by adopting the attitude he did he escaped a snare from which it is practically impossible to extricate oneself.

As he held that the intellect knows directly the essence, the universal, St. Thomas drew the logical conclusion that the human mind does not know directly singular material things. The emphasis is, of course, on 'mind' and 'know', since it cannot be denied that the human being apprehends particular material objects sensitively: the object of sense is precisely the sensible particular. The intellect, however, comes to know by abstracting the intelligible species from the individualising matter, and in this case it can have direct knowledge of universals only. Nevertheless, even after abstracting the intelligible species, the intellect exercises its activity of knowing only through a 'conversion', a turning of attention to the phantasms in which it apprehends the universals, and in this way it has a reflexive or indirect knowledge of the particular things represented by the phantasms. Thus the sensitive apprehension of Socrates enables the mind to abstract the universal 'man'; but the abstract idea is a means of knowledge, an instrument of knowledge to the intellect only in so far as the latter adverts to the phantasm, and so it is able to form the judgement that Socrates is a man. It is thus not true to say that the intellect, according to St. Thomas, has no knowledge of corporeal particulars: what he held was that the mind has only an indirect knowledge of such particulars, the direct object of knowledge being the universal.[2] But this should not be taken to imply that the primary object of intellectual cognition is the abstract idea as such: the mind apprehends the formal element, the potentially universal element in Socrates, for example, and abstracts this from the individualising matter. In technical language its primary object of knowledge is the direct universal, the universal apprehended in the particular: it is only secondarily that it apprehends the universal precisely as universal, the reflexive universal.

Two explanatory remarks should be added. St. Thomas explains that when he says that the mind abstracts the universal from the corporeal particular by abstracting it from the individualising matter, he means that when the mind abstracts the idea of man, for example, it abstracts it from *this* flesh and *these* bones, that is, from the particular individualising matter, not from matter in general, 'intelligible matter' (i.e. substance as subject to quantity). Corporeality enters into the idea of man as such, though particular matter does not enter into the universal idea of man.[3] Secondly, St. Thomas does not mean to imply that it is the particular thing as such which cannot be the direct object of intellectual cognition, but rather the particular sensible or corporeal object. In other words, the particular corporeal object is debarred from being the direct object of intellectual cognition not precisely because it is particular but because it is material and the mind knows only by abstracting from matter as principle of individuation, that is, from this or that matter.[4]

3. According to St. Thomas, then, the human mind is originally in potentiality to knowledge; but it has no innate ideas. The only sense in which ideas are innate is that the mind has a natural capacity for abstracting and forming ideas: as far as actual ideas go, the mind is originally a *tabula rasa*. Moreover, the source of the mind's knowledge is sense-perception, since the soul, the form of the body, has as its natural object of knowledge the essences of material objects. The rational soul knows itself only by means of its acts, apprehending itself, not directly in its essence but in the act by which it abstracts intelligible species from sensible objects.[5] The soul's knowledge of itself is not, therefore, an exception to the general rule that all our knowledge begins with sense-perception and is dependent on sense-perception. This fact St. Thomas expresses by saying that the intellect, when united to a body in the present life, cannot come to know anything *nisi convertendo se ad phantasmata*.[6] The human mind does not think without the presence of a phantasm, as is clear from introspection, and it is dependent on the phantasm, as is shown by the fact that a disordered power of imagination (as in mad people) hinders knowledge; and the reason for this is that the cognitive power is proportioned to its natural object.[7] In brief, the human soul, as Aristotle said, understands

nothing without a phantasm, and we can say, *nihil in intellectu quod prius non fuerit in sensu.*

4. From this it obviously follows that the human mind cannot in this life attain a direct knowledge of immaterial substances, which are not and cannot be the object of the senses.[8] But the problem also arises whether there can be metaphysical knowledge at all on these premisses, whether the human mind can rise above the things of sense and attain any knowledge of God, for example, since God cannot be an object of sense. If our intellects are dependent on the phantasm, how can they know those objects of which there are no phantasms, which do not act on the senses?[9] On the principle, *nihil in intellectu quod prius non fuerit in sensu,* how can we attain knowledge of God when we cannot say *quod Deus prius fuerit in sensu?* In other words, once given the Thomist psychology and epistemology, it would appear that the Thomist natural theology is inevitably invalidated: we cannot transcend the objects of sense and are debarred from any knowledge of spiritual objects.

In order to understand St. Thomas's reply to this serious objection, it is necessary to recall his doctrine of intellect as such. The senses are necessarily determined to one particular kind of object, but the intellect, being immaterial, is the faculty of apprehending being. Intellect as such is directed towards all being. The object of the intellect is the intelligible: nothing is intelligible except in so far as it is in act, partakes of being, and all that is in act is intelligible in so far as it is in act, i.e. partakes of being. If we consider the human intellect precisely as intellect, we must admit, then, that its primary object is being. *Intellectus respicit suum obiectum secundum communem rationem entis; eo quod intellectus possibilis est quo est omnia fieri.*[10] *Primo autem in conceptione intellectus cadit ens; quia secundum hoc unumquodque cognoscibile est, inquantum est actu . . . Unde ens est proprium obiectum intellectus.*[11] The first movement of the intellect is thus towards being, not towards sensible being in particular, and the intellect can know the essence of a material thing only in so far as it is being: it is only in the second place that a particular kind of intellect, the human intellect, is directed towards a particular kind of being. Owing to its embodied state and the necessity of the *conversio ad phantasma* the human intellect has, in its embodied state, the sensible object as the natural and 'proper' object of its apprehension, but it does not lose its orientation towards being in general. As *human* intellect it must start from sense, from material beings, but as human *intellect* it can proceed beyond sense, not being confined to material essences, though it can do this only in so far as the immaterial objects are manifested in and through the sensible world, in so far as the material things have a relation to immaterial objects. As embodied intellect, as a *tabula rasa*, the natural object of which is the material essence, the intellect does not and cannot by its own power apprehend God directly; but sensible objects, as finite and contingent, reveal their relation to God, so that the intellect can know that God exists. Moreover, sensible objects, as the effects of God, manifest God to some extent, so that the intellect can come to know something of God's nature, though this knowledge cannot (naturally) be more than analogical. The necessity of the *conversio ad phantasma* means that we cannot know God directly, but we can know Him in so far as sensible objects manifest His existence and enable us to attain an analogical, indirect and imperfect knowledge of His nature: we can know God *ut causam, et per excessum, et per remotionem.*[12]

A presupposition of this position is the activity of the human intellect. If the human intellect were merely passive, if the *conversio ad phantasma* meant that ideas were caused simply passively, there could obviously be no natural knowledge of God, since sensible objects are not God and of God and other immaterial beings *non sunt phantasmata*. It is the active power of the intellect which enables it to read off, as it were, the relation to immaterial being in sensible being. Sensible cognition is not the total and perfect cause of our intellectual cognition, but is rather the *materia causa* of intellectual cognition: the phantasm is made actually intelligible by the active intellect through its abstractive operation. Inasmuch, then, as sensitive cognition is not the total cause of intellectual cognition, 'it is nothing to be astonished at if intellectual cognition extends farther than sensitive cognition'.[13] The human intellect, as united to a body, has as its natural object the essences of material things, but by means of these essences it can ascend to 'some sort of knowledge of invisible things'. These immaterial objects we can know only *per remotionem*, by denying of them the characteristics peculiar to sensible objects, or analogically; but we could not know them at all, were it not for the active power of the intellect.[14]

A further difficulty, already mentioned, remains. How can there be any positive content to our idea of God, or indeed of any spiritual object? If we say, for example, that God is personal, we obviously do not mean to ascribe to God human personality. If, however, we simply mean that God is not less than what we know as personal, is there any positive content to our idea of divine personality? Is 'not-less-than-personal' a positive idea? If we state it in affirmative terms, 'more-than-personal', has it a positive content? If it has not, then we are confined to the *via negativa* and can know God only *per remotionem*. But St. Thomas does not adhere simply to the *via negativa*: he utilises also the *via affirmativa*, maintaining that we can know God *per excessum*. Now, if when we ascribe wisdom, for instance, to God, we say that we are ascribing wisdom *modo eminentiori*, it is difficult to see what the content of our idea of divine wisdom actually is. It must be based on human wisdom, which is the only wisdom we experience naturally and directly; and yet it cannot be precisely human wisdom. But if it is human wisdom without the limitations and forms of human wisdom, what positive content does the idea possess, when we have no experience of wisdom without limitations? It would seem that if one is determined to maintain that the idea has a positive content, one must say either that the idea of human wisdom plus a negation of its limitations is a positive idea or, with Scotus, that we can attain an idea of the essence of wisdom, so to speak, which can be predicated univocally of God and man. The latter theory, though helpful in some ways, is not altogether satisfactory, since neither St. Thomas nor Scotus would hold that wisdom or any other perfection is realised univocally in God and creatures. As to the first answer, it may seem at first hearing to constitute an evasion of the difficulty; but reflection will show that to say that God is wise, meaning that God is more than wise (in the human sense), is not at all the same thing as saying that God is not wise (in the human sense). A stone is not wise (in the human sense), neither is it more than wise: it is less than wise. It is true that if we use the word 'wise' as signifying precisely the wisdom we experience, namely human wisdom, we can say with truth not only that the stone is not wise, but also that God is not wise; but the meaning of the two statements is not the same, and if the meaning is not the same, there must be a positive content in the statement that God is not wise (i.e. that God is more than wise in the specifically human sense). The statement, therefore, that God is wise ('wise' meaning infinitely more than wise in the human sense) has a positive content. To demand that the content of analogical ideas should be perfectly clear and expressible, so that they could be understood perfectly in terms of human experience, would be to misunderstand altogether the nature of analogy. St. Thomas was no rationalist, though he allowed that we can attain to *aliqualis cognitio Dei*. The infinity of the object, God, means that the finite human mind can attain no adequate and perfect idea of God's nature; but it does not mean that it cannot attain an imperfect and inadequate notion of God's nature. To know that God understands is to know something positive about God, since it tells us at the very least that God is not irrational like a stone or a plant, even though to know what the divine understanding is in itself exceeds our power of comprehension.

To return to the example of personality. The assertion that God is personal depends on the argument that the necessary Being and first Cause cannot be less perfect than what proceeds from it and depends on it. On the other hand, the Aristotelian-Thomist psychology and epistemology prevent one from saying that an argument of this kind will afford any adequate idea of what the divine personality is in itself. If one claimed that one had such an idea, it would be derived from experience and it would inevitably represent the data of experience. In practice this would mean that one would affirm that God is *a* Person, and the consequence would be a contradiction between revelation and philosophy. If, however, one realises that one can by philosophical argument alone attain no adequate idea of the divine personality, one will realise that all one is entitled to say from the philosophical viewpoint is that God is personal, not that God is *a* Person. When revelation informs us that God is three Persons in one Nature, our knowledge of God is extended, but no contradiction between theology and philosophy is involved. Moreover, when we say that God is personal, we really mean that He is not less than what we experience as personality, in the sense that the perfection of personality must be in Him in the only manner in which it can be in an infinite Being. If it is objected that this is to beg the question, since the question is precisely whether personality and infinity are compatible, one can reply that the proofs of God's personality and of His infinity are independent, so that we know that personality and infinity must be compatible, even though we have no direct experience of the divine personality or of the divine infinity. That there is a positive content of some sort to our idea of divine personality is shown by the fact that the meaning in the statement 'God is super-personal' (i.e. more than that which we directly experience as personality) is different from the meaning in the statement 'God is not personal' (i.e. in any sense, just as a stone is not personal). If we had reason to believe that God were not personal in the sense in which a stone is not personal, we should see the uselessness of worship and prayer; but the statement that God is personal suggests immediately that worship and prayer are in place, even though we have no adequate idea of what the divine personality is in itself. Of an infinite Being we can have but a finite and analogical natural knowledge, precisely because we ourselves are finite; but a finite and imperfect knowledge is not the same thing as no knowledge at all.

Chapter Thirty-nine

ST. THOMAS AQUINAS—IX:
MORAL THEORY

Eudaemonism—The vision of God—Good and bad—The virtues—The natural law—The eternal law and the foundation of morality in God—Natural virtues recognised by St. Thomas which were not recognised by Aristotle; the virtue of religion.

To treat the moral theory of St. Thomas in detail would be impracticable here, but a discussion of some important points may help to show its relation to the Aristotelian ethic.

1. In the *Nicomachean Ethics* Aristotle argues that every agent acts for an end and that the human agent acts for happiness, with a view to the acquisition of happiness. Happiness, he says, must consist in an activity, primarily in the activity which perfects the highest faculty in man directed to the highest and noblest objects. He comes to the conclusion, therefore, that human happiness consists primarily in *theoria*, in contemplation of the highest objects, chiefly in the contemplation of the unmoved Mover, God, though he held that the enjoyment of other goods, such as friendship and, in moderation, external goods, is necessary to perfect happiness.[1] Aristotle's ethic was thus eudaemonistic in character, teleological, and markedly intellectualist, since it is clear that for him contemplation meant philosophical contemplation: he was not referring to a religious phenomenon, such as the ecstasy of Plotinus. Moreover, the end (*telos*) of moral activity is an end to be acquired in this life: as far as the ethics of Aristotle are concerned there is no hint of any vision of God in the next life, and it is indeed questionable whether he believed in personal immortality at all. Aristotle's truly happy man is the philosopher, not the saint.

Now, St. Thomas adopted a similar eudaemonological and teleological standpoint, and his theory of the end of human conduct is in some respects intellectualist; but a change of emphasis soon becomes visible which marks a very considerable difference between his ethical theory and that of Aristotle. The only acts of man which fall properly within the moral sphere are free acts, acts which proceed from man precisely as man, as a rational and free being. These human acts (*actiones humanae*, as distinguished from *actiones hominis*) proceed from man's will, and the object of the will is the good (*bonum*). It is the prerogative of man to act for an end which he has apprehended, and every human act is performed for an apprehended end; but the particular end or good, for the attainment of which a particular human act is performed, does not and cannot fully perfect and satisfy the human will, which is set towards the universal good and can find its satisfaction only in the attainment of the universal good. What is the universal good in the concrete? It cannot consist in riches, for example, for riches are simply a means to an end, whereas the universal good is necessarily the final end and cannot be itself a means to a further end. It cannot consist in sensible pleasure, since this perfects only the body, not the whole man; nor can it consist in power, which does not perfect the whole man or satisfy the will completely and which, moreover, can be abused, whereas it is inconceivable that the ultimate and universal good can be abused or employed for an unworthy or evil purpose. It cannot consist even in consideration of the speculative sciences, since philosophic speculation certainly does not satisfy completely the human intellect and will. Our natural knowledge is drawn from sense-experience; yet man aspires to a knowledge of the ultimate cause as it is in itself, and this cannot be acquired by metaphysics. Aristotle may have said that the good of man consists in the consideration of the speculative sciences, but he was speaking of imperfect happiness, such as is attainable in this life. Perfect happiness, the ultimate end, is not to be found in any created thing, but only in God, who is Himself the supreme and infinite Good. God is the universal good in the concrete, and though He is the end of all things, of both rational and irrational creatures, it is only rational creatures who can attain this final good by way of knowledge and love: it is only rational creatures who can attain the vision of God in which alone perfect happiness lies. In this life man can know that God exists and he can attain an imperfect and analogical notion of God's nature, but it is only in the next life that he can know God as He is in Himself and no other end can fully satisfy man.[2]

Aristotle, says St. Thomas, was speaking of imperfect happiness such as is attainable in this life; but Aristotle, as I have already mentioned, says nothing in the *Ethics* of any other happiness. His ethic was an ethic of human conduct in this life, whereas St. Thomas has not proceeded far before he has brought in consideration of the perfect happiness attainable only in the next life, this happiness consisting principally in the vision of God, though it also includes, of course, satisfaction of the will, while other goods, such as the society of friends, contribute to the *bene esse* of beatitude, though no good save God is *necessary* for happiness.[3] At once, therefore, St. Thomas's moral theory is seen to move on a different plane from that of Aristotle, since however much St. Thomas may use Aristotle's language, the introduction of the next life and of the vision of God into moral theory is foreign to the thought of Aristotle.[4] What Aristotle calls happiness, St. Thomas calls imperfect happiness or temporal happiness or happiness as attainable in this life, and this imperfect happiness he regards as ordered to perfect happiness, which is attainable only in the next life and consists principally in the vision of God.

2. St. Thomas's statement that the perfect happiness of man consists in the vision of God raises a very difficult problem for any interpreter of the Saint's moral theory, a problem which is of much greater importance than might at first appear. The ordinary way of presenting the Thomist ethic has been to assimilate it to the ethic of Aristotle so far as is consistent with St. Thomas's position as a Christian, and to say that St. Thomas as moral philosopher considers man 'in the natural order' without reference to his supernatural end. When he speaks of beatitude as a moral philosopher he would, therefore, be speaking of natural beatitude, that attainment of the supreme Good, God, which is open to man in the natural order, without supernatural grace being necessary. His difference from Aristotle would lie in the fact that he, unlike the latter, introduces consideration of the next life, concerning which Aristotle is silent. Beatitude would consist principally in the natural knowledge and love of God attainable in this life (imperfect natural beatitude) and in the

next life (perfect natural beatitude). Those actions would be
good which lead to or are compatible with the attainment of
such beatitude, while those actions would be bad which are
incompatible with the attainment of such beatitude. The
fact that St. Thomas speaks of the attainment of the vision of
the divine essence (which is man's supernatural end and is
unattainable without supernatural grace) when we would
expect him to continue speaking as a moral philosopher
would, then, be due to the fact that he makes in practice no
very methodical separation between the rôles of philosopher
and theologian and speaks sometimes as the one, sometimes
as the other, without any clear indication of the change. Al-
ternatively one would have to explain away references to the
vision of God as meaning not the supernatural vision of the
divine essence, but merely the knowledge of God which would
be attainable by man in the next life, had man no supernatural end. In some such way one would make of St. Thomas
a moral philosopher who completed the Aristotelian ethic
by introducing consideration of the next life.

Unfortunately for upholders of this interpretation not only
does St. Thomas seem to refer to the vision of God in the
proper sense, but he even speaks of a 'natural desire' for the
vision of God. 'Ultimate and perfect beatitude can consist
only in the vision of the divine essence.' This, say some commentators, does not refer to the vision of God as supreme
good, as He is in Himself, but only to the vision of God as
first cause. But how could St. Thomas speak of knowledge of
God as first cause as though such knowledge were or could
be a vision of the divine essence? By the natural light of
reason we can know that God is first cause, but St. Thomas
states that 'for perfect beatitude it is required that the intellect should arrive at the very essence of the first cause'.[5]
Again, 'Ultimate beatitude consists in the vision of the divine essence, which is the very essence of goodness.'[6] For the
attainment of that vision there is in man a natural desire, as
man naturally desires to know the essence, the nature of the
first cause.[7] Whether or not St. Thomas was right in saying
this, it is to me inconceivable that he meant to refer only to
what Cajetan calls a *potentia obedientialis*: what can a 'natural desire' be, if it is not something positive? On the other
hand, it is out of the question to suppose that St. Thomas
meant to deny the supernatural and gratuitous character of
the beatific vision of God. Some commentators (Suarez, for

example) have got rid of the difficulty by saying that St. Thomas meant to affirm the presence in man of a *conditional* natural desire, that is, conditional on God's elevating man to the supernatural order and giving him the means to attain the supernatural end. This is a reasonable position, no doubt; but is it necessary to suppose that by a natural desire St. Thomas meant more than a desire to know the nature of the first cause, a desire which *in the concrete*, that is, given man's elevation to the supernatural order and his being destined for a supernatural end, means a desire for the vision of God? In other words, I suggest that St. Thomas is considering man in the concrete and that when he says that there is in man a 'natural desire' to know God's essence, and so to attain the vision of God, he means that man's natural desire to know as much as possible of the ultimate cause is, in the concrete and actual order, a desire to see God. Just as the will is naturally set towards the universal good and this movement of the will can reach satisfaction and quiescence only in the possession of God, so the intellect is made for truth and can be satisfied only by the vision of the absolute Truth.

It may be objected that this implies either that man has a natural desire for the beatific vision (using the word natural as opposed to supernatural), and in this case it is difficult to safeguard the gratuity of the supernatural order, or that by 'natural' St. Thomas means simply natural in the sense in which we frequently use the word, as opposed to 'unnatural' rather than supernatural, which is to interpret him in an arbitrary and unjustifiable fashion. But what I am suggesting is that St. Thomas is speaking pretty well as St. Augustine might speak, that he is considering man in the concrete, as called to a supernatural end, and that when he says that man has a natural desire to know the essence of God, he does not mean to imply that man in a hypothetical state of nature would have had such a natural desire, whether absolute or conditional, of seeing God, but simply that the term of the natural movement of the human intellect towards truth is *de facto* the vision of God, not because the human intellect can of itself see God, whether in this life or the next, but because *de facto* the only end of man is a supernatural end. I do not think that St. Thomas is considering the hypothetical state of nature at all, when he speaks of the *desiderium naturale*, and if this is so, it obviously means that his moral theory is not and cannot be a purely philosophical theory.

His moral theory is partly theological and partly philosophical: he utilises the Aristotelian ethic but fits it into a Christian setting. After all, Aristotle was himself considering man in the concrete, as far as he knew what man in the concrete actually is, and St. Thomas, who knew much better than Aristotle what man in the concrete actually is, was fully justified in utilising the thought of Aristotle when he believed it to be correct and found it compatible with his Christian standpoint.

It is perfectly true that St. Thomas speaks of imperfect beatitude, of man's temporal good, and so on; but that does not mean that he is considering man in a hypothetical state of pure nature. If St. Thomas says that the Church is instituted to help man to attain his supernatural good, and the State to help man to attain his temporal good, it would be absurd to conclude that in considering man in relation to the State he is considering man in a purely hypothetical condition: he is considering actual man in certain aspects and functions. It is not that St. Thomas ignores the fact that the attainment of man's true end exceeds man's unaided powers, but that in his moral theory he considers man as set towards, as called to that end. When answering the question if beatitude, once attained, can be lost, he answers that the imperfect beatitude of this life can be lost, but that the perfect beatitude of the next life cannot be lost, since it is impossible for anyone who has once seen the divine essence to desire not to see it.[8] This shows clearly enough that he is speaking of supernatural beatitude. In the reply to the second objection he says that the will is ordered to the last end by a natural necessity;[9] but this does not mean either that the last end in question is purely natural or, if it is supernatural, that God *could not* have created man without directing him to this end. The will necessarily desires happiness, beatitude, and *de facto* this beatitude can be found only in the vision of God: we can say, therefore, that the concrete human being necessarily desires the vision of God.

It seems to me that this interpretation is confirmed by the doctrine of the *Summa contra Gentiles*. First of all[10] St. Thomas argues that the end of every intellectual substance is to know God. All creatures are ordered to God as to their last end,[11] and rational creatures are ordered to God principally and peculiarly by way of their highest faculty, the intellect. But though the end and happiness of man must consist principally in the knowledge of God, the knowledge in question is not that knowledge which is obtained philosophically, by demonstration. By demonstration we come to know rather what God is not than what He is, and man cannot be happy unless he knows God as He is.[12] Nor can human happiness consist in the knowledge of God which is obtained through faith, even though by faith we are able to know more about God than we can learn through philosophical demonstration. The 'natural desire' is satisfied by the attainment of the final end, complete happiness, but 'knowledge by faith does not satisfy the desire, but rather inflames it, since everyone desires to see what he believes'.[13] Man's final end and happiness must consist, therefore, in the vision of God as He is in Himself, in the vision of the divine essence, a vision which is promised us in the Scriptures and by which man will see God 'face to face'.[14] It is only necessary to read St. Thomas in order to see that he is talking of the vision of the divine essence properly speaking. On the other hand, it is only necessary to read St. Thomas in order to see that he is perfectly aware that 'no created substance can by its natural power come to see God in His essence'[15] and that to attain this vision supernatural elevation and aid are required.[16]

What, then, of the 'natural desire'? Does not St. Thomas explicitly say that 'since it is impossible for a natural desire to be in vain (inane), and since this would be the case if it were not possible to arrive at the knowledge of the divine substance, which all minds naturally desire, it is necessary to say that it is possible for the substance of God to be seen by the intellect',[17] even though this vision cannot be attained in this life?[18] If there is really a 'natural desire' for the vision of God, is not the gratuitous character of supernatural beatitude endangered? In the first place it may be pointed out once again that St. Thomas explicitly states that man cannot attain to the vision of God by his own efforts: its attainment is made possible only through the grace of God, as he clearly affirms.[19] But there certainly is a difficulty in seeing how the grace of God, which alone makes possible the attainment of the final end, is not in some sense due to man, if there is a 'natural desire' for the vision of God and if it is impossible for a natural desire to be in vain. To come to a definitive conclusion as to what St. Thomas precisely understood by desiderium naturale in this connection may not be possible;

but it seems legitimate to suppose that he was regarding the natural desire of the intellect to know absolute Truth in the light of the actual and concrete order. Man's intellect has a natural orientation towards happiness, which must consist primarily in the knowledge of the absolute Truth; but man in the concrete actual order has been destined for a supernatural end and cannot be satisfied with anything less. Regarding the natural desire in the light of the facts known by revelation, one can say, then, that man has a 'natural desire' for the vision of God. In the *De Veritate*[20] St. Thomas says that man, according to his nature, has a natural appetite for *aliqua contemplatio divinorum*, such as it is possible for a man to obtain by the power of nature, and that the inclination of his desire towards the supernatural and gratuitous end (the vision of God) is the work of grace. In this place, then, St. Thomas does not admit a 'natural desire' in the strict sense for the vision of God, and it seems to me only reasonable to suppose that when in the *Summa Theologica* and the *Summa contra Gentiles* he speaks of a natural desire for the vision of God, he is not speaking strictly as a *philosopher*,[21] but as a theologian and philosopher combined, that is, presupposing the supernatural order and interpreting the data of experience in the light of that presupposition. In any case what has been said should be sufficient to show the difference between Aristotle's and St. Thomas's views of the end of man.[22]

3. The will, therefore, desires happiness, beatitude, as its end, and human acts are good or bad in so far as they are or are not means to the attainment of that end. Happiness must, of course, be understood in relation to man as such, to man as a rational being: the end is that good which perfects man as a rational being, not indeed as a disembodied intellect, for man is not a disembodied intellect, but in the sense that the perfecting of his sensitive and vegetative tendencies must be accomplished in subordination to his primary tendency, which is rational: the end is that which perfects man as such, and man as such is a rational being, not a mere animal. Every individual human act, that is to say, every deliberate act, is either in accordance with the order of reason (its immediate end being in harmony with the final end) or out of accordance with the order of reason (its immediate end being incompatible with the final end), so that every human act is either good or bad. An indeliberate act, such as the reflex act

of brushing away a fly, may be 'indifferent'; but no human, deliberate act, can be indifferent, neither good nor bad.[23]

4. St. Thomas follows Aristotle in treating the moral and intellectual virtues as habits, as good qualities or habits of the mind, by which a man lives rightly.[24] The virtuous habit is formed by good acts and facilitates the performance of subsequent acts for the same end. It is possible to have the intellectual virtues with the exception of prudence without the moral virtues, and it is possible to have the moral virtues without the intellectual virtues, with the exception of prudence and of understanding.[25] Moral virtue consists in a mean (*in medio consistit*). The object of moral virtue is to secure or facilitate conformity to the rule of reason in the appetitive part of the soul; but conformity implies the avoidance of the extremes of excess and defect, it means that the appetite or passion is reduced to the rule of reason. Of course, if one is considering simply conformity to reason, virtue is an extreme and all difformity with the rule of reason, whether by excess or defect, constitutes the other extreme (to say that virtue consists in a mean is not to say that it consists in mediocrity); but if one considers moral virtue in regard to the matter with which it is concerned, the passion or appetite in question, it is then seen to consist in a mean. The adoption of this theory of Aristotle might seem to make it difficult to defend virginity or voluntary poverty, for example, but St. Thomas points out that complete chastity, for instance, is virtuous only when it is in conformity with reason enlightened by God. If it is observed in accordance with God's will or invitation and for man's supernatural end, it is in accord with the rule of reason and so is, in St. Thomas's use of the word, a mean: if, however, it were observed out of superstition or vainglory, it would be an excess. In general, a virtue may be looked at as an extreme in relation to one circumstance, as a mean in regard to another.[26] In other words, the fundamental factor in virtuous action is conformity to the rule of reason, directing man's acts to his final end.

5. The rule and measure of human acts is the reason, for it belongs to the reason to direct a man's activity towards his end.[27] It is reason, therefore, which gives orders, which imposes obligation. But this does not mean that the reason is the arbitrary source of obligation or that it can impose whatever obligations it likes. The primary object of the practical reason is the good, which has the nature of an end, and the practical

reason, recognising the good as the end of human conduct, enunciates its first principle, *Bonum est faciendum et prosequendum, et malum vitandum*, good is to be done and pursued, and evil avoided.[28] But the good for man is that which befits his nature, that to which he has a natural inclination as a rational being. Thus man, in common with all other substances, has a natural inclination to the preservation of his being, and reason, reflecting on this inclination, orders that the means necessary to the preservation of life are to be taken. Conversely, suicide is to be avoided. Again, man, in common with other animals, has a natural inclination to the propagation of the species and the bringing up of children, while as a rational being he has a natural inclination to seek out the truth, especially concerning God. Reason, therefore, orders that the species is to be propagated and children educated, and that truth is to be sought, especially that truth which is necessary to the attainment of man's end. Obligation, therefore, is imposed by reason, but it is founded immediately on human nature itself; the moral law is rational and natural, in the sense of not being arbitrary or capricious: it is a natural law, *lex naturalis*, which has its basis in human nature itself, though it is enunciated and dictated by reason.

As the natural law is founded in human nature as such, in that nature which is the same in all men, it has regard primarily to those things which are necessary to human nature. There is an obligation, for example, to preserve one's life, but that does not mean that every man has to preserve his life in exactly the same way: a man must eat, but it does not follow that he is under an obligation to eat this or that, this much or that much. In other words, acts may be good and according to nature without being obligatory. Moreover, though reason sees that no man can preserve his life without eating and that no man can order his life rightly without knowledge of God, it also sees that the precept of propagating the species falls not on the individual, but on the multitude, and that it is fulfilled, even though not all individuals actually fulfil it. (This would be St. Thomas's answer to the objection that virginity is contrary to the natural law.)[29]

From the fact that the natural law is founded on human nature itself it follows that it cannot be changed, since human nature remains fundamentally the same, and that it is the same for all. It can be 'added to', in the sense that precepts useful for human life can be promulgated by divine law and by human law, even though these precepts do not fall directly under the natural law; but it cannot be changed, if by change is meant subtraction from the law.[30]

The primary precepts of the natural law (e.g. life is to be preserved) are entirely unchangeable, since their fulfilment is absolutely necessary for the good of man, while the proximate conclusions from the primary precepts are also unchangeable, though St. Thomas admits that they may be changed in a few particular cases on account of special reasons. But St. Thomas is not thinking here of what we call 'hard cases': he is thinking rather of cases like that of the Israelites who made off with the goods of the Egyptians. His meaning is that in this case God, acting as supreme lord and owner of all things rather than as legislator, transferred the ownership of the goods in question from the Egyptians to the Israelites, so that the Israelites did not really commit theft. Thus St. Thomas's admission of the changeability of the secondary precepts of the natural law in particular cases refers rather to what the Scholastics call a *mutatio materiae* than to a change in the precept itself: it is rather that the circumstances of the act are so changed that it no longer falls under the prohibition than that the prohibition itself is changed.

Moreover, precisely because the natural law is founded on human nature itself, men cannot be ignorant of it in regard to the most general principles, though it is true that they may fail on account of the influence of some passion to apply a principle to a particular case. As regards the secondary precepts men may be ignorant of these through prejudice or passion, and that is all the more reason why the natural law should be confirmed by positive divine law.[31]

6. Obligation, as we have seen, is the binding of the free will to perform that act which is necessary for the attainment of the last end, an end which is not hypothetical (an end which may or may not be desired) but absolute, in the sense that the will cannot help desiring it, the good which must be interpreted in terms of human nature. So far the ethic of St. Thomas follows closely that of Aristotle. Is there nothing further? Is the natural law, promulgated by reason, without any transcendental foundation? Aristotle's eudaemonological ethic fitted in, of course, with his general finalistic outlook; but it was not grounded in God and could not be, since the Aristotelian God was not Creator nor did He

exercise providence: He was final cause, but not first efficient cause or supreme exemplary cause. In St. Thomas's case, however, it would be extremely strange were ethics to be left without demonstrable connection with metaphysics, and in fact we find that connection insisted on.

On the supposition that God created and rules the world (the proof of this does not pertain to ethics), it follows that the divine wisdom must be conceived as ordering man's actions towards his end. God, to speak somewhat anthropomorphically, has an exemplar idea of man and of the acts which fulfil man's nature and which are required for the attainment of man's end, and the divine wisdom as directing man's acts to the attainment of that end constitutes the eternal law. As God is eternal and His idea of man eternal, the promulgation of the law is eternal *ex parte Dei*, though it is not eternal *ex parte creaturae*.[32] This eternal law, existing in God, is the origin and fount of the natural law, which is a participation of the eternal law. The natural law is expressed passively in man's natural inclinations, while it is promulgated by the light of reason reflecting on those inclinations, so that inasmuch as every man naturally possesses the inclinations to the end of man and possesses also the light of reason, the eternal law is sufficiently promulgated for every man. The natural law is the totality of the universal dictates of right reason concerning that good of nature which is to be pursued and that evil of man's nature which is to be shunned, and man's reason could, at least in theory, arrive by its own light at a knowledge of these dictates or precepts. Nevertheless, since, as we have seen, the influence of passion and of inclinations which are not in accordance with right reason may lead men astray and since not all men have the time or ability or patience to discover the whole natural law for themselves, it was morally necessary that the natural law should be positively expressed by God, as was done by the revelation of the Decalogue to Moses. It must also be added that man has *de facto* a supernatural end, and in order that he should be able to attain this supernatural end, it was necessary that God should reveal the supernatural law, over and above the natural law. 'Since man is destined to the end of eternal beatitude, which exceeds the capacity of the human natural faculty, it was necessary that besides the natural law and human law he should also be directed to his end by a divinely given law.'[33]

It is very important to realise clearly that the foundation of the natural law in the eternal law, the metaphysical foundation of the natural law, does not mean that the natural law is capricious or arbitrary; that it could be otherwise than it is: the eternal law does not depend primarily on the divine will but on the divine reason, considering the exemplar idea of human nature. Given human nature, the natural law could not be otherwise than it is. On the other hand, we must not imagine that God is subject to the moral law, as something apart from Himself. God knows His divine essence as imitable in a multiplicity of finite ways, one of those ways being human nature, and in that human nature He discerns the law of its being and wills it: He wills it because He loves Himself, the supreme Good, and because He cannot be inconsistent with Himself. The moral law is thus ultimately founded on the divine essence itself and so cannot change: God wills it certainly, but it does not depend on any arbitrary act of the divine will. Hence to say that the moral law does not depend primarily on the divine will is not at all equivalent to saying that there is a moral law which in some mysterious way stands behind God and rules God: God is Himself the supreme Value and the source and measure of all value: values depend on Him, but in the sense that they are participations or finite reflections of God, not in the sense that God arbitrarily confers on them their character as values. St. Thomas's doctrine of the metaphysical foundation, the theistic foundation, of the moral law in no way threatens its rational or necessary character: ultimately the moral law is what it is because God is what He is, since human nature, the law of whose being is expressed in the natural law, itself depends on God.

7. Finally one can point out that St. Thomas's realisation of God as Creator and supreme Lord led him, in company, of course, with other Scholastics, to recognise natural values which Aristotle did not envisage and could not envisage once given his view of God. To take one example, that of the virtue of religion (*religio*). Religion is the virtue by which men pay to God the worship and reverence which they owe Him as 'first Principle of the creation and government of things'. It is superior to the other moral virtues, inasmuch as it is more closely concerned with God, the last end.[34] It is subordinate to the virtue of justice (as a *virtus annexa*), inasmuch as through the virtue of religion a man pays to God his debt of

worship and honour, a debt which is owing in justice.[35] Religion is thus grounded in man's relationship to God, as creature to Creator, as subject to Lord. As Aristotle did not look upon God as Creator nor as exercising conscious government and providence, but regarded Him as the final Cause alone, wrapped up in Himself and drawing the world unconsciously, he could not envisage a personal relationship between man and the unmoved Mover, though he expected, of course, that man would recognise and in a sense honour the unmoved Mover, as the noblest object of philosophic contemplation. St. Thomas, however, with his clear idea of God as Creator and as provident Governor of the universe, could and did envisage as man's primary duty the expression in act of the relationship which is bound up with his very being. The virtuous man of Aristotle is, in a sense, the most independent man, whereas the virtuous man of St. Thomas is, in a sense, the most dependent man, that is, the man who realises truly and fully expresses his relation of dependence on God.

Chapter Forty

ST. THOMAS AQUINAS–X:
POLITICAL THEORY

*St. Thomas and Aristotle—The natural origin of human so-
ciety and government—Human society and political authority
willed by God—Church and State—Individual and State—Law
—Sovereignty—Constitutions—St. Thomas's political theory an
integral part of his total system.*

1. St. Thomas's ethical theory or theory of the moral life
was based philosophically on the moral theory of Aristotle,
though St. Thomas supplied it with a theological basis which
was lacking in Aristotle's theory. In addition, the Thomist
theory is complicated by the fact that St. Thomas believed,
as a Christian, that man has *de facto* only one end, a supernatural end, so that a purely philosophical ethic was bound
to be in his eyes an insufficient guide to practice: he could not
simply adopt Aristotelianism lock, stock and barrel. The same
is true of his political theory, in which he adopted the general
framework of Aristotle's treatment, but had at the same time
to leave the political theory 'open'. Aristotle certainly supposed that the State satisfied or ideally could satisfy all the
needs of man;[1] but St. Thomas could not hold this, since he
believed that man's end is a supernatural end and that it is
the Church and not the State which caters for the attainment
of that end. This meant that a problem which was not, and
could not be, treated by Aristotle had to be considered by
St. Thomas, as by other mediaeval writers on political
theory, the problem of the relations of Church and State. In
other words, though St. Thomas borrowed largely from Aristotle in regard to the subject-matter and method of treat-

ment of political theory, he considered the matter in the light of the Christian mediaeval outlook and modified or supplemented his Aristotelianism in accordance with the exigencies of his Christian faith. The Marxist may like to point to the influence of mediaeval economic, social and political conditions on St. Thomas's theory, but the important difference between Aristotle and St. Thomas is not that the former lived in a Greek City-state and the latter in the feudal epoch; it is rather that for the former the natural end of man is self-sufficient and is attained through life in the State, whereas for the latter the end of man is supernatural and is fully attainable only in the next life. Whether the amalgamation of Aristotelianism with the Christian view of man and his end constitutes a fully consistent and coherent synthesis or a somewhat fragile partnership, is a further question; what is insisted on at the moment is that it is a mistake to place a greater emphasis on the influence of mediaeval conditions on St. Thomas than on the influence of the Christian religion as such, which did not grow up in the Middle Ages and is not confined to the Middle Ages. The precise form taken by the problem of the relations of Church and State must of course be seen in the light of mediaeval conditions; but ultimately the problem arises from the confrontation of two different conceptions of man and his destiny; its precise formulation at any given time or by one thinker is incidental.

2. The State is for St. Thomas, as for Aristotle, a natural institution, founded on the nature of man. At the beginning of the De regimine principum[2] he argues that every creature has its own end, and that whereas some creatures attain their end necessarily or instinctively, man has to be guided to its attainment by his reason. But man is not an isolated individual who can attain his end simply as an individual by using his own individual reason; he is by nature a social or political being, born to live in community with his fellows. Indeed, man needs society more than other animals do. For whereas nature has provided the animals with clothing, means of defence, etc., she has left man unprovided, in a condition where he has to provide for himself by the use of his reason, and this he can do only through co-operation with other men. Division of labour is necessary, by which one man should devote himself to medicine, another to agriculture, and so on. But the most evident sign of the social nature of man is his faculty of expressing his ideas to other men through the

medium of language. Other animals can express their feelings only through very general signs, but man can express his concepts completely (*totaliter*). This shows that man is naturally fitted for society more than any other gregarious animal, more even than the ants and the bees.

Society, therefore, is natural to man; but if society is natural, so also is government. Just as the bodies of men and animals disintegrate when the controlling and unifying principle (the soul) has left them, so would human society tend to disintegrate owing to the number of human beings and their natural preoccupation with self, unless there was someone to take thought for the common good and direct the activities of individuals with a view to the common good. Wherever there is a multitude of creatures with a common good to be attained there must be some common ruling power. In the body there is a principal member, the head or the heart; the body is ruled by the soul, and in the soul the irascible and concupiscible parts are directed by the reason; in the universe at large inferior bodies are ruled by the superior, according to the disposition of divine providence. What is true, then, of the universe at large, and of man as an individual, must be true also of human society.

3. If human society and government are natural, are prefigured in human nature, it follows that they have a divine justification and authority, since human nature has been created by God. In creating man God willed human society and political government, and one is not entitled to say that the State is simply the result of sin. If no one did wrong, then obviously some activities and institutions of the State would be unnecessary; but even in the state of innocence, if it had persisted, there would have to have been an authority to care for the common good. 'Man is by nature a social animal. Hence in the state of innocence men would have lived in society. But a common social life of many individuals could not exist, unless there were someone in control, to attend to the common good.'[3] Moreover, there would have been some inequality of gifts even in the state of innocence, and if one man had been supereminent in knowledge and righteousness, it would not have been proper that he should have no opportunity to exercise his outstanding talents for the common good by direction of common activities.

4. By declaring the State a natural institution St. Thomas gave it, in a sense, a utilitarian foundation, but his utilitarian-

ism is Aristotelian; he certainly did not consider the State
simply the creation of enlightened egoism. He recognised the
force of egoism, of course, and its centrifugal tendency in
regard to society; but he also recognised the social tendency
and impulse in man, and it is this social tendency which
enables society to endure in spite of the tendency to egoism.
As Hobbes regarded egoism as the only fundamental impulse,
he had to find the practical principle of cohesion in force,
once society had been founded by the prudential dictates of
enlightened egoism; but in point of fact neither force nor enlightened egoism would be sufficient to make society endure,
if man had no social tendency implanted by nature. In other
words, the Christianised Aristotelianism of St. Thomas enabled him to avoid both the notion that the State is the result
of original sin, a notion to which St. Augustine seems to have
tended, and the notion that the State is simply the creation
of egoism: it is prefigured in human nature, and since human
nature is God's creation, it is willed by God. From this there
follows the important consequence that the State is an institution in its own right, with an end of its own and a sphere
of its own. St. Thomas could not, then, adopt an extremist
position in regard to the problem of the relations between
Church and State: he could not, if he was to be logical,
turn the Church into a super-State and the State into a kind
of dependency of the Church. The State is a 'perfect society'
(*communitas perfecta*), that is, it has at its disposal all the
means necessary for the attainment of its end, the *bonum
commune* or common good of the citizens.[4] The attainment
of the common good postulates first of all peace within the
State, among the citizens, secondly the unified direction of
the activities of the citizens *ad bene agendum*, thirdly the
adequate provision for the needs of life; and the government
of the State is instituted to secure these necessary conditions
of the common good. It is also necessary for the common
good that hindrances to the good life, such as danger from
foreign enemies and the disintegrating effects of crime
within the State, should be averted, and the monarch has at
his disposal the means necessary to avert these hindrances,
namely armed force and the judiciary system.[5] The end of
the Church, a supernatural end, is higher than that of the
State, so that the Church is a society superior to the State,
which must subordinate itself to the Church in matters bearing upon the supernatural life; but that does not alter the

fact that the State is a 'perfect society', autonomous within its own sphere. In terms of later theology, then, St. Thomas must be reckoned as an upholder of the *indirect power* of the Church over the State. When Dante in his *De Monarchia* recognises the two spheres of Church and State, he is at one with St. Thomas, as far at least as the Aristotelian aspect of the latter's political theory is concerned.[6]

However, the attempted synthesis between the Aristotelian idea of the State and the Christian idea of the Church was somewhat precarious. In the *De regimine principum*[7] St. Thomas declares that the end of society is the good life and that the good life is a life according to virtue, so that a virtuous life is the end of human society. He then goes on to observe that the *final* end of man is not to live virtuously, but by living virtuously to attain to the enjoyment of God, and that the attainment of this end exceeds the powers of human nature. 'Because man does not attain the end of enjoyment of God by human power, but by divine power, according to the words of the Apostle "the grace of God, life eternal",[8] to lead man to this end will pertain not to human but to divine rule': the leading of man to his final end is entrusted to Christ and His Church, so that under the new Covenant of Christ kings must be subject to priests. St. Thomas certainly recognises that the king has in his hands the direction of human and earthly matters, and he cannot be rightly interpreted as meaning to deny that the State has its own sphere; but he insists that it pertains to the king to procure the good life of his subjects with a view to the attainment of eternal beatitude: 'he should order those things which lead to heavenly beatitude and prohibit, as far as possible, their contraries.'[9] The point is that St. Thomas does not say that man has, as it were, two final ends, a temporal end which is catered for by the State and a supernatural, eternal end which is catered for by the Church: he says that man has one final end, a supernatural end, and that the business of the monarch, in his direction of earthly affairs, is to facilitate the attainment of that end.[10] The power of the Church over the State is not a *potestas directa*, since it is the business of the State, not the Church, to care for economic concerns and the preservation of peace; but the State must care for these concerns with an eye on the supernatural end of man. In other words, the State may be a 'perfect society', but the elevation of man to the supernatural order means that the State is very much a handmaid of the Church. This point of view is based not so much on mediaeval practice as on the Christian faith, and it is, needless to say, not the view of Aristotle who knew nothing of man's eternal and super-natural end. That there is a certain synthesis between the Aristotelian political theory and the demands of the Christian faith in the thought of St. Thomas, I should not attempt to deny; but I do think that the synthesis is, as I have already suggested, somewhat precarious. If the Aristotelian elements were pressed, the result would be a theoretical separation of Church and State of a kind which would be quite foreign to the thought of St. Thomas. In fact, his view of the rela-tion of Church and State is not unlike his view of the rela-tion between Faith and Reason. The latter has its own sphere, but philosophy is none the less inferior to theology: similarly, the State has its own sphere, but it is none the less, to all intents and purposes, the handmaid of the Church. Con-versely, if one adheres to the historic Aristotle so closely as to make philosophy absolutely autonomous in its own sphere, one will naturally, in political theory, tend to make the State absolutely autonomous within its own sphere: this is what the Averroists did, but St. Thomas was most emphatically not an Averroist. One may say, then, that St. Thomas's po-litical theory does represent to some extent the actual situa-tion, in which the nation-State was becoming self-conscious but in which the authority of the Church had not yet been expressly repudiated. St. Thomas's Aristotelianism allowed him to make the State a perfect society, but his Christianity, his conviction that man has but one ultimate end, effectually prevented him from making the State an absolutely autono-mous society.

5. A similar ambiguity shows itself in St. Thomas's doc-trine of the relation of the individual to the State. In the *Summa Theologica*[11] he remarks that since the part is or-dered to the whole as what is imperfect to what is perfect, and since the individual is a part of the perfect society, it is necessary that law should properly be concerned with the common happiness. It is true that he is trying to show simply that law is concerned primarily with the common good rather than with the good of the individual, but he does speak as though the individual citizen were subordinated to the whole of which he forms a part. The same principle, that the part exists for the whole, is applied by St. Thomas in more than

one place to the individual's relation to the community. For example,[12] he argues that it is right for the public authority to deprive an individual citizen of life for the graver crimes on the ground that the individual is ordered to the community, of which he forms a part, as to an end. And it is really an application of this principle when he insists in the Commentary on the *Ethics*[13] that courage is shown by giving one's life for the best things, as is the case when a man dies in defence of his country.

If this principle, that the part is ordered to the whole, which represents St. Thomas's Aristotelianism, were pressed, it would seem that he subordinates the individual to the State to a remarkable degree; but St. Thomas also insists that he who seeks the common good of the multitude seeks his own good as well, since one's own good cannot be attained unless the common good is attained, though it is true that in the *corpus* of the article in question he remarks that right reason judges that the common good is better than the good of the individual.[14] But the principle should not be over-emphasised, since St. Thomas was a Christian theologian and philosopher as well as an admirer of Aristotle, and he was well aware, as we have already seen, that man's final end is outside the sphere of the State: man is not simply a member of the State, indeed the most important thing about him is his supernatural vocation. There can, then, be no question of 'totalitarianism' in St. Thomas, though it is obvious that his Aristotelianism would make it impossible for him to accept such a theory of the State as that of Herbert Spencer: the State has a positive function and a moral function. The human being is a person, with a value of his own; he is not simply an 'individual'.

6. That totalitarianism is foreign to St. Thomas's thought is shown clearly by his theory of law and of the origin and nature of sovereignty. There are four kinds of law: the eternal law, the natural law, the divine positive law and human positive law. The divine positive law is the law of God as positively revealed, imperfectly to the Jews, perfectly through Christ,[15] while the law of the State is human positive law. Now, the function of the human legislator is primarily to apply the natural law[16] and to support the law by sanctions.[17] For example, murder is forbidden by the natural law, but reason shows the desirability of positive enactments whereby murder is clearly defined and whereby sanctions are added,

since the natural law does not of itself clearly define murder in detail or provide immediate sanctions. The legislator's primary function is, therefore, that of defining or making explicit the natural law, of applying it to particular cases and of making it effective. It follows that human positive law is derived from the natural law, and that every human law is a true law only in so far as it is derived from the natural law. 'But if it disagrees with the natural law in something, it will not be a law, but the perversion of law.'[18] The ruler is not entitled to promulgate laws which go counter to or are incompatible with the natural law (or, of course, the divine law): he has his legislative power ultimately from God, since all authority comes from God, and he is responsible for his use of that power: he is himself subject to the natural law and is not entitled to transgress it himself or to order his subjects to do anything incompatible with it. Just human laws bind in conscience in virtue of the eternal law from which they are ultimately derived; but unjust laws do not bind in conscience. Now, a law may be unjust because it is contrary to the common good or because it is enacted simply for the selfish and private ends of the legislator, thus imposing an unjustifiable burden on the subjects, or because it imposes burdens on the subjects in an unjustifiably unequal manner, and such laws, being more acts of violence than laws, do not bind in conscience, unless perhaps on occasion their non-observance would produce a greater evil. As for laws which are contrary to the divine law, it is never licit to obey them, since we ought to obey God rather than men.[19]

7. It will be seen, then, that the legislator's power is very far from being absolute in the thought of St. Thomas; and the same is clear from a consideration of his theory of sovereignty and government. That St. Thomas held that political sovereignty comes from God is admitted by all, and it seems probable that he maintained the view that sovereignty is given by God to the people as a whole, by whom it is delegated to the actual ruler or rulers; but this latter point does not seem to me to be quite so certain as some writers have made out, since texts can be alleged to show that he held otherwise. Yet it is undeniable that he speaks of the ruler as representing the people[20] and that he states roundly[21] that the ruler possesses legislative power only in so far as he stands in place (*gerit personam*) of the people,[22] and such statements may reasonably be taken to imply that he did hold that sovereignty

comes to the ruler from God *via* the people, though at the same time it must be admitted that St. Thomas scarcely discusses the question in a formal and explicit manner. In any case, however, the ruler possesses his sovereignty only for the good of the whole people, not for his private good, and if he abuses his power, he becomes a tyrant. Assassination of a tyrant was condemned by St. Thomas and he speaks at some length of the evils which may attend rebellions against a tyrant. For example, the tyrant may become more tyrannical, if the rebellion fails, while if it is successful, it may simply result in the substitution of one tyranny for another. But deposition of a tyrant is legitimate, especially if the people have the right of providing themselves with a king. (Presumably St. Thomas is referring to an elective monarchy.) In such a case the people do no wrong in deposing the tyrant, even if they had subjected themselves to him without any time limit, for he has deserved deposition by not keeping faith with his subjects.[23] Nevertheless, in view of the evils which may attend rebellion, it is far preferable to make provision beforehand to prevent a monarchy turning into a tyranny than to have to put up with or to rebel against tyranny once established. If feasible, no one should be made ruler if he is likely to turn himself into a tyrant; but in any case the power of the monarch should be so tempered that his rule cannot easily be turned into a tyranny. The best constitution will in fact be a 'mixed' constitution, in which some place is given to aristocracy and also to democracy, in the sense that the election of certain magistrates should be in the hands of the people.[24]

8. In regard to classification of forms of government St. Thomas follows Aristotle. There are three good types of government (law-abiding democracy, aristocracy and monarchy) and three bad forms of government (demagogic and irresponsible democracy, oligarchy and tyranny), tyranny being the worst of the bad forms and monarchy the best of the good forms. Monarchy gives stricter unity and is more conducive to peace than other forms: moreover, it is more 'natural', bearing an analogy to the rule of reason over the other functions of the soul and of the heart over the other members of the body. Moreover, the bees have their monarch, and God rules over all creation.[25] But the ideal of the best man as monarch is not easily attainable, and in practice the best constitution, as we have seen, is a mixed constitution, in

which the power of the monarch is tempered by that of magistrates elected by the people. In other words and in modern terms St. Thomas favours limited or constitutional monarchy, though he does not regard any particular form of decent government as divinely ordained: it is not the precise form of government which is of importance, but the promotion of the public good, and if in practice the form of government is an important consideration, it is its relation to the public good which makes it of importance. St. Thomas's political theory, therefore, is flexible in character, not rigid and doctrinaire, and while he rejects absolutism, he also implicitly rejects the *laissez-faire* theory. The ruler's task is to promote the public good, and this he will not do unless he promotes the economic well-being of the citizens. In fine, St. Thomas's political theory is characterised by moderation, balance and common sense.

9. In conclusion one may point out that St. Thomas's political theory is an integral part of his total philosophical system, not just something added on. God is supreme Lord and Governor of the universe, but He is not the only cause, even though He is the first Cause and the final Cause; He directs rational creatures to their end in a rational manner through acts the fitness and rightness of which are shown by reason. The right of any creature to direct another, whether it be the right of the father of the family over the members of the family or of the sovereign over his subjects, is founded on reason and must be exercised according to reason: as all power and authority is derived from God and is given for a special purpose, no rational creature is entitled to exercise unlimited, capricious or arbitrary authority over another rational creature. Law is defined, then, as 'an ordinance of reason for the common good, made by him who has care of the community, and promulgated'.[26] The sovereign occupies a natural place in the total hierarchy of the universe, and his authority must be exercised as part of the general scheme by which the universe is directed. Any idea of the sovereign being completely independent and irresponsible would thus be essentially alien to St. Thomas's philosophy. The sovereign has his duties and the subjects have their duties: 'legal justice', which should exist both in the sovereign and in his subjects, directs the acts of all the virtues to the common good;[27] but these duties are to be seen in the light of the relationship of means to end which obtains in all creation. As man is a social being,

there is need for political society, in order that his nature may be fulfilled; but man's vocation to live in political society must itself be seen in the light of the final end for which man was created. Between the supernatural end of man and the natural end of man there must be due harmony and the due subordination of the latter to the former; so that man must prefer the attainment of the final end to anything else, and if the sovereign orders him to act in a manner incompatible with the attainment of the final end, he must disobey the sovereign. Any idea of the complete and total subordination of the individual to the State would be necessarily abhorrent to St. Thomas, not because he was an extreme 'Papalist' in political affairs (he was not), but because of his total theological-philosophical system, in which order, proportion and subordination of the lower to the higher reign, though without the enslavement or moral annihilation of the lower. In the whole scheme of creation and providence man has his place: abuses and practical exaggerations cannot alter the ideal order and hierarchy which are ultimately based on God Himself. Forms of government may alter; but man himself has a fixed and abiding essence or nature, and on that nature the necessity and moral justification of the State are grounded. The State is neither God nor Antichrist: it is one of the means by which God directs the rational embodied creation to its end.

Note on St. Thomas's aesthetic theory.

One cannot say that there is a formal discussion of aesthetic theory in the philosophy of St. Thomas, and what he does have to say on the matter is mostly borrowed from other writers, so that though his remarks may be taken as the starting-point of an aesthetic theory, it would be a mistake to develop an aesthetic theory on the basis of his remarks and then attribute that theory to him, as if he had himself developed it. Nevertheless, it may be as well to point out that when he remarks that *pulchra dicuntur quae visa placent*,[28] he does not mean to deny the objectivity of beauty. The beautiful consists, he says, in proper proportion and belongs to the formal cause: it is the object of the cognitive power, whereas the good is the object of desire.[29] For beauty three elements are required, integrity or perfection, proper proportion and clarity:[30] the form shines out, as it were, through colour, etc., and is the object of disinterested (non-appetitive) apprehension. St. Thomas recognises, therefore, the objectivity of beauty and the fact that aesthetic appreciation or experience is something *sui generis*, that it cannot be identified simply with intellectual cognition and that it cannot be reduced to apprehension of the good.

Chapter Forty-one

ST. THOMAS AND ARISTOTLE:
CONTROVERSIES

St. Thomas's utilisation of Aristotle—Non-Aristotelian elements in Thomism—Latent tensions in the Thomist synthesis—Opposition to Thomist 'novelties'.

1. Although St. Albert had gone some way in the utilisation of the Aristotelian philosophy, it was left to St. Thomas to attempt the full reconciliation of the Aristotelian system with Christian theology. The desirability of attempting this reconciliation was clear, since to reject the Aristotelian system would mean rejecting the most powerful and comprehensive intellectual synthesis known to the mediaeval world. Moreover, St. Thomas, with his genius for systematisation, saw clearly the use that could be made of the principles of the Aristotelian philosophy in achieving a systematic theological and philosophical synthesis. But when I say that St. Thomas saw the 'usefulness' of Aristotelianism, I do not mean to imply that his approach was pragmatic. He regarded the Aristotelian principles as true and, because true, as useful; he did not regard them as 'true' because they were useful. It would be absurd, of course, to suggest that the Thomist philosophy is simply Aristotelianism, since he makes use of other writers like St. Augustine and the Pseudo-Dionysius, as also of his mediaeval predecessors and of Jewish (Maimonides in particular) and Arabian philosophers; but none the less the Thomist synthesis is unified by the application of fundamental Aristotelian principles. A great deal of St. Thomas's philosophy is indeed the doctrine of Aristotle, but it is the doctrine of Aristotle re-thought by a powerful mind,

not slavishly adopted. If St. Thomas adopted Aristotelianism, he adopted it primarily because he thought it true, not simply because Aristotle was a great name or because an 'unbaptised' Aristotle might constitute a grave danger to orthodoxy: a man of St. Thomas's serious mind, devoted to truth, would certainly not have adopted the system of a pagan philosopher, had he not considered it to be in the main a true system, especially when some of the ideas he put forward ran contrary to tradition and created some scandal and lively opposition. Yet his conviction as to the truth of the philosophy which he adopted did not lead St. Thomas to ✓ adopt mechanically an ill-digested system: he gave a great deal of thought and attention to Aristotelianism, as can be seen from his commentaries on Aristotle's works, and his own works bear evidence of the care with which he must have considered the implications of the principles he adopted and their relation to Christian truth. If I suggest presently that the synthesis of Christianity and Aristotelianism in St. Thomas's thought was in some respects rather precarious, I do not mean to take back what I have just said and to imply that the Saint adopted Aristotelianism purely mechanically, though I think it is true that he did not fully realise the latent tension, in regard to certain points, between his Christian faith and his Aristotelianism. If this is really the case, however, it need cause no surprise; St. Thomas was a great theologian and philosopher, but he was not infinite mind, and a much smaller intellect can look back and discern possibly weak points in the system of a great mind, without the latter's greatness being thereby impugned.

Of St. Thomas's utilisation of Aristotelian themes for the purpose of systematisation one can afford space for only one or two examples. One of the fundamental ideas in the Aristotelian philosophy is that of act and potency or potentiality. St. Thomas, like Aristotle before him, saw the interplay, the correlation of act and potency in the accidental and substantial changes of the material world and in the movements (in the broad Aristotelian sense) of all creatures. Adopting the Aristotelian principle that nothing is reduced from potentiality to act, save by the agency of that which is itself in act, he followed Aristotle in arguing from the observed fact of movement, of change, to the existence of the unmoved Mover. But St. Thomas saw deeper than Aristotle: he saw that in every finite thing there is a duality of principles, of essence and existence, that the essence is in potency its existence, that it does not exist necessarily, and so he was enabled to argue not merely to the Aristotelian unmoved Mover, but to the necessary Being, God the Creator. He was able, moreover, to discern the essence of God as existence, not simply as self-thinking thought but as *ipsum esse subsistens*, and thus while following in the footsteps of Aristotle he was able to go beyond Aristotle. Not distinguishing clearly essence and existence in finite being, Aristotle could not arrive at the idea of Existence itself as the essence of God, from whom all limited existence comes.

Again, a fundamental idea in the Aristotelian philosophy is that of finality; indeed, this idea is in one sense more fundamental than that of act and potency, since all reduction from potentiality to act takes place in view of the attainment of an end, and potency exists only for the realisation of an end. That St. Thomas uses the idea of finality in his cosmological, psychological, ethical and political doctrines is a point which needs no labouring; but one may point out the help it was to him in explaining creation. God, who acts according to wisdom, created the world for an end, but that end can be none other than God Himself: He created the world, therefore, in order to manifest His own perfection, by communicating it to creatures by participation, by diffusing His own goodness. Creatures exist *propter Deum*, for God, who is their ultimate end, though He is not the ultimate end of all creatures in the same way; it is only rational creatures who can possess God by knowledge and love. Creatures have, of course, their proximate ends, the perfecting of their natures, but this perfecting of creatures' natures is subordinate to the final end of all creation, the glory of God, the manifestation of His divine perfection, which is manifested precisely by the perfecting of creatures, so that the glory of God and the good of creatures are by no means antithetical ideas. In this way St. Thomas was able to utilise the Aristotelian doctrine of finality in a Christian setting or rather in a way which would harmonise with the Christian religion.

Among the individual ideas borrowed by St. Thomas from Aristotle or thought out in dependence on the philosophy of Aristotle one may mention the following. The soul is the form of the body, individualised by the matter it informs; it is not a complete substance in its own right, but soul and body together make up a complete substance, a man. This stressing of the close union of soul and body, with the rejection of the Platonic theory on this point, makes it much easier to explain why the soul should be united to the body (the soul is by nature the form of the body), but it suggests that, granted the immortality of the soul, the resurrection of the body is demanded by the soul.[1] As for the doctrine of matter as the principle of individuation, which has as its consequence the doctrine that angelic beings, because devoid of matter, cannot be multiplied within the same species, this doctrine excited the hostility of critics of Thomism, as we shall see presently. The same can be said of the doctrine that there is only one substantial form in any substance, a doctrine which, when applied to the human substance, means the rejection of any *forma corporeitatis*.

The adoption of Aristotelian psychology naturally went hand in hand with the adoption of Aristotelian epistemology and with insistence on the fact that human knowledge is derived from sense-experience and reflection thereon. This meant the rejection of innate ideas, even in a virtual form, and the rejection of the theory of divine illumination or rather the interpretation of divine illumination as equivalent to the natural light of the intellect with the ordinary and natural concurrence of God. This doctrine raises difficulties, as we have seen earlier on, in regard to man's analogical knowledge of God.

But though St. Thomas did not hesitate to adopt an Aristotelian position even when this led him into conflict with traditional theories, he did so only when he considered that the Aristotelian positions were true in themselves and were thus compatible with Christian revelation. When it was a question of positions which were clearly incompatible with the Christian doctrine, he rejected them, or maintained that the Averroistic interpretation of Aristotle on such points was not the true interpretation or at least was not rendered necessary by Aristotle's actual words. For example, commenting on Aristotle's description of God as self-thinking Thought, St. Thomas observes that it does not follow that things other than God are unknown to Him, for by knowing Himself He knows all other things.[2] Probably, however, the historic Aristotle did not think of the unmoved Mover as knowing the world or as exercising any providence: He is the cause of movement as final, not as efficient, cause. Similarly, as already mentioned, when commenting on the very obscure words of Aristotle in the *De Anima* concerning the active intellect and its persistence after death, St. Thomas interprets the passage *in meliorem partem* and not in the Averroistic sense: it is not necessary to conclude that for Aristotle the intellect is one in all men and that there is no personal immortality. St. Thomas was anxious to rescue Aristotle from the toils of Averroes and to show that his philosophy did not necessarily involve the denial of divine providence or of personal immortality, and in this he succeeded, even if his interpretation of what Aristotle actually thought on these matters is probably not the correct one.

2. St. Thomas's Aristotelianism is so obvious that one sometimes tends to forget the non-Aristotelian elements in his thought, though such elements certainly exist. For example, the God of Aristotle's *Metaphysics*, though final cause, is not efficient cause; the world is eternal and was not created by God. Moreover, Aristotle envisaged the possibility at least of a multiplicity of unmoved movers corresponding to the different spheres, the relation of which to one another and to the highest unmoved mover he left in obscurity.[3] The God of St. Thomas's natural theology on the other hand is first efficient cause and Creator, as well as final cause: He is not simply wrapped in splendid isolation, the object of *eros*, but He acts *ad extra*, creating, preserving, concurring, exercising providence. St. Thomas made a certain concession to Aristotle perhaps in allowing that the possibility of creation from eternity had not been disproved; but even if the world could have had no beginning in time, its creation, its utter dependence on God, can none the less be proved. All that St. Thomas admits is that the idea of *creatio ab aeterno* has not been shown to be self-contradictory, not that creation cannot be demonstrated. It may be said that St. Thomas's position in natural theology constituted a supplement to or a completion of Aristotle's position and that it cannot be said to be non-Aristotelian; but it must be remembered that for St. Thomas God creates according to intelligence and will and that He is efficient cause, Creator, as exemplary cause: that is to say, He creates the world as a finite imitation of His divine essence, which He knows as imitable *ad extra* in a multiplicity of ways. In other words, St. Thomas utilises the position of St. Augustine in regard to the divine ideas, a position which, philosophically speaking, was derived from neo-Platonism, which in turn was a development of the Platonic

philosophy and tradition. Aristotle rejected the exemplary ideas of Plato, as he rejected the Platonic Demiurge; both of these notions, however, are present in the thought of St. Augustine, transmuted and rendered philosophically consistent, coupled also with the doctrine of *creatio ex nihilo*, at which the Greeks did not arrive; and St. Thomas's acceptance of these notions links him on this point with Augustine, and so with Plato through Plotinus, rather than with Aristotle.

Again, St. Thomas's Christian faith frequently impinges on or has some effect on his philosophy. For instance, convinced that man has a supernatural final end, and a supernatural final end alone, he was bound to envisage the term of man's intellectual ascent as the knowledge of God as He is in Himself, not as the knowledge of the metaphysician and astronomer; he was bound to place the final goal of man in the next life, not in this, thus transmuting the Aristotelian conception of beatitude; he was bound to recognise the insufficiency of the State for fulfilling the needs of the whole man; he was bound to acknowledge the subordination of State to Church in point of value and dignity; he was bound, not only to allow for divine sanctions in the moral life of man, but also to link up ethics with natural theology, and indeed to admit the insufficiency of the natural moral life in regard to the attainment of beatitude, since the latter is supernatural in character and cannot be attained by purely human means. Instances of this impinging of theology on philosophy could no doubt be multiplied; but what I want to draw attention to now is the latent tension on some points between St. Thomas's Christianity and his Aristotelianism.

3. If one looks on the philosophy of Aristotle as a complete system, a certain tension is bound to be present when one attempts to combine it with a supernatural religion. For the Aristotelian philosopher it is the universal and the totality which really matters, not the individual as such: the viewpoint is what one might call that of the physicist, and partly that of the artist. Individuals exist for the good of the species: it is the species which persists through the succession of individuals; the individual human being attains his beatitude in this life or he does not attain it at all: the universe is not a setting for man, subordinate to man, but man is an item in, a part of, the universe; to contemplate the heavenly bodies is really more worth while than to contemplate man. For the Christian on the other hand the individual human being has

a supernatural vocation and his vocation is not an earthly vocation, nor is his final beatitude attainable in this life or by his own natural efforts; the individual stands in a personal relation to God, and however much one may stress the corporate aspect of Christianity, it remains true that each human person is ultimately of more value than the whole material universe, which exists for the sake of man, though both man and the material universe exist ultimately for God. One can, it is true, legitimately adopt a point of view from which man is regarded as a member of the universe, since he is a member of the universe, rooted in the material universe through his body, and if one adopts, as St. Thomas adopted, the Aristotelian psychology, the doctrine of the soul as by nature the form of the body, individualised by the body and dependent on the body for its knowledge, one emphasises the more man's place as a member of the cosmos. It is from this point of view, for instance, that one is led to regard physical defects and physical suffering, the death and corruption of the individual, as contributing to the good and harmony of the universe, as the shadows that throw into relief the lights of the total picture. It is from this point of view too that St. Thomas speaks of the part as existing for the whole, the member for the whole body, using an analogy taken from the organism. There is, as has been admitted, truth in this point of view, and it has been strenuously defended as a corrective to false individualism and to anthropocentricism: the created universe exists for the glory of God, and man is a part of the universe. No doubt; but there is another point of view as well. Man exists for the glory of God and the material universe exists for man; it is not quantity, but quality which is truly significant; man is small from the point of view of quantity, but qualitatively all the heavenly bodies together pale into insignificance beside one human person; moreover, 'man', existing for the glory of God, is not simply the species man, but a society of immortal persons, each of whom has a supernatural vocation. To contemplate man is more worth while than to contemplate the stars; human history is more important than astronomy; the sufferings of human beings cannot be explained simply 'artistically'. I am not suggesting that the two viewpoints cannot be combined, as St. Thomas attempted to combine them; but I do suggest that their combination involves a certain tension and that this tension is present in the Thomist synthesis.

Since, historically speaking, Aristotelianism was a 'closed' system, in the sense that Aristotle did not and could not envisage the supernatural order, and since it was a production of reason unaided by revelation, it naturally brought home to the mediaevals the potentialities of the natural reason: it was the greatest intellectual achievement they knew. This meant that any theologian who accepted and utilised the Aristotelian philosophy as St. Thomas did was compelled to recognise the theoretical autonomy of philosophy, even though he also recognised theology as an extrinsic norm and criterion. As long as it was a question of theologians, the balance between theology and philosophy was, of course, preserved; but when it was a question of thinkers who were not primarily theologians, the charter granted to philosophy tended to become a declaration of independence. Looking back from the present day and bearing in mind human inclinations, characters, temperaments and intellectual bents, we can see that the acceptance of a great system of philosophy known to have been thought out without the aid of revelation was almost certain sooner or later to lead to philosophy going her own way independently of theology. In this sense (and the judgement is an historical, not a valuational judgement) the synthesis achieved by St. Thomas was intrinsically precarious. The arrival of the full Aristotle on the scene almost certainly meant in the long run the emergence of an independent philosophy, which would first of all stand on its own feet while trying to keep the peace with theology, sometimes sincerely, sometimes perhaps insincerely, and then in the end would try to supplant theology, to absorb the content of theology into itself. At the beginning of the Christian era we find the theologians utilising this or that element of Greek philosophy to help them in their statement of the data of revelation and this process continued during the stages of mediaeval Scholastic development; but the appearance of a fully-fledged system of philosophy, though an inestimable boon in the creation of the Thomist synthesis, could hardly be anything else but a challenge in the long run. It is not the purpose of the present writer to dispute the utility of the Aristotelian philosophy in the creation of a Christian theological and philosophical synthesis or in any way to belittle the achievement of St. Thomas Aquinas, but rather to point out that when philosophic thought had become more or less full-grown and had won a certain autonomy, it was not to be expected that it should for ever be content to sit at home like the elder son in the parable of the prodigal. St. Thomas's baptism of philosophy in the person of Aristotle could not, historically speaking, arrest the development of philosophy, and in that sense his synthesis contained a latent tension.

4. To turn finally, but of necessity briefly, to the opposition caused by the Thomist adoption of Aristotle. This opposition must be looked at against the background of the alarm caused by Averroism, i.e. the Averroistic interpretation of Aristotle, which we shall consider in the next chapter. The Averroists were accused, and certainly not without justice, of preferring the authority of a pagan philosopher to that of St. Augustine and the *Sancti* in general, and of impairing the integrity of revelation; and St. Thomas was regarded by some zealous traditionalists as selling the pass to the enemy. They accordingly did their best to involve Thomism in the condemnations levelled against Averroism. The whole episode reminds us that St. Thomas in his own day was an innovator, that he struck out on new paths: it is useful to remember this at a time when Thomism stands for tradition, for theological soundness and security. Some of the points on which St. Thomas was most bitterly attacked by the hot-heads may not appear particularly startling to us to-day; but the reasons why they were attacked were largely theological in character, so that it is clear that Thomist Aristotelianism was once regarded as 'dangerous' and that the man who now stands before us as the pillar of orthodoxy was once regarded, by hot-heads at least, as a sower of novelties. Nor was the attack confined to people outside his own religious Order; he had to bear the hostility even of Dominicans, and it was only by degrees that Thomism became the official philosophy of the Dominican Order.

One of the principal points attacked was St. Thomas's theory of the unicity of the substantial form. It was combated at a debate in Paris, before the bishop, about 1270, Dominicans and Franciscans, especially the Franciscan Peckham, accusing St. Thomas of maintaining an opinion which was contrary to the teaching of the saints, particularly Augustine and Anselm. Peckham and the Dominican Robert Kilwardby maintained this point of view vigorously in their letters, the chief ground of complaint being that the Thomist doctrine was unable to explain how the dead body of Christ was the same as the living body, since according to St. Thomas there is only one substantial form in the human substance and this form, the soul, is withdrawn at death, other forms being educed out of the potentiality of matter. St. Thomas certainly held that the dead body of a man is not precisely the same as the living body, but is the same only *secundum quid*,[4] and Peckham and his friends regarded this theory as fatal to the veneration of the bodies and relics of the saints. St. Thomas, however, maintained that the dead body of Christ remained united to the Divinity, so that it was, even in the tomb, united to the Word of God and worthy of adoration. The doctrine of the passivity of matter and that of the simplicity of the angels were also among the novel opinions to which exception was taken.

On March 7th, 1277, Stephen Tempier, Bishop of Paris, condemned two hundred and nineteen propositions, threatening with excommunication anyone who should uphold them. This condemnation was levelled chiefly against the Averroists, particularly Siger of Brabant and Boethius of Dacia, but a number of propositions were common to Siger of Brabant and St. Thomas so that Thomism was affected by the bishop's act. Thus the theories of the necessary unicity of the world, of matter as the principle of individuation, of the individualisation of angels and their relation to the universe were condemned, though that of the unicity of substantial form does not appear in the condemnation and seems never to have been formally condemned at Paris, apart from being censured in Scholastic debates and disputation.

The Parisian condemnation was followed, on March 18th, 1277, by a condemnation at Oxford, inspired by Robert Kilwardby, O.P., Archbishop of Canterbury, in which figured, among other propositions, those of the unicity of the substantial form and the passivity of matter. Kilwardby remarked in a letter that he forbade the propositions as dangerous, without condemning them as heretical, and indeed he does not seem to have been oversanguine as to the probable results of his prohibition since he offered an indulgence of forty days to anyone who would abstain from propounding the offending ideas. Kilwardby's condemnation was repeated by his successor in the Archbishopric of Canterbury, the Franciscan Peckham, on October 29th, 1284, though by that time Thomism had been officially approved in the Dominican Order. However, Peckham again prohibited the novel propositions on April 30th, 1286, declaring them to be heretical.

Meanwhile Thomism had been growing in popularity among the Dominicans as was indeed only to be expected in the case of such a splendid achievement by one of their number. In the year 1278 the Dominican Chapter at Milan and in 1279 the Chapter of Paris took steps to counteract the hostile attitude which was evident among the Oxford Dominicans, the Paris Chapter forbidding the condemnation of Thomism, though not enjoining its acceptance. In 1286 another Chapter of Paris declared that professors who showed hostility to Thomism should be relieved of their office, though it was not until the fourteenth century that its acceptance was made obligatory on members of the Order. The growing popularity of Thomism in the last two decades of the thirteenth century, however, naturally led to the publication by Dominican authors of replies to the attacks levelled against it. Thus the *Correctorium Fratris Thomas*, published by William de la Mare, a Franciscan, called forth a series of Corrections of the Correction, such as the *Apologeticum veritatis super corruptorium* (as they called the *Correctorium*), published by Rambert of Bologna near the end of the century, to which the Franciscans replied in their turn. In 1279 the latter, in their General Chapter at Assisi, prohibited the acceptance of the propositions condemned at Paris in 1277, while in 1282 the General Chapter of Strasbourg ordered that those who utilised Thomas's *Summa Theologica* should not do so without consulting William de la Mare's *Correctorium*. However, the attacks of Franciscans and others naturally diminished after the canonisation of St. Thomas on July 18th, 1323, and in 1325 the then Bishop of Paris withdrew the Parisian censures. At Oxford there does not seem to have been any formal withdrawal of this kind, but Peckham's successors did not confirm or repeat his censures and the battle gradually came to an end. Early in the fourteenth century Thomas of Sutton speaks of Aquinas as being, according to the testimony of all, the Common Doctor (*in ore omnium communis doctor dicitur*).

Thomism naturally established itself in the estimation of Christian thinkers owing to its completeness, its lucidity and its depth: it was a closely reasoned synthesis of theology and philosophy which drew on the past and incorporated it into itself, while at the same time it utilised the greatest purely philosophical system of the ancient world. But though the suspicion and hostility which Thomism, or certain aspects of it, at first aroused were destined to die a natural death in face of the undeniable merits of the system, it must not be supposed that Thomism ever acquired in the Middle Ages that official position in the intellectual life of the Church which it has occupied since the Encyclical *Aeterni Patris* of Pope Leo XIII. The *Sentences* of Peter Lombard, for example, continued to be commented upon for very many years, while at the time of the Reformation there existed Chairs in the universities for the exposition of the doctrines not only of St. Thomas and Duns Scotus and Giles of Rome, but also of Nominalists like William of Ockham and Gabriel Biel. Variety was in fact the rule, and though Thomism became at an early date the official system of the Dominican Order, many centuries elapsed before it became in any real sense the official system of the Church. (I do not mean to imply that even after *Aeterni Patris* Thomism, in the sense in which it is distinguished from Scotism, for example, is imposed on all religious Orders and ecclesiastical institutes of higher studies; but Thomism is certainly proposed as a norm from which the Catholic philosopher should dissent only when inspired by reasons which seem to him compelling, and then without disrespect. The singular position now accorded to Thomism must be looked at in the light of the historical circumstances of recent times, in order to be understood; these circumstances were not those obtaining in the Middle Ages.)

Chapter Forty-two

LATIN AVERROISM: SIGER OF BRABANT

Tenets of the 'Latin Averroists'—Siger of Brabant—Dante and Siger of Brabant—Opposition to Averroism; condemnations.

1. The term 'Latin Averroism' has become so common that it is difficult not to make use of it, but it must be recognised that the movement characterised by this name was one of integral or radical Aristotelianism: Aristotle was the real patron of the movement, not Averroes, though the latter was certainly looked on as the commentator *par excellence* and was followed in his monopsychistic interpretation of Aristotle. The doctrine that the passive intellect, no less than the active intellect, is one and the same in all men and that this unitary intellect alone survives at death, so that individual personal immortality is excluded, was understood in the thirteenth century as being the characteristic tenet of the radical Aristotelians, and as this doctrine was supported by the Averroistic interpretation of Aristotle its upholders came to be known as the Averroists. I do not see how exception can really be taken to the use of this term, provided that it is clearly realised that the 'Averroists' regarded themselves as Aristotelians rather than as Averroists. They seem to have belonged to the faculty of arts of Paris and to have pushed their adherence to Aristotle as interpreted by Averroes so far that they taught doctrines in philosophy which were incompatible with Christian dogma. The salient point in their doctrine, and the one which attracted most attention, was the theory that there is only one rational soul in all men. Adopting Averroes's interpretation of Aristotle's obscure and ambiguous teaching on

this matter, they maintained that not only the active intellect, but also the passive intellect is one and the same in all men. The logical consequence of this position is the denial of personal immortality and of sanctions in the next life. Another of their heterodox doctrines, and one which incidentally was an undoubtedly Aristotelian doctrine, was that of the eternity of the world. On this point it is important to note the difference between the Averroists and St. Thomas. Whereas for St. Thomas the eternity of the (created) world has not been proved impossible, though it certainly has not been proved true (and we know from revelation that as a matter of fact the world was not created from eternity), the Averroists held that the eternity of the world, the eternity of change and movement, can be philosophically demonstrated. Again, it appears that some of them, following Aristotle, denied divine providence and followed Averroes in maintaining determinism. It can, therefore, be understood without difficulty why the theologians attacked the Averroists, either, like St. Bonaventure, attacking Aristotle himself or, like St. Thomas, arguing not only that the peculiar Averroistic positions were intrinsically false, but also that they did not represent the real thought, or at least the clear teaching, of Aristotle.

The Averroists or radical Aristotelians were thus forced to reconcile their philosophical doctrines with theological dogmas, unless they were prepared (and they were not prepared) simply to deny the latter. In other words, they had to provide some theory of the relation of reason to faith which would permit them to assert with Aristotle that there is only one rational soul in all men and at the same time to assert with the Church that every man has his own individual rational soul. It is sometimes said that in order to effect this conciliation they had recourse to the theory of the double truth, maintaining that a thing can be true in philosophy or according to reason and yet that its opposite can be true in theology or according to faith; and indeed Siger of Brabant speaks in this way, implying that certain propositions of Aristotle and Averroes are irrefutable, though the opposite propositions are true according to faith. Thus it can be rationally proved that there is but one intellectual soul in all men, though faith makes us certain that there is one intellectual soul to each human body. Looked at from the logical standpoint this position would lead to the rejection of either theology or philosophy, faith or reason; but the Averroists seem to have meant that in the natural order, with which the philosopher deals, the intellectual soul would have been one in all men, but that God has miraculously multiplied the intellectual soul. The philosopher uses his natural reason, and his natural reason tells him that the intellectual soul is one in all men, while the theologian, who treats of the supernatural order and expounds the divine revelation, assures us that God has miraculously multiplied what by nature could not be multiplied. It is in this sense that what is true in philosophy is false in theology and *vice versa*. This mode of self-defence naturally did not appeal to the theologians, who were quite unprepared to admit that God intervened to perform miraculously what was rationally impossible. Nor had they much sympathy with the alternative method of self-defence adopted by the Averroists, namely the contention that they were simply reporting the teaching of Aristotle. According to a contemporary sermon, perhaps by St. Bonaventure, 'there are some students of philosophy who say certain things which are not true according to faith; and when they are told that something is contrary to faith, they reply that Aristotle says it, but that they themselves do not assert it and are only reporting Aristotle's words'. This defence was treated as a mere subterfuge by the theologians, and justifiably, in view of the Averroists' attitude towards Aristotle.

2. The foremost of the Averroists or radical Aristotelians was *Siger of Brabant*, who was born about the year 1235 and became a teacher in the faculty of arts at Paris. In 1270 he was condemned for his Averroistic doctrines, and it appears that he not only defended himself by saying that he was simply reporting Aristotle and did not intend to assert what was incompatible with the Faith, but also somewhat modified his position. It has been suggested that he was converted from Averroism by the writings of St. Thomas, but there is no certain evidence that he definitely abandoned his Averroism. If he did so, it would be difficult to explain why he was involved in the condemnation of 1277 and why in that year the Inquisitor of France, Simon du Val, ordered him to appear before his court. In any case the question of the changes in Siger's opinions cannot be settled with certainty until the chronology of his works has been settled. The works which have been discovered include the *De anima intellectiva, De aeternitate mundi, De necessitate et contingentia causarum, Compendium de generatione et corruptione*, some *Quaes-*

tiones naturales, some *Quaestiones morales*, some *Quaestiones logicales*, *Quaestiones in Metaphysicam*, *Quaestiones in Physicam*, *Quaestiones in libros tres de Anima*, six *Impossibilia*, and fragments of the *De intellectu* and the *Liber de felicitate*. It appears that the *De intellectu* was a reply to St. Thomas's *De unitate intellectus contra Averroistas* and that in his reply Siger maintained that the active intellect is God, and that man's beatitude on earth consists in union with the active intellect. Whether Siger was still a monopsychist at this time or not, depends, however, on what he thought about the unicity or multiplication of the passive intellect: it cannot be concluded without more ado from the identification of the active intellect with God that he was still a monopsychist in the Averroistic sense. If Siger appealed from the Inquisition to Rome, it may be that he felt he had been unjustly accused of heterodoxy. He died at Orvieto about 1282, being assassinated by his mad secretary.

To mention Siger of Brabant simply in connection with the Averroistic controversy is to give a partial view of his thought, since it was a system that he expounded, and not simply isolated points in regard to which he followed Averroes. His system, however, though professedly a system of true Aristotelianism, differed very much in important respects from the philosophy of the historic Aristotle, and this was bound to be so if he followed Averroes. For example, while Aristotle looked on God as the first mover in the sense of ultimate final cause, not in the sense of first efficient cause, Siger followed Averroes in making God the first creative cause. God operates mediately, however, through intermediate causes, the successively emanating intelligences, and in this respect Siger followed Avicenna rather than Averroes, so that, as M. Van Steenberghen has noted, Siger's philosophy cannot, with strict accuracy, be called radical Averroism. Nor for the matter of that can it accurately be termed radical Aristotelianism, if one is thinking of the historic Aristotle, though it is a convenient enough term if one is thinking of Siger's intentions. On the question of the eternity of creation Siger follows 'Aristotle', but rather because the Arabian philosophers followed 'Aristotle' on this point than because of what Aristotle himself said on the matter, since the latter did not envisage creation at all. Similarly, Siger's notion that all terrestrial events are determined by the movements of the heavenly bodies smacks of the Islamic philosophy. Again, while the idea that no species can have had a beginning, so that there can have been no first man, is Aristotelian in origin, the idea of the eternal recurrence or cyclic process of determined events is not found in Aristotle.

As regards the salient Averroistic theses of monopsychism and the eternity of the world, Siger seems to have retracted his heterodox opinions. Commenting on the *De Anima*, for example, he not only admits that the monopsychism of Averroes is not true, but proceeds to admit the weight of the objections brought against it by St. Thomas and others. Thus he allows that it is impossible for two different individual acts in two different human beings to proceed simultaneously from an intellectual faculty or principle which is numerically one. Similarly, in his Questions on the *Physics*, he concedes that motion is not eternal and that it had a beginning, although this beginning cannot be rationally demonstrated. However, as has already been noted, it is difficult to ascertain with certainty whether this apparent change of front involved a real change of opinion or whether it was a prudential course adopted in view of the condemnation of 1270.

3. The fact that Dante not only places Siger of Brabant in Paradise, but even puts his praises on the lips of St. Thomas, his adversary, is difficult to explain. Mandonnet, believing on the one hand that Siger of Brabant was a real Averroist and on the other hand that Dante was an anti-Averroist, was forced to suggest that Dante was probably unacquainted with Siger's doctrines. But, as M. Gilson has pointed out, Dante also places in Paradise and attaches to St. Bonaventure the Abbot Joachim of Flores, whose doctrines were rejected by both St. Bonaventure and St. Thomas, and it is extremely unlikely that Dante was unaware of what he was doing in the case of either Joachim or Siger. M. Gilson himself has suggested that Siger of Brabant, as he appears in the *Divine Comedy*, is not so much the actual historical Siger of Brabant as a symbol. St. Thomas symbolises speculative theology, St. Bernard mystical theology, and while Aristotle represents philosophy in limbo Siger, being a Christian, represents it in Paradise. When, therefore, Dante makes St. Thomas praise Siger of Brabant, he is not intending to make the historic Thomas praise the historic Siger, but rather to make speculative theology pay her compliments to philosophy. (M. Gilson explains in an analogous manner St. Bonaventure's praise of Joachim in the *Divine Comedy*.)

M. Gilson's explanation of the problem seems to me to be reasonable. There are, however, other possibilities. Bruno Nardi argued (and he was followed by Miguel Asín) that the explanation of the problem lies in the fact that Dante was not a pure Thomist, but that he incorporated doctrines not only from other Scholastic sources, but also from the Moslem philosophers, notably Averroes, whom he particularly admired. As Dante could not place Avicenna and Averroes in Paradise, he consigned them to limbo, whereas Mohammed he placed in hell proper; but as Siger was a Christian he placed him in Paradise. Dante would thus have acted with deliberation, showing his appreciation of Siger's devotion to Islamic philosophy.

Even if what Bruno Nardi says of Dante's philosophical sources is true, it seems to me that his explanation could well be combined with that of M. Gilson. If Dante admired the Moslem philosophers and was influenced by them, it would explain why he placed Siger in Paradise; but would it explain why he placed Siger's praises on the lips of St. Thomas? If Dante knew that Siger was an Averroist, he certainly knew also that St. Thomas was an anti-Averroist. May it not have been that Dante made St. Thomas the symbol of speculative theology, as Gilson suggests, and Siger, the Averroist, he made the symbol of philosophy, precisely because Siger was a member of the faculty of arts and not a theologian? In that case, as M. Gilson says, St. Thomas's praise of Siger would simply represent theology's tribute to philosophy.

The question has been complicated by M. Van Steenberghen's contention that Siger of Brabant abandoned Averroism inasmuch as it conflicted with theology and approximated to St. Thomas's position. If this is true, and if Dante were aware of the fact that Siger changed his opinions, the difficulty of explaining how St. Thomas could be made to praise Siger would obviously be greatly lessened. In other words, in order to obtain an adequate explanation of the fact why the poet not only placed Siger in heaven, but also made his adversary, St. Thomas, speak his praises, one would have to obtain first an adequate and accurate idea not only of Dante's philosophical sympathies, but also of the evolution of Siger's opinions.[1]

4. We have seen that the philosophy of St. Thomas aroused considerable opposition on the part of other Scholastic philosophers; but even if an attempt was made to implicate St.

Thomas in the condemnation of Averroistic Aristotelianism, it remains true that the controversy over such Thomist doctrines as the unicity of the substantial form was a domestic controversy which can be distinguished from the Averroistic controversy proper in which the theologians in general, including St. Thomas, were united in a common front against the heterodox philosophers. Thus the Franciscans, from Alexander of Hales and St. Bonaventure to Duns Scotus, were at one with Dominicans like St. Albert and St. Thomas, Augustinians like Giles of Rome and secular clergy like Henry of Ghent, in opposing what they regarded as a dangerous movement. From the philosophic standpoint the most important feature of their opposition was, of course, their critical refutation of the offending theories, and in this respect one may mention St. Albert's *De unitate intellectus contra Averroem* (1256), St. Thomas's *De unitate intellectus contra Averroistas* (1270), Giles of Rome's *De purificatione intellectus possibilis contra Averroem* and his *Errores Philosophorum* (which lists the errors of Aristotle and the Moslem philosophers, but does not treat of Siger of Brabant), and Raymond Lull's *Liber contra errores Boetii et Segerii* (1298), *Liber reprobationis aliquorum errorum Averrois, Disputatio Raymundi et Averroistae* and *Sermones contra Averroistas*.

The theologians were not, however, content with writing and speaking against the Averroists; they also endeavoured to secure their official condemnation by ecclesiastical authority. This was only natural, as can be seen from considering the clash on important points between Averroistic philosophy and the Faith, and also from considering the theoretical and possible practical consequences of such theories as those of monopsychism and determinism. Accordingly, in 1270 the Bishop of Paris, Stephen Tempier, condemned the doctrines of monopsychism, denial of personal immortality, determinism, eternity of the world and denial of divine providence. In spite of this condemnation, however, the Averroists continued to teach in secret ('in corners and before boys', as St. Thomas puts it), although in 1272 the professors of the faculty of arts were forbidden to treat of theological matters, and in 1276 secret teaching in the university was prohibited. This led to a further condemnation on March 7th, 1277, when the Bishop of Paris condemned 219 propositions and excommunicated anyone who should persist in maintaining them. The condemnation was aimed principally at the teaching of Siger of Brabant and Boethius of Dacia, and it involved the 'double truth' subterfuge. Boethius of Dacia, who was a contemporary of Siger of Brabant, upheld the intellectualist idea of beatitude expounded by Aristotle, maintaining that only philosophers can attain true happiness, while non-philosophers sin against the natural order. The condemned propositions, that 'there is no more excellent state than to devote oneself to philosophy' and that 'the wise men of the world are the philosophers alone', seem to have been taken from or to have summarised the teaching of Boethius, who, as professor of the faculty of arts, omitted all mention of the supernatural order and treated the Aristotelian conception of beatitude as adequate, at least from the standpoint of reason.

Chapter Forty-three

FRANCISCAN THINKERS

Roger Bacon, life and works—Philosophy of Roger Bacon—Matthew of Aquasparta—Peter John Olivi—Roger Marston—Richard of Middleton—Raymond Lull.

1. One of the most interesting of mediaeval thinkers is *Roger Bacon* (*c.* 1212 to after 1292), called the *Doctor Mirabilis*. He would be of interest, were it only for his interest in and respect for experimental science and the application of mathematics in science; but what makes him considerably more interesting is that his scientific interests are combined with a lively interest in philosophy proper, and that both these interests were combined with a typically Franciscan emphasis on mysticism. Traditional elements were thus fused with a scientific outlook which was really foreign to the mentality of the majority of contemporary theologians and philosophers.[1] Moreover, Roger Bacon, impulsive, somewhat intolerant and hot-headed, convinced of the truth and value of his own opinions and of the obscurantism of many of the leading thinkers of his time, particularly those of Paris, is interesting not only as philosopher, but also as a man. He was something of a stormy petrel in his Order, but he is at the same time one of the glories of that Order and one of the leading figures of British philosophy. If a comparison were instituted between Roger Bacon and Francis Bacon (1561–1626), the comparison would by no means be to the unqualified advantage of the latter. As Professor Adamson remarked, 'it is more than probable that in all fairness, when we speak of the Baconian reform of science, we should refer to the forgotten monk of the thirteenth century rather than

to the brilliant and famous Chancellor of the seventeenth',[2] while Bridges observes that though Francis Bacon was 'immeasurably superior as a writer, Roger Bacon had the sounder estimate and the firmer grasp of that combination of deductive with inductive matters which marks the scientific discoverer'.[3]

Born at Ilchester, Roger Bacon studied at Oxford under Adam Marsh and Robert Grosseteste. For the latter Bacon had the liveliest admiration, remarking that he knew mathematics and perspective, and that he could have known everything; Grosseteste also knew enough of languages to understand the wise men of antiquity.[4] From Oxford, Bacon went to Paris, where he apparently taught for a few years. For the Parisian professors he had little respect. Thus of Alexander of Hales's *Summa* he remarks that it weighed more than a horse, though he contests its authenticity,[5] while he blames the theologians for their incursions into philosophy, for their ignorance of the sciences, and for the unmerited deference they paid to Alexander of Hales and Albert the Great.[6] Ignorance of the sciences and of languages were his chief charges against contemporary thinkers, though he also found fault with the veneration given to the *Sentences* of Peter Lombard, which, he says, was preferred to the Bible itself, and with faulty Scriptural exegesis. In other words, his criticism (which was often unfair, as in regard to St. Albert) shows the twofold character of his thought, a devotion to science coupled with a traditional or conservative attitude in respect to theology and metaphysics. As regards Aristotle, Bacon was an admirer of the Philosopher, but he detested what he regarded as bad and misleading Latin translations of his works and declared that he would have them all burnt, if it lay in his power to do so.[7]

But though Bacon had little use for the great figures of the University of Paris and contrasted the Parisian thinkers unfavourably with his fellow countrymen, he met at Paris one man at least who had a lasting influence on his thought, Peter of Maricourt, a Picard and author of an *Epistola de magnete* and a *Nova compositio Astrolabii particularis*.[8] According to Roger Bacon[9] he was the one man who could safely be praised for his achievements in scientific research. 'For the last three years he has been working at the production of a mirror which shall produce combustion at a distance; a problem which the Latins have neither solved nor attempted, though books have been written upon the subject.' Peter evidently stimulated Roger Bacon's leaning to experimental science and won his respect by putting his questions to Nature herself instead of attempting to answer them *a priori* and without recourse to experiment.

About the year 1250 Bacon entered the Franciscan Order and taught at Oxford until 1257, when he had to abandon public teaching, having incurred the suspicion or hostility of his superiors. He was still permitted to write, however, though not to publish his works. In June 1266 Pope Clement IV, a friend of Bacon, told the latter to send him his works; but the Pope died shortly afterwards and it is not known with certainty if the manuscripts ever reached Rome and, if they did, what reception was accorded them. In any case Bacon got into trouble in 1277 by writing the *Speculum astronomiae* in order to defend his ideas on astrology and to criticise Stephen Tempier's condemnation of astrology. The Franciscan General of the time, Jerome of Ascoli, had Bacon brought before a Chapter in Paris under suspicion of teaching novelties, and this resulted in Bacon's imprisonment in 1278. He seems to have remained in prison until 1292, and it was in this year or not long afterwards that he died, being buried at Oxford in the Franciscan Church.

Bacon's chief work was the *Opus Maius*, which may have been completed and sent to the Pope. The *Opus Minus* and the *Opus Tertium* are more or less summaries of material incorporated in the *Opus Maius*, though they contain additional matter as well. It is in the *Opus Minus* that Bacon treats of the seven sins of theology, for example. A number of other works, such as the *Quaestiones supra libros octo Physicorum Aristotelis* and the *Quaestiones supra libros Primae Philosophiae*, have been published in the fourteen volumes of the *Opera hactenus inedita Rogeri Baconi* of which sixteen fascicules have so far appeared. Some of these works seem to have been written as parts of a projected *Scriptum Principale*. Bacon also wrote a *Compendium Philosophiae*, a *Compendium studii Philosophiae* and a *Compendium studii Theologiae*.

2. In the first part of the *Opus Maius* Bacon enumerates four principal causes of human ignorance and failure to attain truth: subjection to unworthy authority, the influence of habit, popular prejudice, and making a show of apparent wisdom to cover one's own ignorance. The first three causes of

error were recognised by men like Aristotle, Seneca, Averroes; but the fourth is the most dangerous, as it makes a man conceal his own ignorance by holding up as true wisdom the result of worshipping untrustworthy authority, of habit and of popular prejudice. For example, because Aristotle said something, it is considered true; but Avicenna may have corrected Aristotle on the point, and Averroes may have corrected Avicenna. Again, because the Fathers did not pursue scientific studies, it is taken for granted that such studies are valueless; but the circumstances of that time were quite different, and what was an excuse for them is not necessarily an excuse for us. Men do not realise the value of studying mathematics and languages, and so they belittle these studies out of prejudice.

In the second part Bacon emphasises the dominating character of theology among the sciences: all truth is contained in the Scriptures. But for the elucidation of the Scriptures we need the help of canon law and of philosophy. Philosophy and the use of reason in general cannot be condemned, since reason is of God. God is the active intellect (so Bacon interpreted St. Augustine, appealing also to Aristotle and Avicenna), and He enlightens the individual human mind, concurring with it in its activity. Philosophy has as its purpose to lead man to the knowledge and service of God; it culminates in moral philosophy. The speculative and moral sciences of the pagans were certainly inadequate and find their completion only in Christian theology and the Christian ethic; but it is not right to condemn or to neglect any particle of truth. As a matter of fact, says Bacon, philosophy was not a pagan invention, but was revealed to the Patriarchs. Subsequently the revelation was obscured through human depravity, but the pagan philosophers helped to rediscover it, or part of it. The greatest of these philosophers was Aristotle, and Avicenna is his principal expounder. As for Averroes, he was a man of real wisdom who improved in many points on what his predecessors had said, though his own theories also stand in need of correction. In fine, we should use pagan philosophy in an intelligent manner, without ignorant rejection and condemnation on the one hand or slavish adherence to any particular thinker on the other. It is our business to carry on and perfect the work of our predecessors, remembering that though it is the function of truth to lead man to God, we should not regard as valueless studies which have at first sight no immediate relation to theology: all truth of whatever kind leads ultimately to God.

The third part Bacon devotes to the subject of language, emphasising the practical importance of the scientific study of languages. Without a real knowledge of Hebrew and Greek the Scriptures cannot be properly interpreted and translated, nor can manuscripts be corrected when faulty; and good translations of Greek and Arabian philosophers are also needed. But for purposes of translation something more than a smattering of a language is necessary, if slavish translations are to be avoided.

In the fourth part Bacon discusses mathematics, the 'door and key' of other sciences. Mathematics were studied by the Patriarchs and came to the knowledge of the Greeks by way of the Chaldeans and Egyptians; but among the Latins they have fallen into neglect. Yet mathematical science is *quasi innata*, or at least it is learnt more easily and immediately and with less dependence on experience than other sciences, so that it may be said to be presupposed by other sciences. Logic and grammar are dependent to a certain extent on mathematics, while it is obvious that without mathematics no advance can be made in astronomy, and they are useful even for theology: mathematical astronomy can, for instance, demonstrate the comparative insignificance of the earth as compared with the heavens, not to speak of the facts that mathematics are useful for solving the chronological problems in the Scriptures and that they show the inadequacy of the Julian Calendar, a matter to which the Pope would do well to attend. Bacon proceeds to speak about light, its propagation, reflection and refraction; about eclipses, tides, the spherical shape of the earth, the unicity of the universe, and so on; and then passes to geography and astrology. Astrology is regarded with suspicion as it is thought to involve determinism; but this suspicion is unjust. The influence and movements of the heavenly bodies affect terrestrial and human events and produce even natural dispositions in human beings, but they do not destroy free will: it is only prudent to gain all the knowledge we can and use it for a good end. Bacon approves Aristotle's advice to Alexander concerning the treatment to be meted out to certain tribes of perverse ways: change their climate, that is, change their place of abode and thus change their morals.

Optics form the subject of the fifth part, in which Bacon

treats of the structure of the eye, the principles of vision and the conditions of vision, reflection, refraction, and finally the practical application of the science of optics. Mirrors, he suggests, might be erected in elevated spots in order that the layout and movements of an enemy's camp might be observed, while by the use of refraction we could make small things appear great and distant objects appear near. There is no evidence to show that Bacon actually invented the telescope; but he conceived the possibility of such a thing.

In the sixth part Bacon considers experimental science. Reasoning may guide the mind to a right conclusion, but it is only confirmation by experience which removes doubt. That is one reason why diagrams and figures are employed in geometry. Many beliefs are refuted by experience. Experience, however, is of two kinds. In one kind of experience we employ our bodily senses, aided by instruments and by the evidence of trustworthy witnesses, while the other kind is experience of spiritual things and needs grace. This latter type of experience advances through various stages to the mystical states of rapture. The former type of experience can be used to prolong life (by improving the science of medicine, and discovering antidotes to poisons), to invent explosive substances, to transmute baser metals into gold and to refine gold itself, and so to disabuse the heathen of their false magical beliefs.

Finally, in the seventh part of the *Opus Maius*, Bacon treats of moral philosophy, which stands on a higher level than philology, or mathematics and experimental science. These sciences are related to action of various kinds, whereas moral philosophy is related to the actions by which we become good or bad, and it instructs man about his relations with God, his fellow men and himself. It is thus closely related to theology and shares in the latter's dignity. Supposing the 'principles of metaphysics', which include Christian revelation, Bacon treats of civic morality and then, more at length, of personal morality, making use of the writings of Greek, Roman and Moslem philosophers, particularly of Seneca, the Roman Stoic. In conclusion he treats of the grounds for accepting the Christian religion. Revelation is necessary and the Christian accepts the Faith on authority; but in dealing with non-Christians we cannot appeal simply to authority, but must have recourse to reason. Thus philosophy can prove the existence of God, His unity and infinity, while the credibility of the sacred writers is established by their personal sanctity, their wisdom, the evidence of miracles, their firm steadfastness under persecution, the uniformity of their faith, and their victory in spite of their humble origin and temporal condition. Bacon ends with the doctrine of man's incorporation with Christ and his participation through Christ in the divine life. *Et quid potest homo plus petere in hac vita?* And what more can a man seek in this life?

From what has been said, the twofold character of Bacon's philosophy is clear. His emphasis on the relation of philosophy to theology, on the former's function of leading man to God, and on the practical or moral aspect of philosophy, the place he attributes in his philosophy to inner knowledge of God and spiritual things, culminating in rapture, the close relation he establishes between theology and philosophy, his doctrine of God as the illuminating active intellect,[10] his adoption of the theories of 'seminal reasons' (for the development of which matter has a kind of active appetite), of the universal hylomorphic composition of creatures, and of the plurality of forms (from the form of corporeity up to the *forma individualis*), all mark him as an adherent, to a large extent, of the Augustinian tradition. In spite of his respect for Aristotle he not infrequently misinterprets him and even ascribes to him doctrines which he certainly never held. Thus he discerns elements of the Christian revelation in the philosophy of Aristotle which were actually not there; and though he refers to St. Thomas he does not seem to have been influenced by the Thomist positions or to have been particularly interested in them. On the other hand, the breadth of his interests and the vigour of his insistence on experimental science in general, on the development of astronomy by the aid of mathematics, and on the practical applications of science mark him out as a herald of the future. By temperament he was somewhat self-assured, inclined to impatience and to sometimes unjust criticism and condemnation; but he laid his finger on many weak points in contemporary science as also in contemporary moral and ecclesiastical life. For his scientific theories he depended very much on other thinkers, as was only natural; but he was quick to see the possibility of their development and application, and, as has already been remarked, he had a firmer grasp of scientific method, of the combination of deduction and induction, than was possessed by Francis Bacon, the Chancellor of England, whose insistence on experiment and observation and the practical applications of knowledge has sometimes been depicted as if without parallel or anticipation among philosophers of an earlier period.

3. An Augustinian of a different type was *Matthew of Aquasparta* (c. 1240–1302), who studied at Paris, taught at Bologna and Rome, and became General of the Franciscan Order in 1287, being created a cardinal in 1288. The author of, among other works, a Commentary on the *Sentences*, *Quaestiones disputatae* and *Quaestiones quodlibetales*, Matthew adhered in general to the position of St. Bonaventure, regarding St. Augustine as the great fount of wisdom. Thus, while he admitted that man's ideas of corporeal objects are formed only in dependence on sense-experience, he refused to admit that corporeal objects can affect more than the body: it is the soul itself which is responsible for sensation as such, as St. Augustine had held, though, of course, sensation requires that a sense-organ should be affected by a sensible object. Again, it is the active intellect which transforms the *species sensibilis* and produces the idea in the passive intellect. Matthew appeals explicitly to St. Augustine on this matter.[11] Yet the soul's activity alone is not sufficient to explain knowledge: the divine illumination is required. What is this divine illumination? It is really God's immediate concurrence with the operation of the human intellect, a concurrence by the aid of which the intellect is moved to know the object. God moves us to know the object of which we receive the *species sensibilis*, this movement being the divine illumination. The object is related to its eternal exemplar foundation, the *ratio aeterna* or divine idea, and it is the divine light which enables us to discern this relation, the *rationes aeternae* exercising a regulative effect on the intellect. But we do not discern the divine light or concurrence, nor are the eternal ideas objects directly perceived; we know them rather as principles which move the intellect to know the created essence, *ut obiectum movens et in aliud ducens*, not as *obiectum in se ducens*.[12] There is, then, no difficulty in seeing how the divine light operates in all men, good or bad, since there is no question of a vision of the divine ideas and of the divine essence as such, in themselves. God co-operates in all the activities of creatures; but the human mind is made in the image of God in a special manner and God's concurrence with the mind's activity is rightly termed illumination.

In the same *De cognitione* to which reference has already

been made, Matthew mentions the Thomist doctrine that the intellect knows the singular thing *per quandam reflexionem*, by a certain act of reflection[13] and rejects it. It is difficult to understand this position, he says, for the knowledge of the singular thing *per reflexionem ad phantasma* means that the intellect knows the singular thing either in the phantasm or directly in itself. The latter supposition is ruled out by the Thomist view, while on the other hand the phantasm is not actually intelligible (*intelligibile actu*), but the *species intelligibilis* has to be abstracted. In opposition to the Thomist view Matthew asserts that the intellect knows singular things in themselves and directly, by means of *species singulares*. It is sense intuition which apprehends the object as existing and intellectual intuition which apprehends the individual quiddity or essence; but unless the mind had first of all an intuition of the singular thing, it could not abstract the universal notion. The *species universalis* thus presupposes the *species singularis*. Of course, the singular thing is not intelligible if by intelligible you mean deductively demonstrable, since it is contingent and passing; but if by intelligible you mean what can be apprehended by the intellect, then in this case it must be allowed that the singular thing is intelligible.[14] Otherwise it is not possible to explain satisfactorily the abstraction and real foundation of the universal idea.

Another theory of St. Thomas which Matthew rejects is the theory that the soul while united to the body has no direct intuition of itself and its dispositions and powers, but knows indirectly that it itself and its dispositions exist, through its perception of the act by which it knows objects through *species* abstracted from phantasms. This theory of the soul's purely indirect knowledge of itself Matthew rejects, as being contrary to the teaching of St. Augustine and also to what reason demands. It is unreasonable to suppose that the soul is so immersed in the body that it can apprehend nothing without an image or phantasm and that it can apprehend itself and its dispositions only indirectly. 'It seems altogether absurd to suppose the intellect so blind that it does not see itself, when it is by the intellect that the soul knows all things.'[15] His own theory Matthew states with considerable care. As regards the *beginning* of knowledge 'I say without any doubt that the soul can intuit neither itself nor the habits which are in it, nor can the first act of knowledge be directed to itself or the things which are in it.'[16] The soul needs a stimulus from the bodily senses for the beginning of knowledge, and then by reflecting on its own perceived act of knowing it comes to know its powers and itself as existent. But afterwards the soul turns in on itself, as it were (*quadam spirituali conversione in semetipsam revocata est*),[17] and then it can have a direct intuition of itself and its habits, these being no longer simply the non-intuited conclusions of a process of reasoning, but the direct object of a mental vision. In order that this intellectual vision should take place, four conditions are required, just as for sensitive vision, namely a visible object which is present as visible, a properly disposed power of vision, mutual proportion, and illumination. All these conditions are or can be fulfilled. The soul is an intellectually visible object and it is present to the intellect; the intellect is an immaterial power and is not intrinsically dependent on a sense-organ; both the intellect and the soul itself are intellectual finite objects, and nothing is so proportioned to the soul as the soul itself; lastly the divine illumination is always present.[18]

Matthew of Aquasparta thus adhered closely, though reasonably and with moderation, to the Augustinian tradition, and it is only to be expected that he would maintain the theories of the *rationes seminales* and the *forma corporeitatis*. In addition he upheld the Bonaventurian doctrine of the universal hylomorphic composition of creatures, rejecting the real distinction of essence and existence as an adequate explanation of their finitude and contingence.

4. A much less faithful Augustinian was *Peter John Olivi* (c. 1248–98), a prominent figure among the Franciscan 'spirituals'. Thus while he clung to the theory of the hylomorphic composition of all creatures and the multiplicability of angels in the same species, as also to the doctrine of plurality of forms, he not only denied the existence of *rationes seminales*, but even maintained that this denial was in accordance with the doctrine of St. Augustine. An anticipation of Scotus's *distinctio formalis a parte rei*, intermediate between a real distinction and a conceptual distinction, is to be found in his philosophy; and it exists between the divine attributes, for instance, as Scotus also thought. Olivi is also remarkable for having adopted the *impetus* theory of Joannes Philoponus, i.e. the theory that when a projectile is set in motion, the mover or thrower confers an impetus or *impulsus* on the pro-

jectile which carries the projectile on even when it is no longer in contact with the mover, though it may be overcome by the resistance of the air and other opposing forces. But consideration of this theory, which meant the abandonment of the Aristotelian theory of 'unnatural' motion, is best reserved for the next volume, in connection with those thinkers who drew some novel conclusions from the doctrine and paved the way for a new conception of the corporeal world. Further consideration of the *distinctio formalis a parte rei* will be reserved for the treatment of the Scotist system. My real reason for mentioning Olivi here is to allude briefly to his theory of the soul and its relation to the body. This theory, or part of it, was condemned at the Council of Vienne in 1311, and the matter is worth mentioning since certain writers in the past have claimed that the Council meant to condemn what they certainly did not mean to condemn.

According to Olivi, there are three constitutive 'parts' in the human soul, the vegetative principle or form, the sensitive principle or form, and the intellectual principle or form. These three forms together constitute the one human soul, the rational soul, as constitutive parts of the whole soul. There was no particular novelty in maintaining a doctrine of plurality of forms; but Olivi drew from his theory the peculiar conclusion that the three formal parts are united by the spiritual matter of the soul in such a way that the higher form influences and moves the lower forms only through the mediation of the spiritual matter. He concluded further that while the vegetative and sensitive parts inform the body, the intellectual part does not of itself inform the body, though it moves the other parts as its instruments and subjects. He maintained that the rooting of all three parts in the spiritual matter of the soul safeguarded the unity of man and the substantial union of soul and body; but at the same time he refused to allow that the intellectual part of the soul informs the body directly. This last point aroused opposition among the Franciscans themselves. One of the reasons of their opposition was that if it were true that the intellectual form did not inform the body directly but only mediately, through the sensitive form, it would follow that Christ was not, as Man, composed of a rational soul and a body, as the Faith teaches.[19] The end of the matter was that in 1311 the Council of Vienne condemned as heretical the proposition that the rational or intellectual soul does not inform the body directly (*per se*)

and essentially (*essentialiter*). The Council did not, however, condemn the doctrine of the plurality of forms and affirm the Thomist view, as some later writers have tried to
maintain. The Fathers of the Council, or the majority of
them at least, themselves held the doctrine of the plurality
of forms. The Council simply wished to preserve the unity
of man by affirming that the intellectual soul informs the
body directly. This is shown clearly by the reference to Chris-
tology. The human nature of Christ consists of a passible
human body and a rational human soul which informs the
body, the two together forming human nature. The Council
did not concern itself with the question of the *forma corporeitatis* or with the question whether there are or are not
various 'parts' in the human soul: what it says is simply that
the rational soul informs the body directly and so is a principle integral to man: it was the separation between the intellectual soul and the human body which it condemned, not
the doctrine of the plurality of forms. It is, therefore, quite
erroneous to state that the Council of Vienne declared that
the human soul informs prime matter directly and that the
Thomist theory is imposed by the Church.

5. If Peter John Olivi was an independent thinker who departed on some points from the Augustinian tradition and
prepared the way for later stages in Franciscan thought, *Roger
Marston* (d. 1303), who was for a time Minister of the English Franciscan province, was a whole-hearted Augustinian.
He embraced all the characteristic 'Augustinian' theories,
such as the intellectual apprehension of the singular thing,
the pre-eminence of will over intellect, universal hylomorphic
composition in creatures, plurality of forms, and he criticised
St. Thomas for admitting the apparent possibility of creation
from eternity and for throwing overboard the *rationes seminales*. Indeed, this resolute English conservative found even
Matthew of Aquasparta too accommodating and firmly rejected any attempt to water down what he regarded as the
genuine doctrine of St. Augustine and St. Anselm. We should
prefer the 'saints' to those 'infernal men', the pagan philosophers.

In his *De Anima* Roger Marston gives an uncompromising
interpretation of St. Augustine's teaching on the divine illumination. The active intellect may indeed be called a part of
the soul if by active intellect is meant a natural disposition
in the soul for the knowledge of truth (*sicut perspicuitas*

naturalis in oculo); but if by active intellect is meant the act of illumination, we must say that it is a separate substance, God Himself.[20] The active intellect is the uncreated or eternal light which impresses on the mind, as a seal on the wax, a certain active impression which leaves a passive impression that is the formal principle in the knowledge of unchanging truths.[21] It is not the concepts or terms of the judgement which are provided by the eternal light, God; but the eternal truth.[22] For example, the eternal light does not infuse into the mind the concept of the whole and the concept of the part, but it is the radiation of the eternal light which enables the mind to apprehend infallibly the relation between the terms, the eternal truth that the whole is greater than the part. The eternal ideas are thus the ultimate foundation of the certain and infallible judgement (*rationes aeternae aliqualiter attinguntur*). The explanation of the fact that the human race agrees about the fundamental truths is to be found in the common illumination of all minds by the one divine light, and Roger Marston refuses to allow that this divine light consists simply in the creation of the human intellect as a finite imitation of the divine intellect. Those who deny that the active intellect is the primal and uncreated light are people who are 'drunk with the nectar of philosophy' and who pervert the meaning of St. Augustine and the *Sancti*.[23] If St. Augustine had not intended to say any more than these people make him say, then his arguments would be without point and would beg the question, since if the human intellect was assumed to be the source of its own light, one could not argue to the existence of an uncreated light, as St. Augustine certainly does.[24]

6. Another English Franciscan of note was *Richard of Middleton*, who studied at Oxford and Paris. He went to Paris in 1278, and after taking his degree he occupied one of the Franciscan chairs of theology until 1286, when he became tutor to St. Louis of Toulouse, the son of Charles II of Sicily. The date of his death is uncertain, but it must have occurred about the turn of the century. He composed the customary Commentary on the *Sentences* of Peter Lombard and was responsible for *Quaestiones Disputatae* and *Quodlibets*.

In some points Richard of Middleton followed the general Franciscan tradition, maintaining, for example, the impossibility of creation from eternity, since this would involve a created infinite, universal hylomorphic composition in creatures, the plurality of forms and the primacy of the will. On other points, however, he approximated to the Thomist position, and in this matter he represents the new movement among Franciscan thinkers towards a modified Augustinianism, the greatest exponent of which was Duns Scotus. Thus Richard insists not only that all valid demonstrations of God's existence are *a posteriori*, but also that our intellectual knowledge of spiritual as well as of corporeal beings is abstracted from sense-experience and that it is unnecessary to postulate any special illumination or to identify the active intellect with God. On the other hand, the mind apprehends the singular, though it does so by means of the same concept by which it apprehends the universal.

In addition, Richard maintained some more or less original ideas. One of the less happy of these ideas was the notion that what the mind directly attains is not the individual existent thing itself, but its *esse repraesentatum*. He also invented a *principium pure possibile*, in order to explain how new forms can appear under the action of a created agent. It might appear at first that this is nothing else but prime matter; but matter, which differs in kind in spiritual and corporeal beings and so is not homogeneous, has some actuality of its own in Richard's eyes, whereas the *principium pure possibile* has no actuality of its own, is concreated with matter and cannot exist separately. If matter is understood as the primary foundation of natural change, as that which is common to corrupted and generated bodies and receives form, then it is really distinct from the purely potential principle, which is transmuted into the form itself. The purely potential principle may then be called the potentiality of matter (*potentia materiae*), if the potentiality of matter is understood as meaning the principle out of which the created agent educes the form and which is transmuted into the form educed; but in this case the *potentia materiae* is really distinct from matter itself. Conversely, if by *potentia materiae* is meant matter's power to receive form, it is the same as matter itself; but in this case it is really distinct from the *principium pure possibile*.[25] In other words, the power to receive form is not the same as the power to become form. Besides prime matter as the subject of change, which has some actuality of its own and which receives form, Richard postulates, then, a kind of receptacle of forms, a purely potential principle which is transmuted into those forms which are received in matter. He considered that this theory constituted an improvement on the theory of *rationes seminales*, and he tried to interpret St. Augustine as teaching the existence, not of active forces (which would amount to a *latitatio formarum*), but of a purely potential principle which becomes forms. In virtue of this positive potentiality forms may be said to be created from the beginning in potency, but this must not be taken to imply the presence of 'seeds'. The principle in question is in matter, and Richard calls it the more intimate part of matter and the passive potentiality of matter; but, as we have seen, it is not identical with matter as subject of change and recipient of form.[26] It is not, therefore, something altogether separate from matter, but it is distinct from matter in the ordinary sense. This may appear to involve an approximation to the Thomist view of prime matter, and to a certain extent this seems to be true; but Richard refused to abandon the traditional view of matter as having some actuality of its own, and so he had to distinguish matter as element in the composite thing from the potential principle which becomes forms under the action of the created agent.

In addition to being composed of matter and form every creature is also composed of essence and existence. But existence is not something really distinct from the essence, to which it comes as an accident. On the other hand, existence is not merely conceptually distinct from essence, since it does add something to essence. What does it add? A twofold relation: a *relatio rationis* to itself, inasmuch as existence confers on essence the dignity of being an hypostasis or substance, and a real relation to the Creator.[27] On this matter Richard of Middleton accepted the position of Henry of Ghent.

At the end of his work *Richard de Middleton*[28] Père E. Hocedez, S.J., remarks: *Richard finit une époque*. The last representative of the Seraphic School, he attempted a synthesis (*prudemment nouvelle*) in which the main positions of Bonaventure, deepened and perfected, should be integrated with what he considered best in Aristotelianism and in the theology of St. Thomas. That Richard of Middleton incorporated ideas from outside the Augustinian tradition is clear enough; but I cannot agree with Père Hocedez that this movement of thought 'had no morrow' and that Scotus directed Franciscan philosophy 'in new ways which were soon to end in nominalism'. Rather did Richard's philosophy form a stage on the way to Scotism, which opened the door wider to Aristotelianism, but was certainly not nominalistic or favourable to nominalism.

7. One of the most interesting of the Franciscan philosophers is *Raymond Lull* (1232/35–1315). Born in Majorca, Raymond Lull was for a time at the court of King James II; but about 1265 he underwent a religious conversion and abandoned his family in order to devote himself to what he considered his great task in life, to fight against Islam and to help in the rooting out of Averroism. With this end in view he devoted nine years to the study of Arabic and philosophy, the first fruit of the period of study being his *Ars Magna*, followed by the *Liber principiorum philosophiae*. He joined the Third Order of St. Francis and travelled to Africa to convert the Moors; he taught at Paris and combated Averroism; he wrote logic, philosophy, theology and poetry, writing in his native Catalan and in Arabic, as well as in Latin. Finally he was martyred in Tunisia in 1315. Besides the two above-mentioned works one may mention the *Ars demonstrativa*, the *Ars brevis*, the *Ars generalis ultima*, and the anti-Averroistic works such as the *Liber contra errores Boetii et Segerii* (i.e. against Boethius of Dacia and Siger of Brabant), the *De naturali modo intelligendi*, the *Liber reprobationis aliquorum errorum Averrois*, the *Disputatio Raymundi et Averroistae* and the *Sermones contra Averroistas*. But this forms but a selection of the astonishing literary output of a man who was apostle and traveller, poet and mystic.

The apostolic interests of Raymond Lull were by no means irrelevant to his philosophy; they were partly responsible for the general attitude he adopted towards philosophy, whose ancillary relation to theology he stressed. He was quite aware of the distinction between faith and reason, and he compared faith to oil which continues to rest unmixed on the water, even if the water is increased; but his interest in the conversion of the Moslems naturally led to an insistence, not only on philosophy's subordinate relation to theology, but also on reason's ability to make acceptable the dogmas of the Faith. It is in the light of this general attitude that we must understand his proposal to 'prove' the articles of faith by 'necessary reasons'. He no more proposed to rationalise (in the modern sense) the Christian mysteries than did St. Anselm or Richard of St. Victor, when they spoke of 'necessary reasons' for the Trinity, and he expressly declares that faith treats of objects which the human reason cannot understand; but he wished to show the Moslems that Christian beliefs are not contrary to reason and that reason can meet the objections adduced against them. Moreover, believing that the accusation brought against the Averroists that they held a 'double truth' theory was justified and that the theory in question was contradictory and absurd, he was concerned to show that there is no need to have recourse to any such radical separation of theology and philosophy, but that theological dogmas harmonise with reason and cannot be impugned by reason. In regard to the peculiar theories of the Averroists themselves, he argued that these are contrary both to faith and reason. Monopsychism, for instance, contradicts the testimony of consciousness: we are conscious that our acts of thought and will are our own.

If one looked merely at the familiar 'Augustinian' theories maintained by Lull, such as the impossibility of creation from eternity, universal hylomorphic composition of creatures, plurality of forms, the primacy of will over intellect, and so on, there would not appear to be any particularly interesting feature in his philosophy; but we find such a feature in his *Ars combinatoria*. Raymond Lull supposes first of all that there are certain general principles or categories, which are self-evident and which are common to all sciences, in the sense that without them there can be neither philosophy nor any other science. The most important of these are the nine absolute predicates, goodness, greatness, eternity, power, wisdom, will, virtue, truth, glory. (These predicates express attributes of God.) There are nine other concepts which express relations (between creatures): difference, agreement, contrariety, beginning, middle, end, majority, equality, minority. In addition, there are sets of fundamental questions, such as how, when, where, etc., of virtues and of vices. Lull cannot have attached any particular importance to the number nine, which appears in the *Ars generalis*, as elsewhere he gives other numbers of divine attributes or absolute predicates; for example, in the *Liber de voluntate infinita et ordinata* he gives twelve, while in the *De possibili et impossibili* he gives twenty: the main point is that there are certain fundamental ideas which are essential to philosophy and science.

These fundamental ideas being presupposed, Raymond Lull speaks as though through their combination one could discover the principles of the particular sciences and even discover new truths, and in order that the work of combination might be facilitated, he had recourse to symbolism, the fundamental concepts being symbolised by letters, and to mechanical means of tabulating and grouping. For example, God was represented by the letter A, and, in the later writings, nine *principia*, also symbolised by letters representing the divine attributes, surround Him. These principles could be combined in a hundred and twenty ways through the use of figures and concentric circles. It is not to be wondered at, therefore, that some writers have seen in Lull's scheme an anticipation of Leibniz's dream of the *caracteristica universalis* and *Ars combinatoria*, of an algebraic symbolism, the use of which would permit the deduction from fundamental concepts not only of already ascertained truths, but even of new truths. As already mentioned, Lull does seem to imply such an aim on occasion, and if this had been his real object, he would obviously have to be considered as separating himself from the Scholastic tradition; but in point of fact he expressly asserts[29] that his aim was to facilitate the use of the memory. Moreover, we must remember his apostolic interests, which suggest that his scheme was designed for purposes of exposition and explanation rather than of deduction in the strict sense. The fact that Leibniz was influenced by Lull proves nothing as to the latter's intentions, of course. According to Dr. Otto Keicher, O.F.M.,[30] it is the *principia* which form the essence not only of the *Ars generalis*, but of the whole system of Raymond Lull; but though it is obvious enough that what Lull regarded as fundamental concepts formed in a sense the basis of his system, it does not seem that one can reduce his 'art' to the establishment of certain principles or categories: the philosopher himself regarded it as something more than that. Of course, if one stresses the expository, didactic aspect of the art, it is scarcely necessary to debate what are the essential and unessential elements in it; but if one chooses to regard it as an anticipation of Leibniz, then it would be relevant to make a distinction between Lull's schematism and mechanical technique on the one hand and on the other hand the general notion of deducing the principles of the sciences from a combination of fundamental concepts, since Lull might have anticipated Leibniz in regard to the latter's general principle, even though his 'logical algebra' was radically deficient. This is more or less the view of Dr. Bernhard Geyer,[31] and I believe it to be correct. That

Lull pursues his deduction in reliance on three main principles;[32] to hold as true everything which affirms the greatest harmony between God and created being, to attribute to God that which is the most perfect, and to assume that God has made whatever truly appears to be the better, is no argument against this interpretation: it doubtless shows the spiritual kinship between Lull and the Augustinian tradition, but it also reminds one of important points in the system of Leibniz some centuries later.

Chapter Forty-four

GILES OF ROME AND HENRY
OF GHENT

(*a*) Giles of Rome. *Life and works—The independence of
Giles as a thinker—Essence and existence—Form and matter;
soul and body—Political theory.*
(*b*) Henry of Ghent. *Life and works—Eclecticism, illustrated
by doctrines of illumination and innatism—Idea of metaphysics—Essence and existence—Proofs of God's existence—General spirit and significance of Henry's philosophy.*

(*a*) *Giles of Rome*

1. Giles (Aegidius) of Rome was born in 1247 or a little
earlier and entered the Order of the Hermits of St. Augustine
about 1260. He made his studies at Paris and seems to have
attended the lectures of St. Thomas Aquinas from 1269 to
1272. It appears that he composed the *Errores Philosophorum*
about 1270, in which he enumerates the errors of Aristotle,
Averroes, Avicenna, Algazel, Alkindi and Maimonides. The
Commentaries on the *De generatione et corruptione*, the *De
Anima*, the *Physics*, the *Metaphysics* and the logical treatises
of Aristotle, the Commentary on the first book of the *Sentences* and the works entitled *Theoremata de Corpore
Christi* and *De plurificatione intellectus possibilis* were apparently also written before 1277. In that year occurred the
famous condemnation by Stephen Tempier, Bishop of Paris
(March 7th); but between Christmas 1277 and Easter 1278
Giles wrote the *De gradibus formarum*, in which he came
out strongly against the doctrine of plurality of forms. For
this and similar offences Giles was called upon to make a
retractation; but he refused and was excluded from the Uni-

versity of Paris before he had completed his theological studies. In his period of absence from Paris he wrote the *Theoremata de esse et essentia* and his Commentary on the second and third books of the *Sentences*.

In 1285 Giles returned to Paris and was permitted to receive the licentiate in theology, though he had to make a public retractation first. He then taught theology at Paris, until he was elected General of the Order in 1292. In 1295 he was appointed Archbishop of Bourges. The works he wrote after his return to Paris in 1285 include *Quaestiones disputatae de esse et essentia*, *Quaestiones Quodlibetales*, a Commentary on the *Liber de Causis*, exegetical works such as the *In Hexaëmeron* and political treatises like the *De regimine principum* and the *De potestate ecclesiastica*. Giles died at Avignon in 1316.

2. Giles of Rome has sometimes been represented as a 'Thomist'; but though he found himself in agreement with St. Thomas on some points, as against the Franciscans, he can scarcely be called a disciple of St. Thomas: he was an independent thinker, and his independence shows itself even in matters where he might at first sight appear to be following St. Thomas. For instance, though he certainly maintained a real distinction between essence and existence, he equally certainly went beyond what St. Thomas taught on this question. Moreover, though he rejected the plurality of forms in 1277, going so far as to declare that this doctrine was contrary to the Catholic faith,[1] it has been shown that this had not always been his view. In the Commentary on the *De Anima*[2] he spoke hesitantly and doubtfully on the unicity of the substantial form in man, and the same is true in regard to the *Theoremata de Corpore Christi*,[3] while in the *Errores Philosophorum* he had stated that the doctrine of the unicity of the substantial form in man is false.[4] It is clear, then, that he began with the 'Augustinian' or Franciscan view, and that he advanced to the opposite theory only gradually.[5] No doubt he was influenced by St. Thomas in the matter, but it does not look as though he simply accepted Thomas's doctrine without question. He did not hesitate to criticise Thomist positions or to deviate from them when he wished to; and when he agreed with them, it is evident that he agreed as a result of personal thought and reflection, not because he was or had been a disciple of St. Thomas. The legend of Giles of Rome as a 'Thomist' was really a conclusion from the fact

that he listened to lectures by St. Thomas for a period; but attendance at a professor's lectures is not a sure guarantee of discipleship.

3. Giles of Rome was considerably influenced by the neo-Platonist theory of participation. Existence (*esse*) flows from God and is a participation of the divine existence. It is received by essence and is really distinct from essence. That it is received by essence can be empirically established as regards corporeal things, since they have a beginning of existence and are not always joined to existence, a fact which shows that they are in potentiality to existence, and that existence is really distinct from the essence of the sensible thing. Indeed, if existence were not really distinct from essence in all created things, creatures would not be creatures: they would exist in virtue of their own essence and would thus be independent of God's creative activity. The real distinction is, therefore, an essential safeguard of the doctrine of creation. Needless to say, the statement that created existence is a participation of the divine existence was not meant to imply pantheism. It was precisely the created character of finite things, of the participations, which Giles wanted to uphold. By essence Giles meant, in the case of material things, the composite of form and matter. The composite or corporeal essence possesses a mode of being (*modus essendi*) which is derived from the union of form and matter (in the case of immaterial creatures the mode of being comes from the form alone); but it does not of itself possess existence in the proper sense (*esse simpliciter*), which is received. The attribution of a *modus essendi* to the essence would seem to make of the latter a thing, and this aspect of the theory is accentuated by Giles's explicit teaching that essence and existence are not only really distinct, but also separable. In fact, he does not hesitate to speak of them as separable things.

This exaggerated version of the theory of the real distinction led to a lively controversy between Giles of Rome and Henry of Ghent, who attacked Giles's doctrine in his first *Quodlibet* (1276). The *Quaestiones disputatae de esse et essentia* contained Giles's answer to Henry; but the latter returned to the attack in his tenth *Quodlibet* (1286), to which Giles retorted in his twelfth *Quaestio disputata*, maintaining therein that unless existence and essence were really distinct, in the sense in which he taught the real distinction, annihilation of a creature would be impossible. He continued to hold, therefore, that his real distinction is absolutely necessary, in order to safeguard the creature's total dependence on God. The fact that he taught a real distinction between essence and existence links him with St. Thomas; but St. Thomas certainly did not teach that essence and existence are two separable things: this was an original, if somewhat strange contribution of Giles himself.

4. Giles of Rome was inclined, as his theory of essence and existence shows, to suppose that wherever the mind detects a real distinction there is separability. Thus the mind abstracts the universal from the individual (abstraction being the work of the passive intellect, when the active intellect has illumined the passive intellect and the phantasm) by apprehending the form of the object without the matter. Therefore, form and matter are really distinct and separable. Now, matter, which is found only in corporeal things, is the principle of individuation, and it follows that if matter and all the individual conditions which follow from it could be removed, the individuals of any given species would be one. Perhaps this is a legitimate conclusion from the doctrine of matter as the principle of individuation; but in any case the tendency to ultra-realism is obvious, and Giles's inclination to equate 'really distinct from' with 'separable from' is partly responsible.

Again, form (soul) and body are really distinct and separable. There is nothing novel in this idea, of course; but Giles suggested that the body may remain a body, that is, numerically the same body, after separation from the form, since before actual separation it was separable, and actual separation does not change its numerical identity.[6] Body in this sense would mean extended and organised matter. Incidentally, this theory afforded him a simple explanation of the way in which Christ's body was numerically identical before and after Christ's death on the Cross. He neither had to have recourse to the doctrine of a *forma corporeitatis* (in which he did not believe) nor was he compelled to refer the numerical identity of Christ's body in the sepulchre with His body before death simply to its union with the Divinity. Moreover, one of the reasons why Giles of Rome attacked the doctrine of plurality of forms as incompatible with theological orthodoxy was that, in his opinion, it endangered the doctrine of Christ's death. If there are several forms in man and only one of them, which is peculiar to man and is not found in other animals, is separated at death, then Christ could not be said to have undergone bodily death. The theological reason was not his only reason by any means for attacking the plurality of forms; he believed, for instance, that different forms are contrary and cannot be found together in the same substance.

5. The *De ecclesiastica potestate* is of interest not merely intrinsically, as treating of the relation between Church and State, but also because it was one of the works which were utilised by Pope Boniface VIII in the composition of his famous Bull, *Unam Sanctam* (November 18th, 1302). In his *De regimine principum*, written for the prince who was to become Philip the Fair of France, Giles wrote in dependence on Aristotle and St. Thomas; but in the *De potestate ecclesiastica* he propounded a doctrine of papal absolutism and sovereignty and of the Pope's jurisdiction even in temporal matters which was aimed especially against the pretensions of monarchs and which was most acceptable to Boniface VIII. In this work he relied much more on the attitude shown by St. Augustine towards the State than on the political thought of St. Thomas, and what St. Augustine had said with the pagan empires principally in mind was applied by Giles to contemporary kingdoms, the doctrine of Papal supremacy being added.[7] There are indeed two powers, two swords, that of the Pope and that of the king; but temporal power is subject to the spiritual. 'If the earthly power goes wrong, it will be judged by the spiritual power as by its superior; but if the spiritual power, and especially the power of the supreme pontiff, acts wrongly, it can be judged by God alone.'[8] When Philip IV of France accused Boniface VIII of asserting, in the *Unam Sanctam*, that the Holy See has direct power over kings even in temporal matters, the Pope replied that that had not been his intention: he did not mean to usurp the power of kings, but to make it clear that kings, like any other members of the Church, were subject to the Church *ratione peccati*. It would appear, however, that Giles of Rome, who spoke, of course, simply as a private theologian, went much further in this matter than Boniface VIII. He admits that there are two swords and two powers and that the one power is vested in the monarch, the other in the Church, and especially in the Papacy; but he goes on to say that although priests and especially the supreme pontiff ought not under the new law, that is, in the Christian dispensation, to

wield the material sword as well as the spiritual sword; this is not because the Church does not possess the material sword, but rather because it possesses the material sword, *non ad usum, sed ad nutum.* In other words, just as Christ possessed all power, spiritual and temporal, but did not actually use His temporal power, so the Church possesses power in temporal matters, though it is not expedient for her to exercise this power immediately and continually. Just as the body is ordered to the soul and should be subject to the soul, so the temporal power is ordered to the spiritual power and should be subject to it, even in temporal matters. The Church has, then, supreme jurisdiction even in temporal matters; and the logical consequence is that kings are little more than lieutenants of the Church.[9] 'All temporal things are placed under the dominion and power of the Church and especially of the supreme pontiff.'[10] This theory was followed by James of Viterbo in his *De regimine Christiano* before September 1302.

In 1287 the signal honour was paid to Giles of Rome of being made the Doctor of his Order during his own lifetime, not only in regard to what he had already written, but also in regard to what he should write in the future.

(b) Henry of Ghent

6. Henry of Ghent was born at Tournai or at Ghent at a date which cannot be determined. (His family came originally from Ghent in any case; but it was not a noble family, as legend had it.) By 1267 he was a Canon of Tournai, and in 1276 he became Archdeacon of Bruges. In 1279 he was made principal Archdeacon of Tournai. His archidiaconal duties do not seem to have been very exacting, as he taught at Paris, first in the faculty of arts and later (from 1276) in that of theology. In 1277 he was a member of the commission of theologians which assisted Stephen Tempier, Bishop of Paris. His works include a *Summa Theologica,* fifteen *Quodlibets, Quaestiones super Metaphysicam Aristotelis* (1–6), *Syncathegorematum Liber* and a *Commentum in Librum de Causis;* but it does not appear that the last three works can be attributed to him with certainty, and the same can be said of the Commentary on the *Physics* of Aristotle. It is, therefore, the *Summa Theologica* and the *Quodlibets* which constitute the sure source for our knowledge of Henry's teach-

ing. He died on June 29th, 1293. He was never a member of the Servite Order, as was once maintained.

7. Henry of Ghent was an eclectic thinker and can be called neither an Augustinian nor an Aristotelian. This eclecticism may be illustrated by his theory of knowledge. If one read a proposition such as *omnis cognitio nostra a sensu ortum habet*,[11] one might suppose that Henry was a decided Aristotelian, with little sympathy for Augustinianism, and especially if one read the proposition in conjunction with his statement that man can know that which is true in the creature without any special divine illumination, but simply through his natural powers aided by God's ordinary concurrence.[12] But this is only one aspect of his thought. The knowledge of creatures which we can attain through sense-experience is but a superficial knowledge, and though we can without illumination know what is true in the creature, we cannot without illumination know its truth. The reason why knowledge based simply on sense-experience is superficial, is this. The *species intelligibilis* contains no more than was contained in the *species sensibilis*: by the latter we apprehend the object in its singularity and by the former we apprehend the object in its universal aspect; but neither the one nor the other gives us the intelligible essence of the object in its relation to the divine ideas, and without the apprehension of the intelligible essence we cannot form a certain judgement concerning the object. The 'truth' (*Veritas*) of the object consists in its relation to the unchanging truth, and in order to apprehend this relation we need the divine illumination.[13] Thus when Henry of Ghent says that our knowledge comes from sense, he restricts the extension of 'knowledge': 'it is one thing to know concerning a creature that which is true in it, and it is another thing to know its truth.' The 'truth' of a thing is conceived by him in an Augustinian manner, and to apprehend it illumination is necessary. He may have made comparatively little use of the illumination theory and watered down Augustinianism to a certain extent, but the Augustinian element was certainly present in his thought: the natural operations of sense and intellect explain what one might call man's normal knowledge, which is a comparatively superficial knowledge of objects, but they do not and cannot explain the whole range of possible human knowledge.

A similar eclectic tendency can be seen in his doctrine of innatism. He rejected the Platonic doctrine of innatism and reminiscence and he rejected the theory of Avicenna that in this life ideas are impressed by the *Dator formarum*; but he did not accept the doctrine of Aristotle (as commonly interpreted) that all our ideas are formed by reflection on the data of sense-experience. Henry made his own the statement of Avicenna that the ideas of being, thing, and necessity are of such a kind that they are imprinted immediately on the soul by an impression which owes nothing to anterior and better-known ideas.[14] On the other hand, the primary ideas, of which the most important and the ultimate is that of being, are not innate in the strict sense, but are conceived together with experience of sense-objects, even if they are not derived from that experience.[15] The mind seems to draw these ideas out of itself or rather to form them from within on the occasion of sense-experience.[16] As the idea of being embraces both uncreated and created being,[17] the idea of God may be called innate in a certain sense; but this does not mean that man has from birth an actual idea of God, the origin of which is quite independent of experience: the idea is only virtually innate, in the sense that a man forms it from the idea of being, which is itself presupposed by experience of concrete objects but does not arise in clear consciousness, is not actually formed, until experience is enjoyed. As metaphysics really consist in an investigation of the idea of being and in the realisation of the relation between the intelligible essences of created being and uncreated being, one would expect that the necessity of illumination would be emphasised; but Henry frequently describes the genesis of ideas and of knowledge without any reference to a special illumination, possibly under the influence of Aristotle and of Avicenna. His tendency to eclecticism seems to have led to a certain carelessness in regard to consistency.

8. While the natural philosopher or *physicus* starts with the singular object and then forms by abstraction the universal notion of the sensible object, the metaphysician starts with the idea of being (or *res* or *aliquid*) and proceeds to discover the intelligible essences virtually contained in that idea.[18] There is a certain overlapping, of course, between the provinces of physics and metaphysics, since, for example, when the metaphysician says that man is a rational animal, he apprehends the same object as the physicist, who says that man is a body and a soul; but the starting-point and the mode of approach of the metaphysician is different from that of

the physicist. The metaphysician, proceeding from the more universal to the less universal, from genus to species, defines the intelligible essence of man, whereas the physicist starts from the individual man and by abstraction apprehends and states the physical components of all men.

Being or *res* in the widest sense comprises *res secundum opinionem* (such as a golden mountain) which have only mental being, and *res secundum veritatem*, which have an actual or possible extramental existence,[19] and it is being in the second sense which is *ens metaphysicum*, the object of metaphysics. Just as *ens* in the widest sense is divided analogically, so is *ens metaphysicum* divided analogically into that which is *ipsum esse*, God, and that *cui convenit esse*, creatures. Being is thus not a genus or predicament. Again, being in the last sense, *aliquid cui convenit vel natum est convenire esse*, comprises and is divided analogically into substances, to which it pertains to exist in themselves (*esse in se*) and accidents, to which it pertains to exist in another (*esse in alio*), that is, in a substance. It is quite true that for Aristotle too metaphysics was the science of being as being; but for Aristotle the idea of being was not the starting-point, the analysis of which leads to the discovery of the analogical divisions of being: Henry of Ghent was inspired in this matter by the thought of Avicenna, whose philosophy was also influential in the building of the Scotist system. According to both Henry of Ghent and Scotus the metaphysician studies the idea of being, and metaphysics move primarily on the conceptual level.

It might appear that on this view not only is it difficult to effect a passage from the essential level to the existential level, but also that there would be confusion between the *res secundum opinionem* and the *res secundum veritatem*. However, Henry maintained that essences which are actualised or which are objectively possible have and can be discerned as having a certain reality of their own, an *esse essentiae*, the possession of which distinguishes them from pure *entia rationis*. The theory of *esse essentiae*, which Henry took from Avicenna, must not be understood, however, to imply a kind of inchoate existence, as though the essence had an extramental existence of a rudimentary sort; Henry accused Giles of Rome of maintaining a theory of this kind: it means that the essence exists actually in thought, that it is definable, that it is an intelligible essence.[20] Its intelligibility, its intrinsic possibility, distinguishes it from the *res secundum opinionem*, from the notion, for example, of a being half man and half goat, which is a contradictory notion. As to the relation between the essential level and the existential level, it is evident enough that we can know the existence of the singular only through experience of the singular (there is no question in Henry's philosophy of any deduction of singulars), while the intelligible essence, which is universal in character, is not deduced from the notion of being so much as 'arranged' under the notion of being. As we have seen, the natural philosopher detects in man his physical components, body and soul; but man is defined by the metaphysician as a rational animal, in terms of genus and species, in terms of his intelligible essence. This intelligible essence is thus arranged under the notion of being and its (analogical) 'contractions', as a particular kind of substance; but that man actually exists is known only by experience. On the other hand, the intelligible essence is a reflection (an *exemplatum* or *ideatum*) of the Idea in God, the exemplar or absolute essence, and God knows singular things through essence considered as multipliable in numerically different substances or *supposita*: there are no ideas of singular things as such in God, but the latter are known by Him in and through the specific essence.[21] From this it would seem to follow either that singular things are contained in the universal idea in some way and are, theoretically at least, deducible from it or that one must relinquish any prospect of rendering singular things intelligible.[22] Henry would not allow that individuality adds any real element to the specific essence:[23] individual things differ from one another simply in virtue of the fact that they exist actually and extramentally. If, then, the individuation cannot be explained in terms of a real added element, it must be explained in terms of a negation, a double negation, that of internal or intrinsic division and that of identity with any other being. Scotus attacked this view on the ground that the principle of individuation cannot be a negation and that the negation must presuppose something positive; but, of course, Henry did presuppose something positive, namely existence.[24]

The above may seem a confusing and perhaps somewhat irrelevant account of varied items of Henry's doctrine, but it is meant to bring out a fundamental difficulty in his system. In so far as metaphysics are a study of the idea of being and of intelligible essences and in so far as individuals are considered as intelligible only as contained in the essence, Henry's metaphysic is of a Platonic type, whereas his theory of individuation looks forward to the Ockhamist view that there is no need to seek for any principle of individuation, since a thing is individual by the very fact that it exists. If the first point of view demands an explanation of objects in terms of essence, the second demands an explanation in terms of existence, of creation and making; and Henry juxtaposes the two points of view without achieving any adequate reconciliation.

9. We have seen that Henry of Ghent endowed the intelligible essence with an *esse essentiae*, as distinguished from the *esse existentiae*. What is the nature of the distinction in question? In the first place Henry rejected the theory of Giles of Rome, who transported the distinction on to the physical plane and made it a distinction between two separable things, essence and existence. Against this view Henry argued in his first (9), tenth (7) and eleventh (3) *Quodlibets*. If existence were distinct from essence in the sense postulated by Giles of Rome, existence would itself be an essence and would require another existence in order to exist; so that an infinite process would be involved. Moreover, what would existence, really distinct from essence, be? Substance or accident? One could maintain neither answer. Furthermore, Henry rejected the real distinction understood as a metaphysical distinction: the essence of an existent object is in no way indifferent to existence or non-existence; in the concrete order a thing either is or it is not. Existence is not a constitutive element or principle of a thing, of such a kind that the thing would be a synthesis of essence and existence; any synthesis there may be, that is, by way of addition of existence to essence, is the work of the mind.[25] On the other hand, the content of the concept of essence is not identical with the content of the concept of existence: the idea of an existent essence contains more, to our view, than the mere idea of essence as such. The distinction, therefore, though not a real distinction, is not a purely logical distinction, but an 'intentional' distinction, expressing different *intentiones* concerning the same simple thing.[26]

But if the actualised essence contains more than the essence conceived as possible and if the real distinction between essence and existence is not to be reintroduced, what can this

'more' be? According to Henry of Ghent, it consists in a relation, the relation of effect to Cause, of creature to Creator. It
is one and the same thing for a creature to exist and to depend on God:[27] to be an effect of God and to have *esse
existentiae ab ipso* are the same, namely a *respectus* or relation to God. The essence considered merely as possible is an
exemplatum and depends on the divine knowledge, whereas
the actualised or existent essence depends on the divine creative power,[28] so that the notion of the latter contains more
than the notion of the former; but though the relation of the
actualised essence to God is a real relation of dependence, it
is not distinct from the essence in the concrete order with a
real distinction. From the metaphysical point of view, then,
God alone can be thought without relation to any other being; the creature, apart from the twofold relationship to God
(as *exemplatum* to Exemplar and as effect to Cause), is nothing. Through the first relationship *by itself* the essence does
not exist 'outside' God; by the second relationship it exists as
an actualised essence; but apart from that relationship it has
no *esse existentiae*, since the *esse existentiae* and the *respectus
ad Deum* are the same.

10. Henry of Ghent admitted the *a posteriori* proofs of
God's existence; but he regarded them as physical in character (his ideas of physics or natural philosophy and of metaphysics could lead to no other conclusion) and as inferior to
the *a priori* proof. The physical proofs can lead us to the
recognition of a pre-eminent Being, but they cannot reveal to
us the essence of that Being: as far as these proofs are concerned, the existence of God is an existence of fact, which
is not revealed as also an existence of right. The metaphysical proof, however, makes us see God's existence as necessarily contained in, or rather identical with His essence.[29]
Similarly, it is only the metaphysical proof which can firmly
establish the unicity of God, by showing that the divine essence has an intrinsic repugnance to any multiplication.[30]

The *a priori* idea of God, that of the supreme conceivable
simple Perfection, which cannot not exist, was assumed by
Henry of Ghent as one of the primary notions, namely Being,
thing or essense, and Necessity. One might expect that he
would attempt to deduce the notions of necessary Being and
contingent being from an original univocal concept of being;
but in point of fact he refused to admit the univocal character of the concept of being. Our realisation of what necessary

Being is and our realisation of what contingent being is grow *pari passu*: we cannot have an imperfect knowledge of the latter without an imperfect knowledge of the former, nor a perfect knowledge of the latter without a perfect knowledge of the former.[31] There is no one univocal concept of being common to God and creatures: there are two concepts, that of necessary Being and that of contingent being, and our concept of being must be one or the other. We can, however, confuse the two. There are two sorts of indetermination, negative indetermination and privative indetermination. A being is negatively indeterminate when it excludes all possibility of determination in the sense of finitude, and God alone is indeterminate in this sense, while a being is privatively indeterminate when it can or must be determined but is not yet determined or is considered in abstraction from its determinations.[32] Thus if one considers being in abstraction from its determinations, one is considering *created* being, which must in the concrete be either substance or accident but which can be considered in abstraction from these determinations, and this concept of the *privative indeterminatum* does not comprise God, the *negative indeterminatum*. But the mind can easily confuse the two concepts and conceive them as one, although they are in reality two. In saying this and in excluding any univocal concept of being common to God and creatures Henry of Ghent wished to avoid the Avicennian idea of necessary creation, which would seem to follow if one could deduce from an original univocal concept of being both necessary and created being; but he came perilously near to teaching, and he was accused by Scotus of so teaching, that the two concepts of being are equivocal. It is perfectly true that Henry expounded a doctrine of analogy and asserted that 'being' is not used purely equivocally of God and creatures;[33] but he insisted so much that the concept of being is either the concept of God or the concept of creatures and that there is no positive community between them, but only negative, (without there being any positive foundation whatsoever for the negation, i.e. the 'indetermination') that there would seem to be considerable justification for Scotus's accusation.[34] Scotus objected that on Henry's view every argument from creatures to God must be fallacious, and it would indeed appear that if that aspect of Henry's thought to which Scotus objected is emphasised, the only way of safeguarding man's philosophical knowledge of God would be to recognise the existence of an *a priori* idea of God, not derived from experience of creatures.

11. Henry of Ghent was, it has been said, an eclectic, and of this eclecticism some examples have been given. While he combated the theory of the real distinction put forward by Giles of Rome (and even that of St. Thomas, though Giles was the particular object of attack), while he refused to allow the possibility of creation from eternity, and while he rejected the Thomist theory of individuation, he also rejected the doctrine of universal hylomorphism in creatures and opposed the doctrine of plurality of forms so far as material beings other than man were concerned. In the first *Quodlibet* Henry adopted the Thomist theory of the unicity of the substantial form in man, but in the second *Quodlibet* he changed his opinion and admitted the *forma corporeitatis* in man. On the other hand, while he postulated special illumination of a restricted type and while he maintained the superiority of the free will to the intellect, he borrowed a good deal from Aristotle, was strongly influenced by the philosophy of Avicenna and, in his doctrine of individuation, bears more resemblance to the thinkers of the Ockhamist movement than to his predecessors. Yet to call a philosopher an 'eclectic' without qualification implies that he achieved no synthesis and that his philosophy is a collection of juxtaposed opinions borrowed from various sources. In the case of Henry of Ghent, to picture him in this light would be to commit an injustice. He was certainly not always consistent, nor do his opinions and tendencies of thought always harmonise well with one another; but he belonged definitely to the Platonic tradition in Christian thought and his borrowings from Aristotle and Aristotelian thinkers do not really affect this fact; St. Bonaventure himself had utilised Aristotle, but he was none the less an Augustinian. The main tendency of Henry as metaphysician was to construct a metaphysic of the intelligible, a metaphysic of essences rather than of the concrete, and this marks him off as a philosopher of the Platonic tradition.

But if Henry belonged to the Platonic tradition, he was also a Christian philosopher. Thus he maintained clearly the doctrine of free creation out of nothing. He did not attempt to deduce created existence from the idea of being, and in his desire to avoid making creation necessary he rejected the univocity of the concept of being as a starting-point for metaphysical deduction. Plato himself, of course, never attempted an 'idealist' deduction of this type; but Henry, unlike Plato or any other pagan Greek philosopher, had a clear idea of creation and he stressed the dependence of all created things on God, maintaining that they were nothing apart from their relationship to Him. This prominent Christian element in his thought sets him in the Augustinian tradition, from which he drew his doctrines of illumination and of virtually innate ideas, of ideas which can be formed from within. On the other hand, while he tried to avoid what he considered to be the faults of the philosophy of Avicenna, his metaphysic was strongly influenced by the Moslem philosopher's thought, so that M. Gilson has been able to speak in this connection of an *augustinisme avicennisant*. Apart from the fact that Henry brings together God in His function as illuminator (St. Augustine) with the separate active intellect of Avicenna (a *rapprochement* which was not peculiar to Henry), his doctrine of mitigated innatism naturally inclined him to a metaphysic of intelligible essences rather than to a metaphysic of the concrete, and, like Avicenna, he attributed a certain reality or objectivity, though not independent of God, to essences considered as possible, essences which follow necessarily from the divine intellect and so are, in themselves at least, deducible. But when it was a question of existence, of the concrete existent world of creation, he had to part company with Avicenna. The latter, regarding the divine will as subject to the same necessity as the divine intellect, made the emergence of existences parallel to the emergence of essences, the subordinate Intelligences being responsible for prolonging the activity of the first Cause and bringing about the transition from the universal to the particular; but Henry of Ghent, as a Christian thinker, could not hold this: he had to admit free creation and also creation in time. He saw quite well that the sensible and concrete cannot be rendered fully intelligible, if to render fully intelligible means to explain in terms of essence, and therefore he made a sharp distinction between metaphysics and physics, each of the sciences having its own starting-point and mode of procedure.

In spite, however, of the Platonic and Avicennian tendencies in his thought, Henry of Ghent helped in a certain sense to prepare the way for nominalism. Insistence on illumination easily leads to a certain scepticism concerning the mind's power of achieving a metaphysical system based on experience, while Henry's tendency to simplification when dealing with the created world (for example, by the denial of any real distinction between essence and existence and by his theory of individuation, which involves the rejection of realism) may, if considered by itself, be regarded as heralding the simplifying tendencies and the conceptualism of the fourteenth century. Of course, this is but one aspect of his philosophy and it is not the most important and characteristic, but it is a real aspect none the less. Ockham criticised Henry of Ghent's thought under its other aspects; but that does not mean that Henry's thought was without influence on the movement of which Ockham was the chief figure. Henry has been called an 'intermediary' figure, intermediary between the thirteenth and fourteenth centuries, and this can hardly be denied; but before Ockhamism arose, Duns Scotus, who so frequently criticised Henry, as Henry had criticised Giles of Rome, was to attempt to develop and justify a synthesis of Augustinianism and Aristotelianism, thus endeavouring, in spite of his polemics against Henry of Ghent, to accomplish satifactorily what Henry had not accomplished satisfactorily.

Chapter Forty-five

SCOTUS–I

Life—Works—Spirit of Scotus's philosophy.

1. John Duns Scotus, *Doctor Subtilis*, was born in Scotland, at Maxton in the county of Roxburgh, his family name, Duns, being originally taken from a place in the county of Berwick. That he was a Scotsman can be now taken as certain, not simply from the fact that by his time Scotsmen and Irishmen were no longer called indiscriminately *Scoti*, but also as having been proved by the discovery of a series of documents, the authority of which can scarcely be called in question. But if the country of his birth is certain, the date is not so certain, though it is probable that he was born in 1265 or 1266, and that he entered the Order of Friars Minor in 1278, taking the habit in 1280 and being ordained priest in 1291. The traditional date of his death is November 8th, 1308. He died at Cologne and was buried in the Franciscan Church in that city.

The dates of Scotus's academic career are by no means certain; but it appears that he studied at Paris under Gonsalvus of Spain from 1293 to 1296, after a brief sojourn at Oxford. According to the traditional view Scotus then went to Oxford, where he commented on the *Sentences* and produced the *Opus Oxoniense* or Oxford Commentary on the *Sentences*. The fact that in the fourth book of the *Opus Oxoniense* Scotus quotes a bull of Benedict XI, of January 31st, 1304, is no certain argument against the traditional view, as Scotus certainly retouched and made later additions to the work.[1] In 1302 Scotus returned to Paris and commented there on the *Sentences*; but in 1303 he was banished from

Paris, as he had supported the Papal party against King Philip the Fair. Where he spent the time of banishment is not quite clear: Oxford, Cologne and Bologna have all been suggested. In any case he taught at Oxford in the academic year 1303–4, returning to Paris in 1304 and receiving the doctorate in theology in 1305. It is possible that he returned to Oxford again for a short while, but he was certainly at Paris, engaged in commenting on the *Sentences*, when he was sent to Cologne in the summer of 1307. At Cologne he resumed his work of teaching; but in 1308, as already mentioned, he died, when about forty-two or forty-three years of age.

2. The uncertainty concerning the exact course of Scotus's life is to be regretted; but far more to be regretted is the uncertainty concerning the authentic character of some works attributed to him in the edition of Luke Wadding. Happily, however, the general authenticity of the two great commentaries on the *Sentences* is not in question, though neither the *Opus Oxoniense* nor the *Reportata Parisiensia* in their traditional form can be ascribed in their totality to Scotus. As to the *Opus Oxoniense*, the original text as Scotus left it (the *Ordinatio*, of which no manuscript has yet been discovered) was added to by disciples who wished to complete the work of the master by presenting a complete exposition of his thought, though in some subsequent codices the scribes attempted to note the additions which had been made. A similar situation presents itself in regard to the *Reportata Parisiensia*, since in their case too the desire to give a complete account of Scotus's teaching led the master's disciples to assemble together partial accounts from various sources, without, however, making any serious attempt to discover the respective authority and value of the different parts of the mosaic. The task of the Commission appointed to superintend the production of the critical edition of Scotus's works is, then, no easy one; but although the Oxford and Paris Commentaries represent basically the thought of Scotus, no secure and final picture of that thought can be given until the critical edition of the Commentaries appears, more especially until the original *Ordinatio* or *Liber Scoti* is published, free from accretions.

The authentic character of the *De primo principio* is not in question, though the arguments adduced by Father Ciganotto to show that it was Scotus's last work, written at

Cologne, do not appear to be decisive. The *Quaestiones Quodlibetales* are also authentic,[2] as are also the forty-six *Collationes* (Wadding knew of only forty, but C. Balić discovered another six) and the first nine books of the *Quaestiones subtilissimae super libros Metaphysicorum Aristotelis*. As to the *De Anima*, the question of its authenticity has been a matter for dispute. Pelster maintained that it was authentic, while Longpré tried to show that it was unauthentic, though his arguments were declared insufficient by Fleig. It is now generally accepted as authentic, even by Longpré. On the other hand, the *Grammatica speculativa* is to be attributed to Thomas of Erfurt, while the *De rerum principio* is also unauthentic, being probably, in part at least, a plagiarism from the *Quaestiones Quodlibetales* of Godfrey of Fontaines. Also unauthentic are the *Metaphysica textualis* (probably to be attributed to Antoine André), the *Conclusiones metaphysicae* and the commentaries on Aristotle's *Physics* and *Meteorology*.

To determine with certainty which are and which are not authentic works of Scotus is obviously a matter of importance. Some doctrines which appear in the *De rerum principio*, for example, do not appear in the certainly authentic works, so that if one were to accept the authenticity of the *De rerum principio* (as already mentioned, it is now rejected), one would have to assume that Scotus first taught a doctrine which he later abandoned, since it would clearly be out of the question to assume that his thought contained patent contradictions. To assert a change of opinion on some comparatively minor doctrine when no such change actually took place might not perhaps be a mistake of great importance, even if it resulted in an inaccurate account of Scotus's doctrinal development; but the question of authenticity or unauthenticity is of much greater importance where the *Theoremata* are concerned. In this work the author states that it cannot be proved that there is only one ultimate Principle or that God is infinite or that He is intelligent, and so on, such statements being, at first sight at least, in clear contradiction with the teaching of the certainly authentic works of Scotus. If, then, one were to accept the *Theoremata* as authentic, one would either have to assume an astonishing *volte-face* on Scotus's part or one would have to attempt a difficult task of interpretation and conciliation.

The first attack on the authenticity of the *Theoremata*

was that of Father de Basly in the year 1918, and this attack
was continued by Father Longpré. The latter argued that no
manuscript had yet been discovered which explicitly attributed the work to Scotus, that the teaching contained in the
work is contrary to that contained in Scotus's certainly authentic works, that Ockham and Thomas of Sutton, who
attacked Scotus's natural theology, never quote the work as
his, that the doctrine of the *Theoremata* is nominalistic in
character and must be attributed to the Ockhamist School,
and that John of Reading, who knew Scotus, quotes from the
authentic works when he is dealing with the question whether
God's existence can be proved or not by the natural light of
reason, but does not mention the *Theoremata*. These arguments appeared to be convincing and were generally accepted as settling the question, until Father Balic brought
forward other arguments to contest Longpré's view. Noting
that Longpré's arguments were, for the most part, based on
internal evidence, Balic tried to show not only that the arguments drawn from internal evidence were unconvincing,
but also that there were good arguments drawn from external
evidence to prove that the *Theoremata* were really the work
of Scotus. Thus four codices explicitly attribute the work to
Scotus, while in the fourth chapter of the *De primo principio*
occur the words *In sequenti, scilicet in Theorematibus, po-
nentur credibilia*. The phrase *scilicet in Theorematibus* cannot have been added by Wadding, since it is found in some
codices. In addition, the *Theoremata* are given as the work of
Scotus by, among others, Joannes Canonicus, a fourteenth-
century Scotist. Baudry then tried to show that even if some
of the theories contained in the *Theoremata* betray a nominalistic spirit, the fundamental doctrines of the work are not
of Ockhamist origin, and Gilson (in the *Archives d'histoire
doctrinale et littéraire du moyen âge*, 1937-8) attempted to
prove that the first sixteen *Theoremata* do not stand in contradiction with the certainly authentic works of Scotus. According to Gilson, Scotus speaks in the *Theoremata* (supposing that the work is really by him) as a philosopher showing
what the unaided human reason can achieve, while in the
Opus Oxoniense, which is a theological work, he shows what
can be achieved by metaphysics aided by theology. Even if
the conclusions arrived at in the *Theoremata* seem to approximate to those of Ockham, the spirit is different, since Scotus
believed that the theologian can give metaphysical and de-

monstrative arguments for God's existence and attributes, whereas Ockham denied this and had recourse to faith alone. In the latest edition (1944) of his work, *La philosophie au moyen âge*, Gilson leaves the question of the authenticity or unauthenticity of the *Theoremata* an open question; but he maintains that if the *Theoremata* are the work of Scotus, there is no difficulty in reconciling the doctrine they contain with the doctrine of the *Opus Oxoniense*. The pure philosopher treats of being in a universal sense and can never get beyond a first mover who is first in the chain of causes but who is nevertheless in the chain; he cannot arrive at the conception of God which can be attained by the philosopher who is also a theologian.

I feel rather doubtful of the validity of M. Gilson's contention. In the Oxford Commentary Scotus states that many essential attributes of God can be known by the metaphysician,[3] and in both commentaries he asserts that man can attain a natural knowledge of God, although he cannot *ex puris naturalibus* come to know such truths as that of the Trinity.[4] I find it hard to suppose that when Scotus said that man can come to know truths about God *ex puris naturalibus*, he was thinking of a metaphysician who is also a theologian. Nor do I see that Scotus meant to confine the pure philosopher's knowledge of God to knowledge of Him as first Mover: he says clearly that the metaphysician can proceed further than the *physicus*.[5] Moreover, it seems to me extremely odd, supposing that the *Theoremata* are Scotus's work, that Scotus should prove in the *De primo principio* that God or the first Principle is, for example, intelligent, and that then in the *Theoremata* he should declare that this truth is a *credibile* and cannot be proved. He certainly restricted somewhat the scope of the natural reason in regard to God (he did not think that God's omnipotence is capable of strict proof by the natural reason); but it would seem from the *Commentaries*, from the *De primo principio* and from the *Collationes* that Scotus undoubtedly considered a natural theology to be possible, irrespective of the question whether the philosopher is also a theologian or not.[6] Of course, if it were ever proved conclusively by external evidence that the *Theoremata* are the authentic work of Scotus, one would have to have recourse to some such theory as that of M. Gilson in order to explain the apparently flat contradiction between the *Theoremata* and the other works of Scotus;

but meanwhile it seems to me to be pressing conciliation too far to suggest that there is no contradiction, and I propose in my exposition of Scotus's natural theology to disregard the *Theoremata*. But, while disregarding the *Theoremata*, I admit, as just mentioned, that in the event of the work's authenticity being satisfactorily proved, one would be compelled to say with Gilson that in that work Scotus is considering simply the power of the natural philosopher (the *physicus*) in regard to the attainment of natural knowledge of God. My point is, however, that until the authenticity of the *Theoremata* is proved, there does not seem to be any adequate or compelling reason for affirming that the metaphysician of the certainly authentic works is necessarily a metaphysician who possesses the background of faith. I shall, therefore, treat the *Theoremata* for practical purposes as unauthentic, without, however, pretending to settle the question definitively or to add any further grounds than those already alleged by other writers for rejecting the work as spurious.

The problem of the *Theoremata* has been discussed at some length in order to show the difficulty there is in interpreting accurately the mind of Scotus. Even if one maintains that the doctrines of the *Theoremata* and of the *Opus Oxoniense* are not at variance, but can be reconciled, the very reconciliation results in a picture of Scotus's philosophy which would hardly be that suggested by a first acquaintance with the *Opus Oxoniense*. Still, even if the authenticity of the *Theoremata* has not been demonstrated and even if it would appear preferable to reject it, convenience of exposition is no sure criterion of authenticity or unauthenticity, and one cannot, in view of recent attempts to rehabilitate the work, exclude the possibility that it may at some future date be shown to be certainly authentic, even though internal evidence may suggest the contrary.

3. Various general interpretations of Scotus's philosophy have been given, ranging from the interpretation of Scotus as a revolutionary, as a direct precursor of Ockham and of Luther, to the attempt to soften down the sharp differences between Scotism and Thomism and to interpret Scotus as a continuator of the work of St. Thomas. The first interpretation, that of Landry, can be dismissed, in its extreme form at least, as extravagant and insufficiently grounded, while on the other hand it is impossible to deny that Scotism does differ from Thomism. But is Scotus to be regarded as a con-

tinuator of the Franciscan tradition who at the same time adopted a great deal from Aristotle and from non-Franciscan mediaeval predecessors, or is he to be regarded as a thinker who carried on the Aristotelian tradition of St. Thomas but at the same time corrected St. Thomas in the light of what he himself considered to be the truth, or is he simply to be regarded as an independent thinker who at the same time depended, as all philosophers must, on preceding thinkers in regard to the problems raised and discussed? The question is not an easy one to answer, and any attempt to answer it definitively must be postponed until the production of the critical edition of Scotus's works; but it would seem that there is truth in each of the foregoing suggestions. Scotus was, indeed, a Franciscan Doctor, and even if he discarded a number of doctrines which were generally held in common by former Franciscan thinkers, he certainly regarded himself as faithful to the Franciscan tradition. Again, although Scotus certainly criticised St. Thomas's views on important points, he can also be regarded as continuing the work of synthesis to which St. Thomas had devoted himself. Finally, Scotus certainly was an independent thinker; but at the same time he built on already existing foundations. But although Scotism did not involve a complete break with the past, it is only reasonable to lay stress on its comparatively original and independent aspects and thus draw attention to the difference between Scotism and other systems.

In some aspects of his thought Scotus did indeed carry on the Augustinian-Franciscan tradition: in his doctrine of the superiority of will to intellect, for example, as also in his admission of plurality of forms and in his utilisation of the Anselmian argument for God's existence. Moreover, it has been shown that Scotus did not invent the *distinctio formalis a parte rei*, but that it had been employed by some preceding Franciscan thinkers. Nevertheless, Scotus often gave a peculiar stamp or emphasis to the elements he adopted from tradition. Thus in his treatment of the relation of will to intellect he emphasised freedom rather than love, though he held, it is true, to the superiority of love to knowledge, a superiority which is closely connected with his theory that the supreme practical principle is that God should be loved above all things. Again, though he utilised the Anselmian argument, the so-called 'ontological argument', he did not accept it as a conclusive proof of God's existence but maintained, not only that it must be 'coloured' before it can be usefully employed, but also that even then it is not a demonstrative proof of God's existence, since the only demonstrative arguments are *a posteriori*.

But if Scotus in some respects carried on the Augustinian-Franciscan tradition, in other respects he departed from that tradition. It is not quite clear whether he did or did not teach the hylomorphic composition of angels; but he expressly rejected as unnecessary the theories of *rationes seminales* and of a special illumination of the human intellect, while he saw no contradiction, as St. Bonaventure had seen, in the idea of creation from eternity, even though he speaks more hesitantly than St. Thomas on this matter. In Scotism, then, the influence of Aristotelianism had penetrated further than it had in the philosophy of St. Bonaventure, and one must mention in particular the influence of Avicenna. For example, Scotus insists that the object of the metaphysician is being as being, and in his insistence on this point, as in his treatment of the problem of God, he seems to have been influenced by the Islamic philosopher, whose name occurs not infrequently in the pages of Scotus's works. It is true that Aristotle himself had declared that metaphysics, or rather first philosophy, is the science of being as being; but the Aristotelian metaphysic centres in practice round the doctrine of the four causes, whereas Scotus treats at length of the idea and nature of being, and the impulse thereto seems to have been partly derived from Avicenna. Scotus's discussion of universals, for instance, was also not without a debt to Avicenna.

Yet even if Scotus owed much more to Aristotle and his commentators than did St. Bonaventure, and even if he appeals to the authority of Aristotle in support of this or that theory, he was far from being a mere follower of 'the Philosopher', whom he does not hesitate to criticise. But, apart from individual pieces of criticism, Scotus's philosophical inspiration, so to speak, was different from that of Aristotle. In his eyes the conception of God as first Mover was a very inadequate conception, as it does not pass beyond the physical world and attain the transcendent, infinite Being on which all finite beings essentially depend. Again, it follows from Scotus's ethical doctrine that the Aristotelian ethic must be insufficient, as the notion of obligation, depending on the divine will, does not appear therein. It may be said, of course, that any Christian philosopher would find Aristotle deficient

on such matters, and that St. Thomas was compelled to supplement Aristotle with Augustine; but the point is that
Scotus did not go out of his way to 'explain' Aristotle or to
'reconcile' his opinions with what he himself considered to
be the truth. In so far, for example, as there is a moral
philosophy in the strict sense in Scotism, its dependence on
or borrowing from Aristotelianism is far from being con-
spicuous.

Scotus's attitude to St. Thomas has been depicted in recent years in a rather different light to that in which it was
formerly sometimes depicted: there has been, and not un-
naturally, a tendency to minimise his divergences from Thomism. It has been pointed out, for example, that in his
polemics he often has other thinkers in mind, Henry of
Ghent, for example. This is quite true, of course; but the
fact remains that he frequently criticises Thomist positions,
giving St. Thomas's arguments and refuting them. But whatever the justice or injustice of this or that individual criticism
may be, Scotus certainly did not criticise for the sake of
criticism. If he insisted, for example, on some intellectual
intuition of the singular object and if he emphasised the
reality of the 'common nature', without however, falling into
the exaggerated realism of early mediaeval philosophers, he
did so, not simply in order to differ from St. Thomas, but in
order to safeguard, as he believed, the objectivity of knowledge. Similarly, if he insisted on the univocal character of
the concept of being, he did so because he considered his own
doctrine to be absolutely necessary if agnosticism were to be
avoided, that is, in order to safeguard the objective character
of natural theology. If he made extensive use of the *distinctio
formalis a parte rei*, this was not simply in order to display
his subtlety, though he certainly was a subtle and sometimes
a tortuous thinker and dialectician, but because he considered that such use was necessitated by the facts and by the
objective reference of our concepts. In so far, then, as Scotus
can be looked on as a successor of St. Thomas or as a continuator of Thomism, one must recognise that he endeavoured to correct what he regarded, rightly or wrongly, as
dangerous deficiencies and tendencies in the Thomist philosophy.

It is well to bear in mind Scotus's concern for the theoretical safeguarding of the objectivity of human knowledge and
of natural theology in particular, since the realisation of this

concern acts as a counterbalance to the tendency to look on him as predominantly a destructive critic. It is true that Scotus was somewhat rigorous in his idea of what constitutes a proof, and he would not allow that the proofs adduced for the soul's immortality, for example, were conclusive, demonstrative; but all the same his philosophy remains one of the great mediaeval syntheses, an effort of constructive and positive thought. Moreover, it had a religious inspiration, as one can see from the invocations of God which sometimes appear in his writings and which one cannot simply dismiss as literary convention.

Nevertheless, if one looks on Scotism in its position as a stage in the development of mediaeval thought, it would be idle to deny that *de facto* it helped to stimulate the critical movement of the fourteenth century. When Scotus asserted that certain of the divine attributes cannot be proved by natural reason and when he denied the demonstrative character of the arguments adduced for the immortality of the human soul, he did not intend to undermine positive philosophy; but, looking at the matter from the purely historical viewpoint, his criticism obviously helped to prepare the way for the much more radical criticism of Ockham. That the latter regarded Scotism with hostility is not really relevant to the point at issue. Similarly, though it is quite untrue that Scotus made the whole moral law to depend on the arbitrary choice of the divine will, it can hardly be denied that the elements of voluntarism in his philosophy helped to prepare the way for the authoritarianism of Ockham. For example, his doctrine of moral obligation and his assertion that the secondary precepts of the decalogue do not belong, in the strict sense, to the natural law and are subject to divine dispensation in particular cases. I am not suggesting that Ockhamism is the legitimate child of Scotism, but simply that after the attainment of the supreme mediaeval synthesis of Thomism the work of the critical intellect or of the critical function of philosophy was only to be expected, and that the restricted and moderate use of criticism by Scotus prepared the way, as a matter of fact, for the radical and destructive criticism which is characteristic of Ockhamism. An historical judgement of this type does not necessarily mean that Scotus's criticism was not justified and the radical criticism of later thinkers unjustified: that is a matter for the philosopher to decide, not the historian. Of course, if the *Theoremata* were ever proved to be authentic, that would but serve to emphasise the critical aspect of Scotism.

In fine, then, the philosophy of Scotus looks backward as well as forward. As a positive and constructive system it belongs to the thirteenth century, the century which witnessed the philosophies of St. Bonaventure and, above all, of St. Thomas; but in its critical aspects and in its voluntaristic elements, associated though the latter are with the Augustinian-Franciscan tradition, it looks forward to the fourteenth century. A triumph of dialectical skill and of careful and patient thought the philosophy of Scotus is the work of a man who was, though impregnated with tradition, a powerful, vigorous and original thinker, a man who really belonged to the closing epoch of 'dogmatic philosophy' but who at the same time heralded the new movement.

Chapter Forty-six

SCOTUS–II: KNOWLEDGE

*The primary object of the human intellect—Why the intellect
depends on the phantasm—The soul's inability to intuit itself
in this life—Intellectual apprehension of the individual thing
—Is theology a science?—Our knowledge is based on sense-
experience, and no special illumination is required for intellectual activity—Intuitive and abstractive knowledge—Induction.*

1. The primary natural object of our intellect is being as
being, from which it follows that every being, every thing
which is intelligible, falls within the scope of the intellect.[1]
Scotus gives, among other proofs, one taken from Avicenna to
the effect that if being were not the primary object of the
intellect, being could be described or explained in terms of
something more ultimate, which is impossible. But if being
as being is the natural object of the intellect and if being is
taken to include every intelligible object, does it not follow
that infinite Being, God, is a natural object of the human intellect? In a sense the answer must be in the affirmative, since
being includes infinite being and finite being, but it does not
follow that man has an immediate natural knowledge of
God, since man's intellect in its present state is directed immediately to sensible things. But, says Scotus, if we are speaking of the primary object of the intellect, it is only reasonable
to assign as its primary object that which is the primary object of intellect as such, not that which is the primary object
of the intellect in this or that particular case. We do not say,
for example, that the primary object of vision is that which
the eye can see in candlelight; but we assign as its primary

object that which is its object simply as a power or faculty.[2] Therefore, even if man in his present state (*homo viator*) comes first of all to know creatures, this does not mean that the primary adequate object of his intellect is not being as being. It may be added that this doctrine does not mean that the human intellect has a natural power of knowing the divine essence in itself or the divine Persons in the Trinity, since the general (and univocal) concept of being does not include *this particular essence as particular*, while creatures are not such perfect imitations of God that they reveal the divine essence as it is in itself.[3] The divine essence as such moves (*movet*) naturally, is the natural object of the divine intellect only; it can be known by the human intellect only through God's free choice and activity, not through the human intellect's natural power.

But if Scotus in assigning being as being as the primary adequate object of the human intellect certainly did not confuse supernatural and natural knowledge, he equally certainly meant to reject St. Thomas's view, or what he regarded as such, of the primary object of the human mind. St. Thomas[4] maintained that the natural object of the human intellect is the essence of the material thing, which essence becomes intelligible to the intellect when it is abstracted from the individualising matter. It is natural to the angelic intellect to know natures which do not exist in matter; but the human intellect cannot do this in its present state, when united to the body. And to be united to the body is the natural state of the human intellect; to be separated from the body is *praeter naturam*. So St. Thomas argues that, inasmuch as the natural object of the human intellect is the form of the material thing and inasmuch as we know this kind of form by abstracting it from the 'phantasm', the human intellect necessarily depends on the 'phantasm', and so on sense-experience, for its knowledge.[5] Scotus[6] interprets St. Thomas as teaching that the quiddity or essence, known by way of abstraction from the phantasm, is the primary object of the human intellect considered not simply as being in a certain state, that is, in the present life, but in its nature as a power or faculty of a certain kind, and he replies that this opinion is untenable by a theologian, i.e. by a man who accepts the next life and the doctrine of eternal happiness. In heaven the soul knows immaterial things directly. Now, the intellect remains the same power in heaven as it was on earth. Therefore, if it can know immaterial things in heaven, we cannot say that its primary object is the essence of the material thing: its primary object, if we consider the intellect as a power, must embrace both immaterial and material things, even if in this life it cannot know immaterial things directly. Its restriction in this life to a certain type of object must be secondary, not primary. If it is answered that in heaven the intellect is elevated, so that it can know immaterial objects directly, Scotus replies that this knowledge either exceeds the power of the intellect or it does not. If the latter is the case, then the primary object of the intellect considered *ex natura potentiae* cannot be the quiddity of the material thing, whereas, if the former is the case, then the intellect in heaven becomes another power, which St. Thomas certainly does not intend to teach.

Scotus also argues that if St. Thomas's view were correct, metaphysical science would be impossible for our intellects, since metaphysics are the science of being as being. If the primary object of the human intellect were the essence of the material thing, it could no more know being as being than the power of vision could extend further than its natural object, colour and light.[7] If the Thomist view were true, metaphysics would either be impossible, if understood in its proper sense, or it would not transcend physics. In fine, 'it does not seem fitting to confine the intellect, considered as a power, to the sensible thing, so that it transcends the senses only through its mode of cognition', that is, not through its object as well.

Since Scotus also maintains[8] that there is in the human intellect a natural desire to know 'the cause' distinctly and that a natural desire cannot be in vain, and since he concludes that the primary object of the intellect cannot, therefore, be material things, which are the effect of the immaterial cause, it might appear that he is contradicting his assertion that we cannot have a natural knowledge of the divine essence; but it must be remembered that he does not deny that the human intellect in its present state is limited in range, though he insists that the object of a power in a certain condition must not be confused with the object of the power considered in itself. Moreover, he did not consider that an analysis of being as being can yield knowledge of the divine essence as it is in itself, for even if being is the primary and adequate object of the human intellect, it does not follow that we form our idea of being by any other way than abstraction. In general, we may say that Scotus accepted the Aristotelian account of abstraction, though he considered that the active and passive intellects are not two distinct powers, but are two aspects or functions of one power.[9]

2. As to the reason why the human intellect in its present state, in this life, depends on the phantasm, Scotus declares that it is due to the order established by divine wisdom, either as a penalty for original sin or with a view to the harmonious operation of our various powers (*propter naturalem concordiam potentiarum animae in operando*), sense and imagination apprehending the individual thing, the intellect apprehending the universal essence of that thing, or else on account of our infirmity (*ex infirmitate*). The intellect in its present condition, he repeats, is moved immediately only by what is imaginable or sensible, and the reason for this may be punitive justice (*forte propter peccatum, sicut videtur Augustinus dicere*) or it may be a natural cause, inasmuch as the order or harmony of powers may require it so far as this present state is concerned. 'Nature' in this connection means, therefore, nature in a particular state or condition, not nature absolutely considered: on this point Scotus insists.[10] This is not a very satisfactory or a very clear or decided explanation; but what Scotus is quite clear about is that the intellect, absolutely considered, is the faculty of being as being, and he decisively rejects what he regards as the Thomist doctrine. Whether Scotus is fair in his interpretation of St. Thomas is another matter. Sometimes St. Thomas states explicitly that the proper object of the intellect is being.[11]

However, it is true that St. Thomas insists on the natural character of the necessity of the *conversio ad phantasma*,[12] arguing that if this necessity were simply the result of union with a body and not natural to the soul itself, it would follow that the union of soul and body takes place for the good of the body, not of the soul, since the soul would be hampered in its natural operations through its union with the body. Emphasising this aspect of the Thomist doctrine, Scotus concluded that Thomism is unable, logically speaking, to justify the possibility of metaphysical science.

3. Scotus's view on the primary object of the human intellect naturally had its effect on his treatment of the disputed question concerning the soul's knowledge of itself. According to St. Thomas Aquinas, the soul in its present state,

which is its natural state, comes to know by means of ideas abstracted from sensible objects, and from this he concludes that the soul has no immediate knowledge of its own essence, but that it comes to know itself only indirectly, by reflecting on the acts by which it abstracts ideas and knows objects in those ideas.[13] Scotus, however, maintained that though the soul actually lacks an immediate intuition of itself in this life, it is a natural object of intellection to itself and would actually intuit itself, 'were it not hindered'.[14] He then proceeds to suggest the causes of this hindrance which have already been mentioned. The difference between Scotus and St. Thomas concerns, then, the explanation of a fact rather than the fact itself. Both agree that the soul is actually without an immediate intuition of itself in this life; but, whereas St. Thomas explains this fact in terms of the nature of the human soul, attacking the Platonist view of the relation of soul to body, Scotus explains it, not in terms of the soul's nature, absolutely considered, but in terms of a hindrance, even suggesting that this hindrance may be due to sin and quoting St. Augustine in support of this suggestion. St. Thomas's attitude follows from his adoption of the Aristotelian psychology, whereas Scotus's position can be associated with the Augustinian tradition. On this matter one should regard Scotus not as an innovator or revolutionary or a destructive critic of Thomism, but rather as an upholder of the Augustinian-Franciscan tradition.

4. We have seen that Scotus considered his doctrine concerning the primary object of the intellect to be essential for the maintenance and justification of metaphysics: he also considered his doctrine of the intellectual apprehension of the individual thing as essential to the maintenance of the objectivity of human knowledge. According to St. Thomas[15] the intellect cannot know individual material things directly, since the intellect comes to know only by abstracting the universal from matter, the principle of individuation. He admits, however, that the mind has an indirect knowledge of individual things, since it cannot actually know the abstracted universal except through the 'conversion to the phantasm'. The imagination always plays its part, and the image is an image of the individual thing; but the primary and direct object of intellectual knowledge is the universal.

Scotus refused to accept this Thomist doctrine. The vehement repudiation of the doctrine wherein it is declared false and even heretical (on the ground that the Apostles believed that a certain visible, palpable, individual human being was God) comes from an unauthentic work, the *De rerum principio*; but the authentic works of Scotus make the latter's position perfectly clear. He accepted in general the Aristotelian account of abstraction; but he insists that the intellect has a confused primary intuition of the singular thing. His principle is that the higher power knows what the lower power apprehends, though the higher power knows the object in a more perfect manner than the lower power does, so that the intellect, which co-operates in perception, knows intuitively the singular thing apprehended by the senses. The intellect knows true contingent propositions and reasons from them; and such propositions concern individual things known intuitively as existing. Therefore, although abstract and scientific knowledge concerns universals, as Aristotle rightly taught, we must also recognise an intellectual knowledge of the singular thing as existent.[16] As already mentioned, the very vehement repudiation of the Thomist position, which is ascribed to Scotus by Father Parthenius Minges, for example,[17] comes from the unauthentic *De rerum principio*, and certain remarks which are found in the authentic works might lead one to suppose that Scotus's position on the question of the intellectual knowledge of the singular thing is exactly parallel to his position in regard to the soul's intuition of itself. He insists that the singular thing is intelligible in itself and that the human intellect has at least the remote capability of understanding it; but he seems to imply, or even to state explicitly, that in its present condition it is unable to do so. 'The singular thing is intelligible in itself, as far as the thing itself is concerned; but if it is not intelligible to some intellect, to ours, for example, this is not due to unintelligibility on the part of the singular thing itself.'[18] Again, 'it is not an imperfection to know the singular thing', but 'if you say that our intellect does not understand the singular thing, I reply that this is an imperfection (which obtains) in its present state'.[19] However, Scotus seems to mean that while we have no clear knowledge of the singular thing as singular, a deficiency which is due, not to the singular thing's lack of intelligibility, but to the imperfection of our intellectual operations in this life, we none the less have a primary, though confused, intellectual intuition of the singular thing as existent. This seems to be the view expressed in the *Quodli-*

bet[20] where Scotus argues that if it is said that we have an intellectual knowledge of the universal and sense-experience of the singular, this is not to be understood in the sense that the two powers are equal and disparate, so that the intellect would not know the singular at all, but in the sense that the lower power is subordinate to the higher and that though the higher power can operate in a way that the lower cannot, the opposite cannot be assumed as true. From the fact that sense cannot know the universal it does not follow that the intellect cannot know the singular. The intellect can have an intuitive knowledge of the singular as existent, even if its knowledge of the essence is knowledge of the universal.

If we are willing to accept the *De Anima* as authentic, Scotus's opinion is placed beyond doubt. In that work[21] Scotus rejects the Thomist doctrine on our knowledge of the singular, and also the Thomist doctrine of the principle of individuation, on which the first doctrine rests, and argues that the singular thing is (i) intelligible in itself; (ii) intelligible by us even in our present state; (iii) not intelligible by us in our present state so far as clear knowledge is concerned. The singular thing is intelligible in itself, since what is not intelligible in itself could not be known by any intellect, whereas the singular thing is certainly known by the divine and angelic intellects. It is intelligible by us even in our present state, as is shown by the process of induction and by the fact that we can love the individual thing, love presupposing knowledge. It is not, however, intelligible by us in our present state in a complete and clear manner (*sub propria ratione*). If two material things were deprived of all difference of accidents (of place, colour, shape, etc.), neither sense nor intellect could distinguish them from one another, even though their 'singularities' (Scotus's *haecceitas*) remained, and this shows that we have, in our present state, no clear and complete knowledge of the singularity of a thing. We can say, therefore, that the object of sense is the individual thing and the object of intellect the universal, if we mean that the intellect is not moved by singularity as such and does not know it clearly and completely in its present state; but we are not entitled to say that the intellect has no intuition of the individual thing as existent. If we say this, we destroy the objectivity of knowledge. 'It is impossible to abstract universals from the singular without previous knowledge of the singular; for in this case the intellect would abstract without knowing from what it was abstracting.'[22] It is clear that Scotus rejected the Thomist doctrine not merely because he rejected the Thomist idea of individuation, nor even merely because a process like induction seemed to him to prove the Thomist doctrine false; but also because he was convinced that the Thomist doctrine endangered the objectivity of that scientific and universal knowledge on which the Thomist laid such stress. Scotus did not mean to reject (he makes this quite clear) the Aristotelian doctrine that human science is of the universal; but he considered it essential to supplement that doctrine by accepting our intellectual intuition of the singular thing as existent, and he considered that this supplementation was necessitated by the facts. Concern for the safeguarding of the objectivity of human knowledge shows itself also in Scotus's handling of the problem of universals; but consideration of this problem is best left for the chapter on metaphysics, where it can be treated in connection with the problem of individuation.

5. From one point of view it would not be unreasonable to maintain, as has been maintained, that Scotus's ideal of science was mathematical science. If science is understood in the sense in which Aristotle uses the word in the first book of the *Posterior Analytics*, that is, as involving necessity of the object, as well as evidence and certainty, we cannot say that theology, as concerned with the Incarnation and with God's relations with man in general, is a science, since the Incarnation is not a necessary or a deducible event.[23] On the other hand, if we consider theology as concerned with its primary object, with God as He is in Himself, it treats of necessary truths like the Trinity of Persons, and is a science; but we must add that it is a science in itself and not for us, since the truths in question, though certain, are not self-evident to us. If someone were unable to understand the arguments of the geometers, but accepted their conclusions on their word, geometry would be for him an object of belief, not a science, even though it would still be a science in itself.[24] Theology considered as concerned with God in Himself, is thus a science in itself, though not for us, since, in spite of the necessity of the object, the data are accepted on faith. Theology as concerned with God's external operations, however, treats of 'contingent', that is, non-necessary events, and so is not a science in that sense. Scotus is clearly taking geometrical science as the model of science in the strict sense.

It should be added, however, that when Scotus denies that theology is a science in the senses above indicated, he does not intend to disparage theology or to cast doubts upon its certainty. He expressly says that if one understands 'science', not in the strictest sense, but as understood by Aristotle in the sixth book of the *Ethics*, namely as contrasted with opinion and conjecture, it is a science, since it is certain and true, though it is more properly to be termed 'wisdom'.[25] Moreover, theology is not subordinate to metaphysics, since, although its object is in some degree comprised in the object of metaphysics, for God as knowable by the natural light of reason is comprised in the object of metaphysics, it does not receive its principles from metaphysics, nor are the truths of dogmatic theology demonstrable by means of the principles of being as such. The principles of dogmatic theology are accepted on faith, on authority; they are not demonstrated by natural reason nor are they demonstrable by the metaphysician. On the other hand, metaphysics are not, in the strict sense, a subordinate science to theology, since the metaphysician does not borrow his principles from the theologian.[26]

Theology, according to Scotus, is a practical science; but he explains very carefully and at length what he means by this.[27] 'Even necessary theology', that is, theological knowledge of necessary truths concerning God in Himself, is logically prior to the elicited act of will by which we choose God, and the first principles of salutary conduct are taken from it. Scotus discusses the views of Henry of Ghent and others, rejecting them in favour of his own view. He thus parts company with St. Thomas, who says[28] that theology is a speculative science, just as he parts company with St. Thomas when the latter declares that theology is a science.[29] Scotus, as one would expect in view of his doctrine of the priority of will over intellect, emphasises the aspect of theology under which it is a norm of salutary conduct for man.

The foregoing considerations may seem to be irrelevant, referring, as they do, to dogmatic theology; but if one understands Scotus's position in regard to dogmatic theology, one can see how unjust and false are some of the accusations which have been brought against him. If one said simply that whereas St. Thomas considered theology to be a science, a speculative science, Scotus declared that theology is not a science and that, in so far as it can be called a science, it is a practical science, one might conclude that theological doctrines were, for Scotus, postulates having only practical or pragmatic value; and in point of fact, Scotus has actually been compared with Kant. But if one considers Scotus's meaning, such an interpretation is obviously unjust and false. For example, Scotus does not deny that theology is a science as far as certainty is concerned; he simply says that if you define science in the sense in which geometry is a science, then theology cannot be called a science. With this position St. Thomas would agree. Theology, he says, is a science, because its principles are derived from those of a higher science, proper to God and the blessed, so that they are absolutely certain; it is not a science in the same sense in which geometry and arithmetic are sciences, since its principles are not self-evident to the natural light of reason.[30] Again, Scotus says that theology is for us a practical science, mainly because revelation is given as a norm for salutary conduct, that we may attain our last end, whereas for St. Thomas[31] theology is primarily a speculative science, though not exclusively, because it deals more with divine things than with human acts. In other words, the main difference between them on this matter is one of emphasis: it is a difference which one would expect in view of St. Thomas's general emphasis on intellect and theoretic contemplation and Scotus's general emphasis on will and love, and it has to be seen in the light of the Aristotelian and Franciscan traditions rather than in the light of Kantianism and Pragmatism. If anyone wishes to make out that Scotus was a Kantian before Kant, he will find no solid reasons to support his contention in Scotus's doctrine concerning dogmatic theology.

6. Although Scotus insists, as we have seen, that the primary object of the intellect is being in general and not simply material essences, his Aristotelianism leads him also to emphasise the fact that our actual knowledge originates with sensation. There are no innate ideas, therefore. In the *Quaestiones subtilissimae super libros Metaphysicorum*[32] he affirms that the intellect does not, in virtue of its own constitution, possess any natural knowledge, either in simple or in complex notions, 'because all our knowledge arises from sensation'. This applies even to the knowledge of the first principles. 'For first the sense is moved by some simple, and not complex object, and through the movement of the sense the intellect is moved and apprehends simple objects: this is the intellect's first act. Secondly, after the apprehension of simple objects

there follows another act, that of bringing together simple objects, and after this composition the intellect is able to assent to the truth of the complex, if it is a first principle.' Natural knowledge of the first principles means no more than that when the simple terms have been understood and combined, the intellect immediately assents, in virtue of its own natural light, to the truth of the principle; 'but the knowledge of the terms is acquired from sensible objects'. What Scotus means is this. We obtain the notions of 'whole' and 'part', for example, through sense-experience; but when the intellect brings together the terms, it sees immediately the truth of the proposition that the whole is greater than the part. The knowledge of what a whole is and what a part is comes from sense-experience; but the natural light of the intellect enables it to see immediately the truth of the complex object, the first principle. In answer to Averroes's objection that in this case all men would assent to the first principles, whereas in point of fact the Christians do not assent to the principle that 'out of nothing nothing is made', Scotus replies that he is speaking of first principles in the strict sense, such as the principle of contradiction and the principle that the whole is greater than its part, not of principles which some people think to be or which may be conclusions from the first principles. In the Paris Commentary, however,[33] he insists that the intellect cannot err in regard to those principles and conclusions which it sees to follow clearly from the first principles. In the same place he speaks of the intellect as a *tabula nuda*, which has no innate principles or ideas.

Scotus also rejects the doctrine that a special illumination of the intellect is necessary in order that it should apprehend certain truth. Thus he gives the arguments of Henry of Ghent on behalf of the illumination theory[34] and proceeds to criticise them, objecting that Henry's arguments seem to result in the conclusion that all certain and natural knowledge is impossible.[35] For example, if it were true that no certainty can be obtained concerning a continually changing object (and sensible objects are constantly changing, according to Henry), illumination would not help in any way, for we do not attain certainty when we know an object otherwise than it actually is. In any case, Scotus adds, the doctrine that sensible objects are continually changing is the doctrine of Heraclitus and is false. Similarly, if the changing character of the soul and its ideas are an obstacle to certainty, illumination will not remedy the defect. In fine, Henry's opinion would lead to scepticism.

Scotus thus defends the activity and natural power of the human intellect, and a similar preoccupation shows itself in his rejection of St. Thomas's doctrine that the soul, when separated from the body, cannot acquire new ideas from things themselves.[36] He gives the opinion of St. Thomas in more or less the same words that the latter uses in his Commentary on the *Sentences*[37] and argues that it belongs to the nature of the soul to know, to abstract, to will, so that, since the soul is also of such a nature that it can exist in separation from the body, we may legitimately conclude that it can acquire fresh knowledge by natural means in this state of separation. The opinion of St. Thomas, Scotus says, degrades the human soul. Scotus's own opinion is, of course, connected with his view that the soul's dependence on the senses in this life is *pro statu isto, forte ex peccato*. It is also connected with his rejection of the doctrine that the soul is purely passive and that the phantasm causes the idea. The soul in the state of separation from the body is, therefore, not cut off from the acquisition of new knowledge, nor is it even confined to intuition: it can exercise the power of abstraction too.

7. Scotus distinguishes intuitive and abstractive knowledge. Intuitive knowledge is knowledge of an object as present in its actual existence and it is against the nature of intuitive knowledge that it should be knowledge of an object which is not actually existent and present.[38] However, Scotus makes a distinction between perfect intuitive knowledge, which is immediate knowledge of an object as present, and imperfect intuitive knowledge, which is knowledge of an existent object as existing in the future, as anticipated, or as existing in the past, as remembered.[39] Abstractive knowledge on the other hand is knowledge of the essence of an object considered in abstraction from its existence or non-existence.[40] The difference between intuitive and abstractive knowledge is not, then, that the former is knowledge of an existent object, the latter of a non-existent object, but rather that the former is knowledge of an object as existent and actually present, that is, in intuition properly speaking, whereas the latter is knowledge of the essence of an object considered in abstraction from existence, whether the object actually exists or not. 'There can be abstractive knowledge of

a non-existent object as well as of an existent object, but there can be intuitive knowledge only of an existent object as existent.'[41] We should have to add the words 'and present', for 'it is against the nature of intuitive knowledge that it should be of something which is not actually existent and present'.[42] Accordingly Scotus says that though the blessed could see him in God, that is, in the beatific vision, as existing and writing, this knowledge would not be intuitive knowledge, since 'I am not actually present in God, whom the blessed behold in heaven'.[43] Scotus's doctrine of abstractive knowledge, the knowledge of essences in abstraction from existence and non-existence, has led to the comparison of this aspect of his thought with the method of the modern Phenomenological School.

8. Scotus was sufficiently permeated by the spirit of the Aristotelian logic to lay stress on deduction and to have a rigorous idea of demonstrative proof; but he made some interesting remarks on induction. We cannot have experience of all instances of a particular type of natural event; but experience of a number of instances may be sufficient to show the scientist that the event in question proceeds from a natural cause and will always follow that cause. 'Whatever happens in most cases (that is, in the cases we have been able to observe) does not proceed from a free cause, but is the natural effect of the cause.' This proposition is recognised as true by the intellect, which sees that a free cause will not produce the same effect: if the cause could produce another effect, we should observe it doing so. If an effect is frequently produced by the same cause (Scotus means if the same effect is produced by the same cause, so far as our experience goes), the cause cannot be a free cause in that respect, nor can it be a 'casual' cause, but it must be the natural cause of that effect. Sometimes we have experience of the effect and are able to reduce the effect to a self-evident causal relation, in which case we can proceed to deduce the effect and so obtain a still more certain knowledge than we had through experience, while on other occasions we may have experience of the cause in such a way that we cannot demonstrate the necessary connection between cause and effect, but only that the effect proceeds from the cause as a natural cause.[44]

Chapter Forty-seven

SCOTUS–III: METAPHYSICS

Being and its transcendental attributes—The univocal concept of being—The formal objective distinction—Essence and existence—Universals—Hylomorphism—Rationes seminales rejected, plurality of forms retained—Individuation.

1. Metaphysics is the science of being as being. The concept of being is the simplest of all concepts, and it is irreducible to other more ultimate concepts: being, therefore, cannot be defined.[1] We can conceive being distinctly by itself, for in its widest signification it simply means that which includes no contradiction, that which is not intrinsically impossible; but every other concept, every concept of a distinct kind of being, includes the concept of being.[2] Being in its widest sense thus includes that which has extramental being and that which has intramental being,[3] and it transcends all genera.[4]

There are various *passiones entis* (categories of being one might call them, provided that the word 'category' is not understood in the Aristotelian sense), the *passiones convertibiles* and the *passiones disiunctae*. The former are those categories of being which are designated by one name, which do not go in distinct pairs, and are convertible with being. For example, *one, true, good,* are *passiones convertibiles*. Every being is one, true, and good by the very fact that it is being, and there is no real distinction between these *passiones convertibiles* or between them and being, but there is a formal distinction, since they denote different aspects of being.[5] The *passiones disiunctae*, on the other hand, are not simply convertible with being if one takes them singly, though they are convertible if one takes them in pairs. For example, not every being is necessary and not every being is contingent; but every being is either necessary or contingent. Similarly, not every being is simply act and not every being is potency; but every being must be either act or potency or act in one respect and potency in another. Scotus speaks of the *passiones disiunctae* as transcendent,[6] since although no *passio disiuncta* comprises all being or is simply convertible with the notion of being, it does not place an object in any definite genus or category, in the Aristotelian sense. The fact that a being is contingent, for example, does not tell one whether it is substance or accident.

As Scotus held that the concept of being is univocal, in the sense shortly to be discussed, it might appear that he tried to deduce the actuality of the *passiones disiunctae*; but this was not his intention. We can never deduce from the notion of being that contingent being exists, nor can we show that contingent being exists if necessary being exists, though we can show that if contingent being exists, necessary being exists and that if finite being exists, infinite being exists. In other words, we cannot deduce the existence of the less perfect *passio disiuncta* from the more perfect, though we can proceed the other way round. That contingent being actually exists is known only by experience.[7]

2. We have seen that in Scotus's opinion it is necessary to maintain that the primary object of the intellect is being in general, if one wishes to safeguard the possibility of metaphysics. By saying this I do not mean to suggest that Scotus's doctrine of the primary object of the intellect was motivated simply by pragmatic considerations. Rather did he hold that the intellect as such is the faculty of apprehending being in general, and, holding this, he then pointed out what appeared to him to be the unfortunate conclusion which followed from the Thomist position. Similarly, Scotus maintained that unless there is a concept of being which is univocal in respect of God and creatures, no metaphysical knowledge of God is possible; but he did not assert this doctrine of the univocal character of the concept of being for a purely utilitarian reason; he was convinced that there is actually a univocal concept of this kind, and then pointed out that unless its existence is admitted, one cannot safeguard the possibility of any metaphysical knowledge of God. Our concepts are formed in dependence on sense-perception and represent immediately material quiddities or essences. But no concept of a material

quiddity as such is applicable to God, for God is not included among material things. Therefore, unless we can form a concept which is not restricted to the material quiddity as such, but is common to infinite being and to finite being, to immaterial and to material being, we can never attain a true knowledge of God by means of concepts which are proper to Him. If Henry of Ghent's doctrine of the equivocal character of the concept of being as applied to God and to creatures were true, it would follow that the human mind was restricted (in this life at least) to the knowledge of creatures alone; agnosticism would thus be the consequence of Henry's theory.[8] If I have mentioned this aspect of the question first, I have done so not in order to imply that Scotus was motivated simply by utilitarian or pragmatic considerations, but rather in order to show that the question was not a purely academic one in Scotus's eyes.

What did Scotus mean by the univocal concept of being? In the Oxford Commentary[9] he says: *et ne fiat contentio de nomine univocationis, conceptum univocum dico, qui ita est unus, quod ejus unitas sufficit ad contradictionem, affirmando et negando ipsum de eodem. Sufficit etiam pro medio syllogistico, ut extrema unita in medio sic uno, sine fallacia aequivocationis, concludantur inter se unum.* Scotus's first point is, therefore, that a univocal concept means for him a concept the unity of which is sufficient to involve a contradiction if one affirms and denies the idea of the same subject at the same time. If one were to say 'the dog (i.e. the animal) is running' and at the same time 'the dog (meaning the star or the dog-fish) is not running', there would be no real contradiction, since 'running' and 'not running' are not affirmed of the same subject: the contradiction is purely verbal. Similarly, if one were to say 'the unicorn is' (meaning that the unicorn has an intramental existence) and 'the unicorn is not' (meaning that the unicorn has no extramental existence in nature), there would be no real contradiction. Scotus, however, is referring to a word the meaning of which is sufficiently the same to bring about a real contradiction if one were to affirm and deny it of the same subject at the same time. For instance, if one said that the unicorn is and that the unicorn is not, understanding 'is' in both judgements as referring to extramental existence, there would be a real contradiction. Similarly, if one said that God is and that God is not, referring in both cases to real existence, there would be a contradiction. What does Scotus mean by *sufficit*? In the judgements 'God is' and 'God is not' it is sufficient for the production of a contradiction that 'is' should mean opposed to nothingness or not-being. A contradiction is involved in saying both that God is opposed to nothingness and that God is not opposed to nothingness. It must be remembered that Scotus is maintaining the existence of a univocal concept of being which is applicable to God and creatures, so that one can say that God is and the creature is, using the word 'is' in the same sense. He is perfectly well aware, of course, that God and the creature are actually opposed to nothingness in different ways, and he does not mean to deny this; but his point is that if you mean by 'is' simply the opposite of nothingness or not-being, then you can use the word 'being' of God and creatures in the same sense, prescinding from the concrete ways in which they are opposed to nothingness. Accordingly he says *sufficit ad contradictionem* so as not to imply that God and the creatures are opposed to nothingness in the same way. But though they are opposed to nothingness in different ways, they are none the less both opposed to nothingness, and if one forms a concept of being denoting sheer opposition to nothingness, a concept which involves contradiction if affirmed and denied of the same subject at the same time, this concept can be predicated univocally of God and creatures.

As to the remark about the syllogism, Scotus says that a univocal concept, as he understands it, is a concept which, when employed as middle term in a syllogism, has a meaning 'sufficiently' the same in both premisses to prevent the fallacy of equivocation being committed. To take a crude example, if one argued 'every ram is an animal, this object (meaning an instrument for pumping water) is a ram, therefore this object is an animal', the syllogism would involve the fallacy of equivocation and would not be valid. Now take the following argument. If there is wisdom in some creatures, there must be wisdom in God; but there is wisdom in some creatures; therefore there is wisdom in God. If the term 'wisdom' is used equivocally, in completely different senses, in regard to God and in regard to creatures, the argument would be fallacious: if the argument is to be valid, the idea of wisdom as applied to God and to creatures must be sufficiently the same for equivocation to be avoided. Scotus is attacking Henry of Ghent, according to whose opinion the predicates we apply

to God and creatures are equivocal, though the two meanings
so resemble one another that one word can be used for both.
Scotus objects that to admit the truth of Henry's opinion
would be to admit that every argument from creatures to
God employs the fallacy of equivocation and is fallacious.
The univocity which Scotus asserts is not restricted, then, to
the concept of being. 'Whatsoever things are common to God
and the creature are such as belong to being as indifferent to
finite and finite.'[10] If one considers being in abstraction from
the distinction between infinite and finite being, that is, as
signifying mere opposition to nothing, one has a univocal
concept of being, and the transcendental attributes of being,
the *passiones convertibiles*, can also give rise to univocal concepts. If one can form a univocal concept of being, one can
also form univocal concepts of *one, true, good*.[11] What, then,
of wisdom? Goodness is a *passio convertibilis*, inasmuch as
every being is good by the mere fact that it is a being; but
not every being is wise. Scotus answers[12] that the *passiones
disiunctae*, such as *necessary* or *possible*, *act* or *potency*, are
transcendent in the sense that neither member determines its
subject as belonging to any special genus, and that wisdom
and suchlike attributes can also be called transcendent, that
is, as transcending the division of being into genera.

Scotus lays a strong emphasis on this doctrine of univocity.
Every metaphysical investigation concerning God involves the
consideration of some attribute and the removal from our
idea of it of the imperfection which attaches to that attribute as found in creatures. In this way we attain an idea
of the essence or *ratio formalis* of the attribute, and then
we can predicate it of God in a supremely perfect sense.
Scotus takes the example of wisdom, intellect and will.[13]
First we remove from the idea of wisdom, for example, the
imperfections of finite wisdom and attain to a concept of the
ratio formalis of wisdom, what wisdom is in itself. Then we
attribute wisdom to God in the most perfect manner (*per-
fectissime*). 'Therefore every investigation concerning God
supposes that the intellect has the same univocal concept,
which it receives from creatures.'[14] If it is denied that we
can thus form an idea of the *ratio formalis* of wisdom, and so
on, the conclusion would follow that we could arrive at no
knowledge of God. On the one hand our knowledge is
founded on our experience of creatures, while on the other
hand we cannot predicate of God any attribute precisely as it

is found in creatures. Therefore, unless we can attain a common middle term with a univocal meaning, no argument from creatures to God is possible or valid. That we can form a univocal concept of being, without reference to infinite or finite, uncreated or created, Scotus regarded as a fact of experience.[15]

Scotus agrees with Henry of Ghent that God is not in a genus, but he will not agree with his denial of the univocal character of the concept of being. 'I hold my middle opinion, that it is compatible with the simplicity of God that there should be some concept common to Him and to the creature, but this common concept is not a generically common concept.'[16] Now, Henry of Ghent, in Scotus's view, maintained that the concept of being as applied to God and to creatures is equivocal, and it is easily understandable that Scotus rejects this opinion. But what was his attitude towards St. Thomas's doctrine of analogy? In the first place Scotus asserts firmly that God and the creature are completely different in the real order, *sunt primo diversa in realitate, quia in nulla realitate conveniunt*.[17] Hence to accuse Scotus of Spinozism is clearly absurd. In the second place Scotus does not reject the analogy of attribution, since he admits that being belongs primarily and principally to God and teaches that creatures are to God as *mensurata ad mensuram, vel excessa ad excedens*,[18] while in the *De Anima*[19] he says that *omnia entia habent attributionem ad ens primum, quod est Deus*. In the third place, however, he insists that analogy itself presupposes a univocal concept, since we could not compare creatures with God as *mensurata ad mensuram, vel excessa ad excedens*, unless there was a concept common to both.[20] God is knowable by man in this life only by means of concepts drawn from creatures, and unless these concepts were common to God and creatures, we should never be able to compare creatures with God as the imperfect with the perfect: there would be no bridge between creatures and God. Even those masters who deny univocity with their lips, really presuppose it.[21] If there were no univocal concepts, we should have only a negative knowledge of God, which is not the case. We may say that God is not a stone, but we can also say that a chimaera is not a stone, so that in saying that God is not a stone we know no more of God than we do of a chimaera.[22] Further, knowledge that something is an effect of God is not sufficient by itself to give us our knowledge of

God. A stone is an effect of God; but we do not say that God is a stone, because He is the cause of the stone, whereas we do say that He is wise, and this presupposes a univocal concept of widom which is transcendent (in Scotus's sense). In fine, Scotus's teaching is that although all creatures have an essential relation of dependence to God, this fact would not be sufficient to afford us any positive knowledge of God, since we possess no natural intuition of God, unless we could form univocal concepts common to God and creatures. Therefore he says that 'all beings have an attribution to the first being, which is God . . . ; yet in spite of this fact there can be abstracted from all of them one common concept which is expressed by this word *being*, and is one logically speaking, although it is not (one) naturally and metaphysically speaking', that is, speaking either as a natural philosopher or as a metaphysician.[23]

This last remark gives rise to the question whether or not Scotus considered the univocity of the concepts of being to be really restricted to the logical order. Some writers affirm that he did. The passage from the *De Anima* which has just been quoted seems to state it positively, and Scotus's observation, quoted above, that God and creatures *sunt primo diversa in realitate, quia in nulla realitate conveniunt*, would seem to teach the same. But if the univocal concept of being were restricted to the logical order in such a way that it was an *ens rationis*, how would it help to ensure objective knowledge of God? Moreover, in the Oxford Commentary[24] Scotus considers the objection to his theory that matter has an *esse* of its own. The objection is that in the case of analogues a thing or attribute is present really only in the primary analogue: in the other it is not present really, except by way of a relation to the primary analogue. Health is present really in the animal, whereas it is present in urine only *per attributionem ad illud*. *Esse* comes from the form: therefore it is not present really in matter, but only through its relation to the form. In answer to this objection Scotus says that the example given is valueless, since there are a hundred examples to the contrary, and then remarks, 'for there is no greater analogy than that of the creature to God *in ratione essendi*, and yet *esse*, existence, belongs primarily and principally to God in such a way that it yet belongs really and univocally to the creature; and similarly with goodness and wisdom and the like'.[25] Here he uses the words 'really and univocally' (*realiter et univoce*) together. If the doctrine of univocity is meant to ensure an objective knowledge of God from creatures, it would seem to be essential to that doctrine that the univocal concept should not be an *ens rationis* merely, but that it should have a real foundation or counterpart in extramental reality. On the other hand, Scotus is insistent that God is not in a genus and that God and creatures are in the real order *primo diversa*. How can the two sets of statements be reconciled?

The concept of being is abstracted from creatures, and it is the concept of being without any determination; it is logically prior to the division of being into infinite and finite being. But in actual fact every being must be either infinite or finite: it must be opposed to nothingness either as infinite being or as finite being: there is no actually existent being which is neither infinite nor finite. In this sense the univocal concept of being, as logically prior to the division of being into infinite and finite, possesses a unity which belongs to the logical order. The natural philosopher obviously does not consider being in this sense, nor does the metaphysician in so far as he is concerned with actually existent being and with possible being, since the concept of a being which would be neither infinite nor finite would not be the concept of a possible being. On the other hand, even though every actual being is either finite or infinite, every being is really opposed to nothingness, though in different ways, so that there is a real foundation for the univocal concept of being. As *intentio prima* the concept of being is founded on reality, for otherwise it could not be abstracted, and has objective reference, while as *intentio secunda* it is an *ens rationis*; but the concept of being as such, whether considered as *intentio prima* or *intentio secunda*, does not express something which has a formal existence outside the mind. It is, therefore, a logical concept. The logician 'considers second intentions as applied to first intentions', says Scotus when speaking of universals,[26] and what is univocal for the logician is equivocal[27] for the philosopher who is studying real things. One can say, then, that the univocal concept of being is an *ens rationis*. On the other hand, the univocal concept of being has a real foundation in actuality. The case is not without parallel to that of the universal. No doubt, Scotus did not consider adequately all the possible objections against his theory; but the truth of the matter seems to be that he was so intent on refuting the doctrine of Henry of Ghent, which he considered to endanger or render impossible any objective knowledge of God in this life, that he did not give his full attention to all the complexities of the problem and to the difficulties which might be raised against his own theory. It must be remembered, however, that Scotus postulated a formal distinction between the attributes of being and between the attributes and being. 'Being contains many attributes which are not different things from being itself, as Aristotle proves in the beginning of the fourth book of the *Metaphysics*, but which are distinguished formally and quidditatively, that is, by a formal, objectively grounded distinction, from one another, and also from being, by a real and quidditative formality, I say.'[28] In this case the univocal concept of being cannot be a mere *ens rationis*, in the sense of a purely subjective construction. There is no separate or separable thing, existing extramentally, which corresponds to the univocal concept of being; but there is an objective foundation for the concept none the less. One can say, then, that the univocal concept of being is not purely logical, provided that one does not mean to imply that there is any *thing* in extramental reality which corresponds to the concept.

3. I have treated the doctrine of univocity at some length, not only because the doctrine is one of the characteristics of Scotism, but also because Scotus attached very considerable importance to the doctrine, as a safeguard of natural theology. I turn now to a brief consideration of another characteristic doctrine of Scotus, that of the *distinctio formalis a parte rei*, the objective formal distinction, which plays an important rôle in the Scotist system and one use of which has just been mentioned.

The doctrine of the formal distinction was not an invention of Scotus: one finds it in the philosophy of Olivi, for example, and it has been ascribed to St. Bonaventure himself. In any case it became a common doctrine among the Franciscan thinkers, and what Scotus did was to take over the doctrine from his predecessors and make extensive use of it. In brief, the doctrine is that there is a distinction which is less than the real distinction and more objective than a virtual distinction. A real distinction obtains between two things which are physically separable, at least by divine power. It is obvious enough that there is a real distinction between a man's two hands, since these are distinct things; but there is also a real distinction between the form and matter of any material object. A purely mental distinction signifies a distinction made by the mind when there is no corresponding objective distinction in the thing itself. The distinction between a thing and its definition, for example, between 'man' and 'rational animal', is purely mental. A formal distinction obtains when the mind distinguishes in an object two or more *formalitates* which are objectively distinct, but which are inseparable from one another, even by divine power. For instance, Scotus asserted a formal distinction between the divine attributes. Mercy and justice are formally distinct, though the divine justice and the divine mercy are inseparable, since, in spite of the formal distinction between them, each is really identical with the divine essence.

An example from psychology may make Scotus's meaning clearer. There is only one soul in man, and there cannot be a real distinction between the sensitive soul and the intellectual or rational soul in man: it is in virtue of the one vital principle that a man thinks and exercises sensation. Not even God can separate a man's rational soul from his sensitive soul, for it would no longer be a human soul. On the other hand, sensation is not thought: rational activity can exist without sensitive activity, as in the angels, and sensitive activity can exist without rational activity, as in the case of the purely sensitive soul of the brute. In man, then, the sensitive and rational principles are formally distinct, with a distinction which is objective, that is, independent of the mind's distinguishing activity; but they are not really distinct *things*; they are distinct *formalitates* of one thing, the human soul.

Why did Scotus assert the existence of this formal distinction, and why was he not content to call it a *distinctio rationis cum fundamento in re*? The ultimate reason was, of course, that he thought the distinction to be not only warranted, but also demanded by the nature of knowledge and the nature of the object of knowledge. Knowledge is the apprehension of being, and if the mind is forced, so to speak, to recognise distinctions in the object, that is, if it does not simply construct actively a distinction in the object, but finds the recognition of a distinction imposed upon it, the distinction cannot be simply a mental distinction, and the foundation of the distinction in the mind must be an objective distinction in the object. On the other hand, there are cases when the foundation of the distinction cannot be the existence of distinct separable factors in the object. It is necessary, then, to find room for a distinction which is less than a real distinction, such as obtains between soul and body in man, but which at the same time is founded on an objective distinction in the object, a distinction which can be only between different, but not separable formalities of one and the same object. Such a distinction will maintain the objectivity of knowledge, without, however, impairing the unity of the object. It may be objected, of course, that the formal distinction as applied by Scotus does, in some cases at least, impair the requisite unity of the object and that it surrenders too much to 'realism'; but it would appear that Scotus considered the distinction to be necessary if the objectivity of knowledge is to be maintained.

4. One of the questions in which Scotus applies his formal distinction is the question of the distinction which obtains between essence and existence in the creature.[29] He refuses to admit a real distinction between essence and existence: 'it is simply false, that existence (*esse*) is something different from essence'.[30] Similarly, 'the proposition is false, that just as existence stands to essence, so operation (*operari*) stands to potency, for existence is really the same as the essence and does not proceed from the essence, whereas act or operation proceeds from potency and is not really the same as potency'.[31] The assertion, *simpliciter falsum est, quod esse sit aliud ab essentia*, would indeed appear to be directed against such statements of St. Thomas as *Ergo oportet quod omnis talis res, cuius esse est aliud a natura sua, habeat esse ab alio;*[32] but, given Scotus's conception of a real distinction, his denial of a real distinction between essence and existence in creatures is more relevant to the doctrine of Giles of Rome, for whom essence and existence were physically separable, than to that of St. Thomas Aquinas.

But when Scotus discusses the relation of essence and existence, his polemic is directed not so much against St. Thomas or even Giles of Rome as against Henry of Ghent. Henry did not maintain a real distinction between essence and existence in creatures, but he distinguished *esse essentiae* and *esse existentiae*, the former being the state of the essence as known by God, the latter being its state after creation, creation adding no positive element to the essence, but only a relation to God. Henry had asserted this doctrine of the *esse essentiae* in order to account for the fact of science, in the sense of knowledge of timeless truths about essences, irrespective of the actual existence of such objects, but Scotus argued that Henry's doctrine destroyed the Christian idea of creation. For example, creation is production out of nothing; but if a stone formerly, before its creation, had *esse verum reale*, then when it is produced by the efficient cause, it is not produced from nothing.[33] Moreover, as the essence is known eternally by God, it would follow from this notion that the essence before actual existence already possesses *esse reale* and that creation is eternal: one would thus have to admit other necessary beings besides God. Only that which actually exists has *esse reale*; possible existence (*esse possibile*) is only *esse secundum quid*.[34] The essence as known may be said to possess *esse diminutum*; but this existence (*esse*) of an essence in the divine mind before its actual production is simply *esse cognitum*. Scotus and St. Thomas are at one on this point, that creation means the production of the whole object out of nothing and that the essence before creation did not possess any *esse* of its own, though Scotus differed from St. Thomas in his view of the relationship which obtains between the essence and the existence in the created object, since he rejected a real distinction, though, as already remarked, this rejection was actually a rejection of the real distinction maintained by Giles of Rome rather than of that taught by St. Thomas.

5. The formal objective distinction was also employed by Scotus in his discussion of universals. In regard to universals Scotus was certainly not an exaggerated realist, and Suarez's assertion[35] that Scotus taught that the common nature is numerically the same in all individuals of the species, misrepresents Scotus's position, at least if taken out of its setting and out of relation to Suarez's own doctrine. Scotus states unambiguously that 'the universal in act does not exist except in the intellect' and that there is no actually existing universal which is predicable of another object than that in which it exists.[36] The common nature is not numerically the same in Socrates and in Plato; it cannot be compared to the divine essence, which is numerically the same in the three divine Persons.[37] Nevertheless, there is a unity which is less than numerical (*unitas minor quam numeralis*). Though the physical nature of an object is inseparable from the object's *haecceitas* (the object's 'thisness' or principle of individuation, which we shall consider shortly) and though it cannot

exist in any other object, there is a formal objective distinction between the human nature and the 'Socratesness' or *haecceitas* in Socrates, but not a real distinction, so that the human nature can be considered simply as such, without reference to individuality or to universality. Appealing to Avicenna,[38] Scotus observes that horseness is simply horseness (*equinitas est tantum equinitas*) and that of itself it has neither *esse singulare* nor *esse universale*.[39] In other words, there exists between the *haecceitas* and the nature in a concrete object a *distinctio formalis a parte rei*, and it is necessary to suppose such a distinction, since otherwise, that is, if the nature were *of itself* individual, if it were, for example, of itself the nature of Socrates, there would be no objective foundation, no valid ground for our universal statements. The abstraction of the logical universal presupposes a distinction in the object between the nature and the *haecceitas*.

It is, however, important to remember that this distinction is not a real distinction, not, that is, a distinction between two separable entities. Form and matter are separable; but the nature and the *haecceitas* are not separable. Not even the divine power can separate physically the 'Socratesness' of Socrates and the human nature of Socrates. Therefore, even though Scotus's assertion of the formal objective distinction is indeed a concession in one sense to realism, it does not imply that the human nature of Socrates is objectively and numerically identical with the human nature of Plato. Scotus is concerned, not to support exaggerated realism, but rather to account for the objective reference of our universal judgements. Whether or not one agrees with his theory is, of course, another matter; but in any case to accuse him of falling into the early mediaeval form of exaggerated realism is to misunderstand and misrepresent his position. Scotus is willing to say with Averroes,[40] *Intellectus est qui facit universalitatem in rebus*; but he insists that this proposition must not be understood as excluding the *unitas realis minor unitate numerali* which exists prior to the mind's operation, since this exclusion would make it impossible to explain why 'the intellect is moved to abstract one specific concept from Socrates and Plato rather than from Socrates and a stone'.[41] It is the objective reference of science which interests Scotus.

J. Kraus[42] has maintained that Duns Scotus distinguishes three universals. First, there is the physical universal, which is the specific nature existing really in individual objects;

secondly, there is the metaphysical universal, which is the common nature, not as it actually exists in the concrete thing, but with the characteristics which it acquires through abstraction by the active intellect, namely positive indetermination or predicability of many individuals *in potentia proxima*; and thirdly, there is the logical universal, the universal in the strict sense, which is the metaphysical universal conceived reflexly in its predicability and analysed into its constitutive notes. But this threefold distinction must not be understood as implying that the physical universal is separable or really distinct from the individuality of the object in which it exists. The concrete object consists of the nature and the *haecceitas*, and between them there is, not a real distinction but a *distinctio formalis a parte rei*. Scotus's mention of the relation of matter to successive forms[43] should not mislead us, since for Scotus there is a real distinction between matter and form, and the same matter can exist under successive forms, though it cannot exist simultaneously under different ultimately determining forms. The physical universal, however, though indifferent, as considered *in itself*, to this or that *haecceitas*, cannot exist in itself extramentally and is physically inseparable from its *haecceitas*.

6. That Scotus taught the doctrine of hylomorphism is clear enough;[44] but it is not so clear whether or not he accepted the Bonaventurian attribution of hylomorphic composition to angels. If the *De rerum principio* were authentic, there could be no doubt as to Scotus's acceptance of the Bonaventurian view, but the *De rerum principio* is not the work of Scotus, and in his authentic writings the latter nowhere expressly states the Bonaventurian doctrine. Thus Father Parthenius Minges, O.F.M., who draws on the *De rerum principio* in his *Joannis Duns Scoti Doctrina philosophica et theologica*, has to admit that 'in the Commentaries on the *Sentences*, the *Quaestiones quodlibetales* and the *Questions on the Metaphysics of Aristotle* Scotus does not expressly state this doctrine, but only more or less touches on, insinuates or supposes it'.[45] It seems to me that Scotus's treatment of matter in the Commentaries can be said to 'suppose' the doctrine of the hylomorphic composition of rational soul and of angels only if one is determined on other grounds to assume that he held this doctrine, if, for example, one is determined to accept the *De rerum principio* as Scotus's work; but it is true that in the *De Anima*[46] he remarks that 'proba-

bly it can be said that in the soul there is matter'. However, Scotus is here engaged in showing that the presence of matter in the soul can be deduced with probability from the premisses of Aristotle and St. Thomas, even though St. Thomas did not hold the doctrine. For example, he argues that if matter is the principle of individuation, as St. Thomas (but not Scotus) held, then there must be matter in the rational soul. It is useless to say that the soul, when separated from the body, is distinguished from other souls by its relation to the body, first because the soul does not exist for the sake of the body, secondly because the relation or inclination to the body, which no longer exists, would be no more than a *relatio rationis*, and thirdly because the inclination or relation supposes a foundation, i.e. *this* soul, so that the thisness could not be due to the relation. Thus Scotus in the *De Anima* is trying to show that if one maintains with St. Thomas that matter is the principle of individuation, one ought to assert the presence of matter in the rational soul, in order to explain the individuality of the rational soul after death; he does not state that this conclusion represents his own opinion. It may be that it does represent Scotus's own opinion and that he wished to show that the Thomist ought, on his own premisses, to share that opinion; but one is hardly in a position to state positively that Scotus without a doubt maintained the Bonaventurian doctrine, and if one were prepared to reject the authenticity of the *De Anima*, there would seem to be no very cogent reason for stating that Scotus even probably maintained the doctrine.

But whatever Scotus's opinion on universal hylomorphism may have been, he certainly held that matter, really distinct from form, is an entity in its own right and that it is *potentia subjectiva* and not simply *potentia objectiva*, that is, that it is something existing, not something which is merely possible.[47] Moreover, matter is an *ens absolutum*, in the sense that it could exist by itself without form, at least through the divine power.[48] An entity which is distinct from and prior to another entity can exist apart from that other entity without any contradiction being involved. That matter is distinct from form is proved by the fact that together with form it makes a real composite being, while that it is prior to form, logically prior at least, is proved by the fact that it receives form and that what receives form must be logically prior to form.[49] Similarly, since God creates matter immediately, He could conserve it immediately, that is, without any secondary conserving agency. Again, form does not belong to the essence of matter nor does the *esse* which form confers on matter belong to the matter itself, since it is removed in substantial change.[50] In other words, the reality of substantial change postulates the reality of matter. In answer to the Thomist objection that it is contradictory to speak of matter as a real entity, that is, as actually existing without form, since to say that matter actually exists on its own account and to say that it has a form is one and the same, Scotus answers that act and form are not necessarily convertible terms. Of course, if act is taken to mean act which is received and which actuates and distinguishes, then matter, which is receptive, is not act; but if act and potency are understood in a wider sense, every thing which is *extra causam suam* is in act, even privations, and in this sense matter is in act, though it is not form.[51]

7. Scotus rejects the theory of *rationes seminales*, on the ground that the theory is not needed in order to avoid the conclusion that the created efficient agent creates and annihilates in the changes it brings about, and that there is no other cogent reason for accepting it.[52] But though he rejects the theory of *rationes seminales*, he retains that of plurality of forms. Against the assertion of the Thomists that there is no need to postulate a form of corporeity, since *sine necessitate non est ponenda pluralitas*, Scotus replies that in this case there is a need, *hic enim est necessitas ponendi plura*, and he goes on to argue that although the body, when the soul has departed, is continually tending to dissolution, it remains a body, for a time at least, and must possess that form which makes a body a body.[53] Moreover, the Body of Christ in the tomb must have possessed a form of corporeity. From the fact that a human body naturally tends to dissolution when the soul has departed it does not follow that the body, in a state of separation from the soul, has no proper form of its own; it follows only that it has not got a *perfect* subsistence of its own, and the reason of this is that the form of corporeity is an imperfect form which disposes the body for a higher form, the soul.

But though Scotus affirms the existence of a form of corporeity in the human body, and, of course, in every organic body, which is transmitted by the parents at the same time that God infuses the rational soul and which is really distinct from the rational soul, from which it can be separated, it

should not be imagined that he breaks up the human soul
into three really distinct forms or even parts, the vegetative,
sensitive and intellective principles; and he rejects the theories which appear to him to impair the unity of the soul.
The rational soul of man comprises these three powers *uni-
tive*, 'although they are formally distinct'.[54] It would be false
to suggest that Scotus taught the existence of three souls in
man or that he maintained that the vegetative and sensitive
powers are distinct from the rational power in the same way
in which the form of corporeity is distinct. Whereas the distinction between the form of corporeity and the human soul
is a real distinction, that between the powers within the soul
itself is a formal distinction, which obtains between inseparable *formalitates* of one object, not between separable entities
or forms.

8. It is necessary to say something about Scotus's somewhat obscure doctrine of individuation, the obscurity lying
rather on the positive than on the negative side of the
doctrine.

Scotus criticises and rejects St. Thomas's theory that prime
matter is the principle of individuation. Prime matter cannot be the primary reason of distinction and diversity since
it is of itself indistinct and indeterminate.[55] Moreover, if
matter is the principle of individuation, it follows that in the
case of substantial change the two substances, that corrupted
and that generated, are precisely the same substance, since
the matter is the same, even though the forms are different.
St. Thomas's theory seems to imply that quantity is actually
the principle of individuation; but quantity is an accident and
a substance cannot be individuated by an accident. Incidentally, Scotus tries to show that Aristotle is wrongly cited as an
authority for the Thomist view of individuation.

The principle of individuation is thus not prime matter,
nor can it be the nature as such, since it is precisely with the
individuation of the nature that we are concerned. What is
it, then? It is an *entitas individualis*. 'This entity is neither
matter nor form nor the composite thing, in so far as any of
these is a nature; but it is the ultimate reality of the being
which is matter or form or a composite thing.'[56] The *entitas singularis* and the *entitas naturae*, whether the latter is
matter or form or a *compositum*, are formally distinct; but
they are not, and cannot be, two things. They are not separable things; nor does the *entitas singularis* stand to the *entitas*

naturae as specific difference to genus.[57] The word *haecceitas* is not used for the principle of individuation in the Oxford Commentary, though it is so used in the *Reportata Parisiensia*[58] and in the *Quaestiones in libros Metaphysicorum.*[59]

It is not so easy to understand exactly what this *haecceitas* or *entitas singularis vel individualis* or *ultima realitas entis* actually is. It is, as we have seen, neither matter nor form nor the composite thing; but it is a positive entity, the final reality of matter, form and the composite thing. A human being, for instance, is *this* composite being, composed of *this* matter and *this* form. The *haecceitas* does not confer any further qualitative determination; but it seals the being as *this* being. Scotus's view certainly cannot be equated with the theory that every nature is of itself individual, since he expressly denies, though in view of the fact that Scotus, while postulating a formal distinction between *haecceitas* and nature, denies their real distinction from one another, it seems to be implied that a thing has *haecceitas* or 'thisness' by the fact that it exists. His theory is not the same as that of the Nominalists, since he postulates contraction of the nature by the 'ultimate reality'; but the fact that he speaks of 'ultimate reality' would seem to imply that a nature acquires this ultimate reality through existence, though it is not, says Scotus, existence itself.[60]

Chapter Forty-eight

SCOTUS–IV: NATURAL THEOLOGY

Metaphysics and God–Knowledge of God from creatures–Proof of God's existence–Simplicity and intelligence of God–God's infinity–The Anselmian argument–Divine attributes which cannot be philosophically demonstrated–The distinction between the divine attributes–The divine ideas–The divine will–Creation.

1. God is not, properly speaking, an object of metaphysical science, says Scotus,[1] in spite of the fact that metaphysics are the science of being, and God is the first being. A truth belongs properly to that science in which it is known *a priori*, from the principles of that science, and the metaphysician knows truths about God only *a posteriori*. God is, therefore, the proper object of theology, in which science He is known as He is in His essence, in Himself; He is the object of metaphysics only *secundum quid*, inasmuch as the philosopher comes to know God only in and through His effects.

This statement certainly does not mean that for Scotus the philosopher or metaphysician is unable to attain any certain knowledge of God. 'By our natural power (*ex naturalibus*) we can know some truths concerning God', says Scotus,[2] and he goes on to explain that many things (*multa*) can be known about God by the philosophers through a consideration of God's effects. By the natural power of reason one can conclude that God is one, supreme, good, but not that God is three in Persons.[3] Theology deals more properly with the divine Persons than with the essential attributes of God, for most of the essential attributes (*essentialia plurima*) can be known by us in metaphysics.[4] Accordingly, the statement that

God is, strictly speaking, the object of theology rather than of metaphysics does not mean that Scotus excludes the study of God from metaphysics, since although God is not the primary object of metaphysics, He is none the less considered in metaphysics in the noblest way in which He can be studied in any natural science.[5] In the *De primo principio*[6] Scotus recapitulates the perfections which the philosophers have proved to belong to God and distinguishes them from other perfections, such as omnipotence and universal and special providence, which belong more properly to the *credibilia*, truths which have not been proved by the philosophers but which are believed by *Catholici*. These latter truths, says Scotus, will be considered in *sequenti* (*tractatu*) and the words have been added, *scilicet in Theorematibus*. That an attempt was made to disprove this identification of the 'following' treatise with the *Theoremata* and that this attempt was largely due to the at least apparent contradiction between the *Theoremata* and the *De primo principio* has already been mentioned in Chapter XLV, and, as I there explained, I propose to expose the natural theology of Scotus on the supposition that the *Theoremata* is not the authentic work of Scotus, with the proviso that, were the authenticity of the *Theoremata* ever to be satisfactorily proved, one would have to explain the apparent contradiction on some such line as that adopted by M. Gilson. In any case, however, Scotus has made it perfectly clear in his certainly authentic works that the philosopher can prove many truths about God by the light of natural reason, without any actual employment of the data of revelation. Some of the points in regard to which Scotus restricted the scope of the unaided human intellect will be noted in the following pages; but it is important to note that Scotus was neither a sceptic nor an agnostic in regard to natural theology, and the *Theoremata*, even if authentic, would be quite insufficient to dispose of the clear and abundant evidence on this point which is afforded by the Commentaries on the *Sentences* and by the *De primo principio*.

2. Scotus certainly thought that the existence of God stands in need of rational proof and that this rational proof must be *a posteriori*. Of his use of the Anselmian argument I shall speak later.

First of all, man has no intuitive knowledge of God in this life, since the intuition of God is precisely that form of knowledge which places a man *extra statum viae*.[7] Our knowledge starts from the things of sense, and our natural conceptual knowledge of God is arrived at through reflection on the objects of experience.[8] By considering creatures as God's effects the human mind is able to form concepts which apply to God; but one must add that the concepts of God which are formed from creatures are imperfect,[9] in contrast, that is, with concepts based on the divine essence itself. It follows that our natural knowledge of God is indistinct and obscure, since it is not knowledge of God as immediately present to the intellect in His essence.[10]

Our natural knowledge of God rests on our capacity to form univocal concepts, as has been explained in the last chapter. Scotus affirms that 'creatures which impress their own ideas (*species*) on the intellect, can also impress the ideas of transcendent (attributes) which belong in common to them and to God';[11] but it would not be possible to proceed from a knowledge of creatures to the knowledge of God, were we not able to form from creatures univocal concepts. When the intellect has formed these concepts, it can combine them to form a composite quidditative idea of God. Just as the imagination can combine the images of mountain and gold to form the image of a golden mountain, so can the intellect combine the ideas of goodness, supreme and actuality to form the concept of a supremely good and actual being.[12] Needless to say, this comparison should not mislead us into thinking that for Scotus the combining activity of the mind in natural theology is exactly parallel to the combining work of imagination and fancy; the former activity is governed by the objective truth and apprehended logical necessity, whereas the imaginative construction of a golden mountain is 'imaginary', that is, arbitrary or the work of fancy.

3. How does Scotus prove the existence of God? In the Oxford Commentary[13] he states that the existence of the first cause is shown much more perfectly from the attributes (*passiones*) of creatures considered in metaphysics than from those which are considered by the natural philosopher. 'For it is a more perfect and immediate knowledge of the first being to know it as first or necessary being than to know it as first mover.' Scotus does not here deny that the natural philosopher can show that the fact of motion requires a first mover; but his point is that the argument from motion does not, of itself, transcend the physical order and arrive at the necessary being which is the ultimate total cause of its effects.

The first mover, considered as such, is simply the cause of motion; it is not conceived as the cause of the being of all other things, but is a (necessary) hypothesis to explain the physical fact of motion. The argument from motion is thus very far from being Scotus's favourite proof. It may be noted in passing that if the Commentary on the *Physics*, which is now rejected as spurious, were authentic, the difficulty in accepting the *Theoremata* might perhaps be lessened. In the former work[14] the author makes clear his belief that the argument from motion does not, of itself, bring us to a recognisable concept of God, since it merely arrives at a first mover, without indicating the nature of the first mover. Thus if it could be maintained that the author of the *Theoremata* was speaking of natural philosophy when he said that it cannot be proved that God is living or intelligent, it would seem that the apparent contradiction between the *Theoremata* and Scotus's certainly authentic works could be resolved. However, as the *Questions on the Physics of Aristotle* is unauthentic and as the authenticity of the *Theoremata* has not been proved, it is hardly worth while pursuing the matter further. In any case it remains true that Scotus emphasised those proofs for the existence of God which are founded on *passiones metaphysicae*. Moreover, in the Oxford Commentary,[15] Scotus remarks that the proposition that mover and moved must be distinct 'is true only in corporeal things' and 'I also believe that (even) there it is not necessarily true', while 'I say at least that in regard to spiritual beings it is simply false . . .'

In the *De primo principio*[16] Scotus argues from the fact of contingency to the existence of a first cause and a necessary being. That there are beings which can have being after not-being, which can come into existence, which are contingent, is clear; and such beings require a cause of their being, since they can neither cause themselves nor be caused by nothing (*nec a se nec a nihilo*). If A is the cause of the being of a contingent object, it must be itself either caused or uncaused. If it is itself caused, let B be the cause of A. But it is impossible to proceed to infinity; so there must ultimately be a cause which is itself uncaused. Scotus distinguishes clearly between the series of *essentialiter ordinata* and the series of *accidentaliter ordinata*, and he points out that what he is denying is not the possibility of an unending regress of successive causes, each of which, taken in itself, is contingent, but the possibility of an unending (vertical) series of simultaneous total causes. As he observes, even if we grant the possibility of an infinite series of successive causes, the whole chain requires an explanation, and this explanation must be outside the chain itself, since each member of the chain is caused, and so contingent. An infinite series of succeeding contingent beings cannot explain its own existence, since the whole series is contingent if each member is contingent: it is necessary to postulate a transcendent cause. 'The totality of ordered effects (*causatorum*) is itself caused; therefore (it has been caused) by some cause which does not belong to that totality.'[17] If, for example, one postulates that the human race goes back to infinity, there is an infinite succession of fathers and children. The father causes the child; but after the father's death the son continues to exist and continues to be contingent. An ultimate cause is required, not only of the son's being here and now, but also of the whole series of fathers and sons, since the infinite regress does not make the series necessary. The same principle must be extended to the universe of contingent beings in general: the universe of contingent beings requires an *actual* transcendent cause (itself uncaused). An infinite succession 'is impossible, except in virtue of some nature of infinite duration (*durante infinite*), on which the whole succession and every member of it depends'.[18]

Scotus then proceeds to show that the first cause in the essential order of dependence must exist actually and cannot be merely possible,[19] that it is necessary being, that is, that it cannot not exist[20] and that it is one.[21] There cannot be more than one necessary being. Scotus argues, for example, that if there were two beings with a common nature of necessary being, one would have to distinguish formally between the common nature and the individuality, which would be something other than necessary being. If it is answered that there is no such distinction in a necessary being, it follows that the two beings are indistinguishable and hence one. This argument, though based on Scotus's theory of the common nature and of individuation, reminds one of an analogous argument given by St. Anselm. Moreover, the one essential order of the universe postulates only one *primum effectivum*. Scotus then goes on to show that there is a first final cause, *primum finitivum*,[22] and a supreme being in the order of eminence,[23] and proceeds to show that the *primum effectivum*, the *primum finitivum* and the *primum eminens* (or *perfectissimum*) are identical.[24]

In the Oxford Commentary on the *Sentences*[25] Scotus argues in much the same way. We have to proceed from creatures to God by considering the causal relation (in respect of either efficient or final causality) or the relation of *excessum* to *excedens* in the order of perfection. Contingent being, the *effectibile*, is caused by nothing or by itself or by another. As it is impossible for it to be caused by nothing or by itself, it must be caused by another. If that other is the first cause, we have found what we are seeking: if not, then we must proceed further. But we cannot proceed for ever in the vertical order of dependence. *Infinitas autem est impossibilis in ascendendo.*[26] Nor can we suppose that contingent beings cause one another, for then we shall proceed in a circle, without arriving at any ultimate explanation of contingency. It is useless to say that the world is eternal, since the eternal series of contingent beings itself requires a cause.[27] Similarly in the order of final causality there must be a final cause which is not directed to any more ultimate final cause,[28] while in the order of eminence there must be a most perfect being, a *suprema natura*.[29] These three are one and the same being. The first efficient cause acts with a view to the final end; but nothing other than the first being itself can be its final end. Similarly, the first efficient cause is not univocal with its effects, that is, it cannot be of the same nature, but must transcend them; and as first cause, it must be the 'most eminent' being.[30]

4. As the first being is uncaused, it cannot possess essential parts like matter and form nor can it possess accidents: it cannot, in short, be composed in any way but must be essentially simple.[31] It must be intelligent and possessed of will. The natural agents in the world which do not consciously act for an end do nevertheless act for an end; and this means that they do so by the power and knowledge of the agent which transcends them. If the natural agents of the world act teleologically, this supposes that the primary cause knows the end and wills it, since nothing can be directed to an end except in virtue of knowledge and will (as, we might say, the arrow is directed to an end by an archer who knows and wills the end). God loves Himself and wills Himself necessarily; but He does not will necessarily anything outside Himself, since nothing outside Himself is necessary to Him:

He alone is necessary being. It follows that He causes His effects freely and not necessarily. God knows and understands from eternity all that He can produce; He has actual and distinct understanding of every intelligible, and this understanding is identical with Himself (*idem sibi*).[32]

5. But Scotus gave his closest attention to the infinity of God. The simplest and most perfect concept of God which we can form is that of the absolutely infinite Being. It is simpler than the concept of goodness or the like, since infinity is not like an attribute or *passio* of the being of which it is predicated, but signifies the intrinsic mode of that being. It is the most perfect concept, since infinite being includes virtually infinite truth, infinite goodness and every perfection which is compatible with infinity.[33] It is true that every perfection in God is infinite, but 'it has its formal perfection from the infinity of the essence as its root and foundation'.[34] All the divine perfections are grounded in the divine essence, which is best described as the infinity of being: it is not correct, therefore, to state that for Scotus the divine essence consists in will. 'Although the will is formally infinite, it does not, however, include all intrinsic perfections formally in itself . . . but the essence alone includes all perfections in this way.'[35]

In the *Opus Oxoniense*[36] and in the *De primo principio*[37] Scotus gives a series of proofs of the divine infinity. Presupposing the compatibility of infinity with being Scotus takes as the text of his first argument Aristotle's words, *Primum movet motu infinito; ergo habet potentiam infinitam*, and argues that the conclusion is invalid if it is understood as following from motion which is infinite in duration, since length of duration does not make a thing more perfect, though it is valid if it is understood as following from the power to produce by motion infinite effects, that is, successively. God, as first efficient Cause, able to produce an infinity of effects, must be infinite in power. Moreover, as God possesses in Himself in a more eminent way the causality of all possible secondary causes, He must be infinite in Himself, *intensive*.[38] Secondly, God must be infinite since He knows an infinity of intelligible objects. This argument might seem to be a sheer *petitio principii*; but Scotus gives a somewhat singular reason for supposing that God knows an infinity of *intelligibilia*. 'Whatsoever things are infinite in potency, so that if they are taken one after the other they can have no end, are infinite in act, if they are together in act. But it is clear enough that intelligible objects are infinite in potency in respect of the created intellect, and in the uncreated intellect all (the *intelligibilia*) which are successively intelligible by the created intellect are actually understood together. Therefore, there are there (in the uncreated intellect) an infinite number of actually apprehended objects.'[39] Thirdly, Scotus argues from the finality of the will. 'Our will can desire and love an object greater than any finite object . . . and what is more, there seems to be a natural inclination to love above all an infinite good. . . . It thus appears that in the act of loving we have experience of an infinite good; indeed, the will seems to find no perfect rest in any other object . . .' The infinite good must, therefore, exist.[40] The fourth argument of the Oxford Commentary[41] is to the effect that it is not incompatible with finite being that there should be a more perfect being, but that it is incompatible with the *ens eminentissimum* that there should be a more perfect being. But infinity is greater and more perfect than finitude, and infinity and being are compatible. The *ens eminentissimum* must, therefore, be infinite. The proof that infinity is compatible with being amounts to little more than saying that we can discern no incompatibility. In the *De primo principio*[42] Scotus also proves God's infinity from the fact that His intellect is identical with His substance, arguing that such identification is impossible in a finite being.

Having proved, to his satisfaction at least, God's infinity, Scotus is able to show that God must be one and one alone.[43]

6. In his discussion of the divine infinity Scotus introduces the so-called ontological argument of St. Anselm.[44] He has just remarked that the intellect, the object of which is being, finds no mutual repugnance between 'being' and 'infinite', and that it would be astonishing, supposing the two to be incompatible, if the intellect did not discern the incompatibility, 'when a discord in sound so easily offends the hearing'. If there is such an incompatibility, why does not the intellect 'shrink back' from the idea of the infinite, if it is incompatible with its own proper object, being? He then proceeds to state that the argument of St. Anselm in the first chapter of the *Proslogium* can be 'coloured' (*potest colorari*) and that it should be understood in this way: 'God is that than which, having been thought without contradiction, a greater cannot be thought without contradiction. That (the words) "with-

out contradiction" must be added is clear, for that in the thought of which a contradiction is included (that is, involved), is unthinkable . . .' It has been asserted that since Scotus admits that the Anselmian argument must be 'coloured', he rejects it. But he obviously does not reject it without more ado. Why should he 'colour' it, except to use it? And in point of fact he does use it. First he tries to show that the idea of the *summum cogitabile* is without contradiction, i.e. that the essence or *esse quidditativum* is possible, and then he observes that if the *summum cogitabile* is possible, it must exist, that it must have *esse existentiae. Majus igitur cogitabile est, quod est in re quam quod est tantum in intellectu.* That which really exists is *majus cogitabile* than that which does not really exist but is merely conceived, inasmuch as that which really exists is 'visible' or capable of being intuited, and that which can be intuited is 'greater' than that which can be merely conceived or can be known by abstractive thought alone. It follows, then, that the *summum cogitabile* must really exist. Scotus is not saying that we have a natural intuition of God; he is giving a reason for the judgement that that which really exists is greater or more perfect than that which does not really exist extramentally.

There is no doubt, then, that Scotus makes use of the Anselmian argument. Two questions arise, therefore. First, in what does the *coloratio* of the argument consist? Secondly, how did Scotus think that his use of the argument was consistent with his clear assertion that we can demonstrate God's existence only *a posteriori?* First the *coloratio* consists in an attempt to show that the idea of the most perfect being is the idea of a possible being, and he does this primarily by observing that no contradiction is observable in the idea of the most perfect being. In other words, he anticipates Leibniz's attempt to show that the idea of God is the idea of a possible being, inasmuch as the idea does not involve any contradiction, and the idea of a being which does not involve a contradiction constitutes the idea of a possible being. On the other hand, Scotus did not consider that the fact that we cannot observe any contradiction in the idea of the most perfect being is a demonstrative proof of the fact that no contradiction is involved. We cannot show apodeictically and *a priori* that the most perfect being is possible, and that is why he states elsewhere that the Anselmian argument belongs to the proofs which amount to no more than *persua-*

siones probabiles.[45] This supplies the answer to our second question. Scotus considered his use of the Anselmian argument to be compatible with his assertion that we can demonstrate God's existence only *a posteriori* because he did not regard the Anselmian argument as a demonstration, but only as a 'probable persuasion', a probable proof. He did not simply reject the argument as St. Thomas did; but he was dissatisfied with the argument as it stood and thought that it needed 'colouring'. On the other hand, he did not think that the 'colouring', the proof that the idea of God is the idea of a possible being, is a demonstrative proof, and so he put forward the argument as probable. He used it as an auxiliary argument to show what is involved or implied in the idea of God rather than as a strict demonstration of God's existence. It is as though he had said: 'This is the best we can make of the argument, and it has its uses if you accept the premisses; but I do not regard the argument as a demonstration. If a strict demonstration of God's existence is wanted, it will have to proceed *a posteriori*.'

7. Scotus did not consider that we can demonstrate by the natural reason all God's essential attributes. Thus in the *De primo principio*[46] he says that consideration of the attributes of omnipotence, immensity, omnipresence, truth, justice, mercy and providence directed to all creatures, to intelligent creatures in particular, will be postponed until the next treatise, as they are *credibilia*, that is, revealed objects of faith. It might well appear strange to read that omnipotence, for instance, cannot be philosophically demonstrated as a divine attribute, when Scotus does not hesitate to conclude God's infinity from His infinite power; but he distinguishes between omnipotence in the proper theological sense (*proprie theologice*), which cannot be demonstrated with certainty by philosophers, and infinite power (*potentia infinita*), which can be demonstrated by philosophers.[47] The distinction consists in this. God's power to produce every possible effect, immediately *or* mediately, can be proved philosophically, but not His power to produce all possible effects immediately. Even though the first cause possesses in itself *eminentius* the causality of the secondary cause, it does not necessarily follow, says Scotus, that the first cause can produce the effect of the secondary cause immediately, without the co-operation of the secondary cause, not because the causality of the first cause needs adding to, so to speak, but because the imperfection

of the effect may require, so far as the philosopher can see, the causal operation of the finite cause as its explanation. Scotus is thus not attacking the demonstrability of God's creative power: what he is saying is that the proposition, 'whatever the first efficient cause can do with the co-operation of a secondary cause, that it can do immediately by itself', is neither self-evident nor philosophically demonstrable, but is known by faith (*non est nota ex terminis neque ratione naturali, sed est tantum credita*). The objection that God's universal immediate causality would destroy the proper causality of creatures cannot be solved by reason alone.[48]

As to the divine immensity and omnipresence, Scotus's denial of the demonstrability of this attribute of God depends on his denial of St. Thomas's rejection of *actio in distans*, action at a distance. According to St. Thomas[49] *actio in distans* is impossible, while for Scotus the greater the efficacy of the agent, the greater its power to act at a distance. 'Therefore, since God is the most perfect agent, it cannot be concluded concerning Him through the nature of action that He is together with (essentially present to) any effect caused by Him, but rather that He is distant.'[50] It is difficult to see what *actio in distans* could possibly mean in regard to God; but, as far as Scotus is concerned, he is not denying that God is omnipresent or that omnipresence is a necessary attribute of God, but only that God's omnipresence is philosophically demonstrable and, in particular, that the supposed impossibility of *actio in distans* is a valid reason for showing that God is omnipresent.

Probably 'truth' must be taken together with mercy and justice, as meaning in the context much the same as justice. At least, if this suggestion of commentators is not accepted, it is extremely difficult to see what Scotus did mean, since truth and veracity are listed among the divine attributes which are known by the natural reason.[51] As to justice, Scotus sometimes seems to say that the divine justice can be known by the natural light of reason;[52] but when he denies that the justice of God is philosophically demonstrable he appears to mean that it cannot be proved that God rewards and punishes in the next life, since it cannot be proved strictly by the philosopher that the soul is immortal,[53] or that we cannot justify by our reason all the ways of God in regard to man. That God is merciful, in the sense of forgiving sins and forgoing the exaction of punishment, cannot be philosophically demonstrated. Finally, as to divine providence, when Scotus says this cannot be philosophically proved, he appears to mean, not that no providence at all can be demonstrated, but that immediate or special providential action on the part of God, without the employment of secondary causes, cannot be philosophically demonstrated. Scotus certainly held that divine creation, conservation and government of the world can be demonstrated.

8. Scotus rejected the theories of St. Thomas and Henry of Ghent concerning the absence in God of any distinction other than the real distinction between the divine Persons and postulated a formal objective distinction between the divine attributes. The *ratio formalis* of wisdom, for example, is not identical with the *ratio formalis* of goodness. Now, 'infinity does not destroy the *ratio* of that to which it is added'.[54] If, therefore, the formal character of the univocal concept of wisdom is not the same as the formal character of the univocal concept of goodness, infinite wisdom will be formally distinct from infinite goodness. It follows, then, that the divine attributes of wisdom and goodness will be formally distinct, independently of the human mind's operation. On the other hand, there can be no composition in God, nor any real distinction in the technical sense between the divine attributes. The distinction between the divine attributes must be, therefore, not a real distinction, but a *distinctio formalis a parte rei*, and the formula will be that the attributes are really or substantially identical (*in re*), but formally distinct. 'So I allow that truth is identical with goodness *in re*, but not, however, that truth is formally goodness.'[55] Scotus contends that the distinction between the divine essence and the divine attributes and between the attributes themselves does not impair the divine simplicity, since the attributes are not accidents of God, nor do they inform God as finite accidents inform finite substances. As infinite they are really identical with the divine essence, and God can be called Truth or Wisdom or Goodness; but the fact remains that the *rationes formales* of truth, wisdom and goodness are formally and objectively distinct.[56]

9. It has been maintained in the past that the divine ideas depend, according to Scotus, on God's free will, so that the exemplar ideas are God's arbitrary creation. But as a matter of fact Scotus explicitly teaches that it is the divine intellect which produces the ideas: 'the divine intellect, precisely as

intellect, produces in God the *rationes ideales*, the ideal or intelligible natures'.[57] The divine essence, however, is the foundation of the ideas. 'God first knows His essence, and in the second instant He understands (*intelligit*) creatures by means of His essence, and then in that way the knowable object depends on the divine understanding in regard to its being known (*in esse cognito*), since it is constituted in its *esse cognito* by that understanding.'[58] The divine ideas do not, then, depend on the divine will. 'The divine intellect, as in some way, that is, logically prior to the act of the divine will, produces those objects in their intelligible being (*in esse intelligibili*), and so in respect of them it seems to be a merely natural cause, since God is not a free cause in respect of anything but that which presupposes in some way His will or an act of His will.'[59] Possibles are not produced by the divine omnipotence, but by the divine intellect, which produces them *in esse intelligibili*.[60]

The divine ideas are infinite in number, and they are substantially identical with the divine essence; but they are not formally identical with the divine essence:[61] they are necessary and eternal, but they are not formally necessary and eternal in precisely the same sense as the divine essence, since the divine essence has a certain logical priority. Again, 'although the divine essence was from eternity the exemplary cause of the stone in its intelligible being, yet by a certain order of priority the Persons were "produced" before the stone in its intelligible being . . . even though it is eternal.'[62] Logically speaking, the divine essence is imitable before the divine intellect apprehends it as imitable.[63] The ideas are participations or possible imitations of the divine essence, apprehended by the divine intellect, and it is because the divine essence is infinite, because it is imitable in an infinite number of ways, that the ideas are infinite, though the presence of the ideas does not compel God to create corresponding objects.[64]

10. Scotus did not teach that the divine will acts in a simply capricious and arbitrary manner, though this doctrine has been ascribed to him. 'Will in God is His essence really, perfectly and identically',[65] and the divine volition is one act in itself.[66] The divine will and the act of the divine will, which are one *in re*, cannot change, therefore, though it does not follow that what God wills eternally must necessarily exist eternally. 'The operation (of the will) is in eternity, and the

production of *esse existentiae* is in time.'[67] Logically speaking, even in God understanding precedes will, and God wills most rationally (*rationabilissime*). Although there is, ontologically, but one act of the divine will, we can distinguish the primary act by which God wills the end or *finis*, Himself, the secondary act by which He wills what is immediately ordered to the end, for example, by predestinating the elect, the third act by which He wills those things which are necessary to attain this end (e.g. grace), and the fourth act by which He wills more remote means, such as the sensible world.[68] But although the divine understanding logically precedes the divine volition, the divine will does not need direction as though it could err or choose something unsuitable, and *in this sense* the divine will is its own rule. Scotus sometimes states, indeed, that the divine will wills because it wills and that no reason can be given; but he makes his meaning clear enough. After citing Aristotle to the effect that it is the mark of an uneducated man to seek a demonstrative reason for everything, Scotus argues that it is not only ultimate priciples which cannot be demonstrated, but also contingent things, because contingent things do not follow from necessary principles. The idea of human nature in God is necessary; but why God willed human nature to be represented in this or that individual, at this or that time, is a question to which no answer can be given save that 'because He willed it to be, therefore it was good that it should be'.[69] Scotus's point is that contingent things cannot be deduced by necessary demonstrations, since they would be necessary, and not contingent, if they could be so deduced. If you ask, he says, why heat heats, the only answer is that heat is heat: so the only answer to the question why God willed a contingent thing is that He willed it.[70] Scotus is not denying that God acts for an end, Himself, that He acts 'most rationally'; but he wants to show the absurdity of seeking a necessary reason for what is not necessary. 'From a necessary (principle) there does not follow something contingent.'[71] The free choice of God is the ultimate reason of contingent things, and we cannot legitimately go behind God's free choice and seek a necessary reason determining that choice. God's intellect does not determine His creative work by necessary reasons, since creation is free, nor is He determined by the goodness of objects, since the objects do not yet exist: rather are they good because He wills them to be. That God can create only what is an imitation of His essence and that He cannot, therefore, create anything evil, is understood.

Scotus thus insisted on God's freedom of will in regard to His operations *ad extra*; but he also maintained that though God loves Himself necessarily and cannot not will and love Himself, that love is none the less free. This theory certainly seems rather singular. That God's will is free in regard to finite objects other than Himself follows from the infinity of the divine will, which can have as its necessary object only an infinite object, God Himself; but that God should love Himself necessarily and freely at the same time would certainly appear, at first sight at least, to involve a contradiction. Scotus's position is as follows. Liberty belongs to the perfection of volition, and it must be present formally in God. As volition directed to the final end is the most perfect kind of volition, it must include what belongs to the perfection of volition. It must, therefore, be free. On the other hand, the divine will, identical with God, cannot but will and love the final end, God Himself. The principle of reconciliation of the two seemingly contradictory propositions is that necessity in the supreme act of the will does not take away, but rather postulates, what belongs to the perfection of will. 'The intrinsic condition of the power itself whether absolutely or in order to a perfect act is not incompatible with perfection in operation. But liberty is an intrinsic condition of the will absolutely or in order to the act of willing. Therefore liberty is compatible with a perfect possible condition in operation, and such a condition is necessity, especially when it is possible.'[72] Scotus gives an example to show what he means. 'If someone voluntarily hurls himself over a precipice (*voluntarie se praecipitat*) and, while falling, always continues to will it, he falls indeed necessarily by the necessity of natural gravity, and yet he freely wills that fall. So God, although He necessarily lives by His natural life, and that with a necessity which excludes all liberty, wills none the less freely that He should live by that life. Therefore, we do not place the life of God under necessity (i.e. we do not attribute necessity to God's life) if we understand by "life" life as loved by God by free will.'[73] Scotus appears to mean, then, that we can distinguish in God the natural necessity by which He loves Himself and His free ratification, as it were, of that necessity, so that necessary love of Himself and free love of Himself are not incompatible. One may think that this distinction is not particularly helpful; but in any case it is clear that Scotus's voluntaristic and libertarian doctrine does not imply that God could refrain from willing Himself or that His love for Himself is arbitrary. The truth of the matter is that Scotus attached so much value to liberty as a perfection of will that he was reluctant to exclude it even from those acts of will which he was compelled to regard as necessary. This will be apparent when we come to consider his doctrine concerning the human will.

11. Scotus maintained that God's power to create out of nothing is demonstrable by the natural light of reason. God as first efficient cause must be able to produce some effect immediately, since otherwise He would not be able to produce effects even mediately (taking as proved that He is *first* efficient cause). 'Therefore it is clear to the natural intellect that God can cause in such a way that something should be from Him (i.e. should have its being from God) without any element of itself being presupposed or any receptive element in which it is received. It is clear, then, to the natural reason that, although the Philosopher (Aristotle) did not say so, something can be proved to be capable of being caused by God in this way.' 'And I say that Aristotle did not affirm that God creates something in this way; but it does not thereby follow that the contrary (i.e. of Aristotle's opinion) cannot be known by the natural reason. . . .'[74] Moreover, it can be proved that God can create out of nothing.[75] But the relationship involved by creation is not mutual: the relation of the creature to God is a real relation, whereas the relation of God to the creature is a mental relation only (*relatio rationis*), since God is not essentially Creator and cannot be called Creator in the same sense in which He is called wise or good. He is really Creator; but His relationship to the creature is not a real relation, since He is not Creator by essence, in which case He would create necessarily, nor on the other hand can He receive an accidental relation.

As to the question whether creation in time can be proved, Scotus inclined to the opinion of St. Thomas, though he did not accept St. Thomas's reasons, that creation in time cannot be proved philosophically. The logical priority of *nihil* can be proved, 'since otherwise creation could not be admitted'; but it is not necessary that logical priority should involve temporal priority. Scotus speaks, however, with hesitation. 'It does not seem to be necessary that *nihil* should precede the world temporally; but it seems sufficient if it precedes the world logically.'[76] In other words, Scotus rejected the opinion of St. Bonaventure that the impossibility of creation from eternity can be philosophically demonstrated, and he inclined to the opinion of St. Thomas that creation in time is also incapable of philosophic demonstration; but he speaks more hesitantly on the point than does St. Thomas.

Chapter Forty-nine

SCOTUS–V: THE SOUL

The specific form of man—Union of soul and body—Will and intellect—Soul's immortality not strictly demonstrated.

1. That the rational soul is the specific form of man can be philosophically proved,[1] and the opinion of Averroes that the intellect is a separate principle is unintelligible. 'All philosophers, generally speaking, have included "rational" in the definition of man as his special *differentia*, understanding by "rational" that the intellectual soul is an essential part of man.' No philosopher of note denies this, 'although that accursed Averroes in his fiction *On the Soul*, which, however, is intelligible neither to himself nor to anyone else, affirms that the intellect is a certain separate substance, which can be joined to us by means of the *phantasmata*; a union which neither he himself nor any disciple of his has hitherto been able to explain, nor has he been able by means of that union to preserve (the truth that) man understands. For according to him man would not be formally anything else but a kind of superior irrational animal, more excellent than other animals in virtue of his type of irrational, sensitive soul.'[2]

That the rational soul is the form of man Scotus proves by an enthymeme. 'Man understands (*intelligit*, apprehends intellectually) formally and properly; therefore the intellectual soul is the proper form of man.'[3] The antecedent, he says, seems to be clear enough through the authority of Aristotle; but in case anyone wantonly denies it, a rational proof must be given. To understand properly (*intelligere proprie*) means to understand by an act of knowledge which transcends every kind of sensitive knowledge, and that man understands in this sense can be proved as follows. To exercise intellectual activity in the proper sense is, as remarked, to exercise an activity transcending the power of sense. Now, sensitive apprehension is an organic function, since each of the senses has a determinate kind of object, the object of the special sense in question. Thus vision is determined to the perception of colour, hearing to that of sound. But the intellect is not determined in this way: its object is being, and it is not bound to a bodily organ in the sense in which sensation is bound. It can apprehend objects which are not immediately given to sensation, such as generic and specific relations. Intellectual cognition, therefore, transcends the powers of sense, and it follows that man can *intelligere proprie*.[4]

That the conclusion of the original enthymeme ('therefore the intellectual soul is the proper form of man') follows from the antecedent can be shown in two ways. Intellectual cognition, as a function of man, must be 'received' in something in man himself which is not extended and which is neither a part nor the whole of the corporeal organism. If it was received in something extended, it would be itself extended and a purely organic function, which it has been proved not to be. When Scotus talks about intellectual cognition being 'received', he means that it is not identical with our substance, since we are not always exercising the power of intellectual cognition; so it must be the act of some principle in us. But it cannot be the act of the material part of man: therefore it must be the act of a spiritual formal principle, and what can this be but the intellectual soul, the principle which has the power of exercising intellectual activity? Secondly, man is master of his voluntary acts, he is free, and his will is not determined to any one kind of appetible object. Therefore it transcends organic appetite, and its acts cannot be the acts of any material form. It follows that our free, voluntary acts are the acts of an intellectual form, and if our free acts are *our* acts, as they are, then the form of which they are the acts must be *our* form. The intellectual soul is, then, the form of man: it is his specific form, which differentiates man from the brutes.[5]

2. In man there is only one soul, though there is, as already mentioned, a form of corporeity. There are, as we also saw earlier, various 'formalities' in the one human soul, which, though not really distinct (separable) from one another, are distinct with a *distinctio formalis a parte rei*, since the intel-

lectual, sensitive and vegetative activities are formally and objectively distinct; but they are formalities of the one rational soul of man. This one rational soul is, therefore, not only the principle of man's rational cognition, but it is also the principle of his sensitive activity and of his life. It gives *esse vivum*, and it is the formal principle by which the organism is a living organism:[6] it is the substantial form of man.[7] The soul is, therefore, a part of man, and it is only improperly that it can be called subsistent, since it is part of a substance rather than a substance by itself; it is the composite being, soul and body, which is a *per se unum*.[8] The soul in the state of separation from the body is not, properly speaking, a person.[9] The soul perfects the body only when the latter is properly disposed for it, and *this* soul has an aptitude for *this* body. This means, says Scotus,[10] that the soul cannot be individuated by the matter it informs, since the soul, that is, a particular soul, is infused into a body, and the creation of that soul is logically prior to its union with the body.

Scotus differs also from St. Thomas in holding that the rational soul does not confer *esse simpliciter*, but rather *esse vivum* and *esse sensitivum*: there is, as already mentioned, a form of corporeity. If the rational soul were to confer *esse simpliciter* on man, man could not really be said to die. Death involves the corruption of the 'entity' of man, and this implies that both soul and body have a reality of their own, that the being of man as man is his being as a *compositum*, not his being as a soul. If the soul conferred *esse simpliciter* and there were no other form in the body, the separation of soul from body would not mean a corruption of the being of man as man. For death to take place, man must have a being as *compositum*, a being distinct from that of his component parts, taken separately or together, for it is this being of man as a *compositum* which is corrupted at death. Moreover, St. Thomas, according to Scotus, contradicts himself. 'Elsewhere he says that the state of the soul in the body is more perfect than its state outside the body, since it is a part of the *compositum*'; yet at the same time he asserts that the soul confers, and therefore possesses, *esse simpliciter*, and that it is not less perfect merely by the fact that it does not communicate that *esse* to any thing other than itself. 'According to you the soul possesses the same *esse* totally in a state of separation which it possessed when united with the body . . . therefore it is in no way more imperfect by the fact that it does not communicate that *esse* to the body.'[11]

The soul is united to the body for the perfection of the whole man, who consists of soul and body. According to St. Thomas,[12] the soul is united to the body for the good of the soul. The soul is naturally dependent on the senses for its cognition, the *conversio ad phantasma* being natural to it,[13] and therefore the soul is united to the body for the soul's good, in order that it may operate according to its nature. For Scotus, however, as we have already seen, the direction of the human intellect towards material things and its *de facto* dependence on the senses originate not so much in the nature of the human reason as such as in the present state of the soul, its condition in the body as wayfarer (with the alternative suggestion that sin may possibly be the responsible factor). St. Thomas would object that in this case its union with the body is for the good of the body, not of the soul, and that this is irrational, 'since matter is for the sake of form, and not conversely'. To such an objection Scotus's answer is that the soul is united to the body, not for the good of the body simply, but for the good of the composite being, man. It is man, the composite being, who is the term of the creative act, not soul taken by itself or body taken by itself, and the union of soul and body is effected in order that this composite being may be realised: the union exists, therefore, for the good of the whole man, *propter perfectionem totius*. The union of soul with body does not take place 'for the perfection of the body, nor for the perfection of the soul alone, but for the perfection of the whole which consists of these parts; and so although no perfection may accrue to this or that part which it would not have possessed without such a union, the union does not, however, take place in vain, since the perfection of the whole, which is principally intended by nature, could not be had except in that way.'[14]

3. Of Scotus's idea of human intellectual activity something has already been said in the chapter on knowledge; but a brief discussion must be given of his doctrine concerning the relation of will to intellect, as this has given rise to some misunderstanding concerning his general position.

The intellect is not, like the will, a free power. 'It is not in the power of the intellect to restrain its assent to the truths which it apprehends; for in so far as the truth of principles becomes clear to it from the terms or the truth of conclusions from principles, in so far must it give its assent on account of its lack of liberty.'[15] Thus if the truth of the proposition that the whole is greater than the part becomes clear to the intellect from the realisation of what a whole is and what a part is, or if the truth of the conclusion that Socrates is mortal becomes clear to the intellect from a consideration of the premisses that all men are mortal and that Socrates is a man, then the intellect is not free to withhold its consent to the proposition that the whole is greater than the part or the proposition that Socrates is mortal. The intellect is thus a *potentia naturalis*.

The will, however, is free, a *potentia libera*, and it is essentially free, its *ratio formalis* consisting more in its freedom than its character as appetite.[16] It is necessary to distinguish between will in the sense of a natural inclination and will as free, and it is only free will that is will in the proper sense; from which it follows that will is free of its very nature and that God could not, for example, create a rational will which would be *naturally* incapable of sinning.[17] By an elicited act of his free will, says Scotus, St. Paul willed 'to be dissolved and to be with Christ'; but this elicited act was contrary to his natural 'will', in the sense of natural inclination.[18] The two, therefore, are distinct, and this distinction is of importance when one considers man's desire of happiness or of his last end. The will as natural appetite or inclination to self-perfection necessarily desires happiness above all things, and since happiness or beatitude is, as a matter of concrete fact, to be found in God alone, there is in man a natural inclination to beatitude 'in particular', to God. But it does not follow that the will as free necessarily and perpetually desires the last end, nor that it necessarily elicits a conscious and deliberate act in regard to that object.[19] Scotus protests that he does not mean to imply that the will can choose misery *as such* or evil *as such*: 'I do not will beatitude' is not the same as 'I will the opposite of beatitude'; it means that I do not here and now elicit an act in its regard, not that I elicit a choice of its opposite, which cannot be an object of will. If I do elicit an act, however, that is, an act of willing beatitude, that act will be free, since every elicited act of the will is free.[20] Moreover, Scotus does not hesitate to draw the conclusion from his doctrine of the essential freedom of the will that the blessed in heaven will and love God freely.[21] He rejects, then, the doctrine of St. Thomas that when the *sum-*

mum bonum is clearly presented, the will chooses and loves it necessarily, and he even goes so far as to say that the blessed retain the power to sin. But when he says this, he does not mean to say any more than that the will as such remains free in heaven, since it is essentially free and heaven does not destroy its freedom: morally speaking, the blessed in heaven not only will not sin, but cannot sin, though this necessity is only *secundum quid*, proceeding from the 'habit of glory' (*habitus gloriae*) and the inclination produced in the will, not from a physical determination of the will.[22] The will of the blessed is thus morally impeccable, though not physically impeccable. Scotus does not differ from St. Thomas as to the actual fact that the blessed will not sin and he is willing to say that they cannot sin, provided that 'cannot' is not understood in a sense which would imply that the essence of the will is in any way impaired.[23]

The intellect, then, is a *potentia naturalis*, the will a *potentia libera*, and, given Scotus's insistence on liberty as a perfection, his position in the controversy regarding the primacy of intellect over will or of will over intellect cannot be in doubt. Knowledge certainly precedes every elicited act of the will, since the will cannot exercise choice in regard to an entirely unknown object (Scotus was no 'irrationalist'), and it is difficult, he says, though not impossible, for the will not to incline itself to what is finally dictated by the practical reason; but, on the other hand, the will can command the intellect. Scotus does not mean, of course, that the will can command the intellect to assent to propositions which are seen to be false: the will does not add anything to the act of understanding as such,[24] nor is it the cause of the intellect's act.[25] But the will can co-operate mediately, as an efficient cause, by moving the intellect to attend to this or that intelligible object, to consider this or that argument.[26] It follows that 'the will, by commanding the intellect, is a superior cause in respect of its act. But the intellect, if it is the cause of volition (that is, as a partial cause, by supplying the knowledge of the object) is a cause subservient to the will'.[27]

Scotus gives other reasons for affirming the primacy of the will. The will is more perfect than the intellect since the corruption of the will is worse than the corruption of the intellect; to hate God is worse than not to know God or not to think of God. Again, sin means willing something evil, whereas to think of something evil is not necessarily a sin: it is only a sin when the will gives some consent to or takes some pleasure in the evil thought of.[28] Again, love is a greater good than knowledge, and love resides in the will,[29] while it is the will which plays the principal part in final beatitude, uniting the soul with God, possessing and enjoying God. Though both powers, intellect and will, are involved in beatitude, the higher faculty, will, is the more immediate means of union with God.[30] Scotus thus rejected the Thomist doctrine of the primacy of the intellect and of the essence of beatitude and remained true to the tradition of the Augustinian-Franciscan School. It does not seem to be a matter of great moment, indeed, whether one adopts the Thomist or Scotist viewpoint, for both sides agree that beatitude, taken *extensive*, involves both powers; but it is necessary to explain Scotus's position, in order to show how foolish are accusations of irrationalism and of unmitigated voluntarism.

4. One might have expected, in view of Scotus's clear teaching, not only that the soul's intellectual activity transcends the powers of sense, but also that it can be proved philosophically to transcend the powers of sense and matter, that he would attempt to demonstrate the immortality of the human soul; but actually he did not believe that this truth can be strictly demonstrated in philosophy, and he criticised the proofs adduced by his predecessors. Of the three propositions, first that the rational soul is the specific form of man, secondly that the soul is immortal, and thirdly that the soul after death will not remain in a perpetual state of separation from the body (that is, that the body will rise again), the first is known by the natural light of reason, the error opposed to it, that of Averroes, being 'not only against the truth of theology, but also against the truth of philosophy' (that is, the Averroistic doctrine is not only against the truth as known by faith, but can also be philosophically refuted). 'But the other two (propositions) are not sufficiently known by the natural reason, although there are certain probable and persuasive arguments (*persuasiones probabiles*) for them. For the second, indeed, there are several more probable (arguments); hence the Philosopher seems to have held it *magis expresse*.' But for the third there are fewer reasons, and consequently the conclusion which follows from those reasons is not thereby sufficiently known through the natural reason.[31] Scotus's general position is, therefore, that we can prove philosophically that the rational soul is the specific form

of man; but that we cannot prove demonstratively in philosophy either that the soul is immortal or that the body will rise again. The philosophical arguments for the soul's immortality have greater weight than those for the resurrection of the body, but they are none the less only probable arguments, the *a priori* arguments, namely those based on the soul's nature, being better than the *a posteriori* arguments, for example, those based on the need for sanctions in a future life. The soul's immortality may be said to be morally provable, *ex inductione*, and it is certainly more probable, philosophically speaking, than its opposite; but the arguments adduced for it are not demonstrative and necessary arguments, enjoying absolute certainty.[32]

As regards the authority of Aristotle, Scotus declares that his opinion is not really clear. 'For he speaks in various ways in different places, and he had different principles, from some of which one opposite (one opinion) seems to follow, from others another. It is probable, then, that he was always doubtful about that conclusion, and at one time he would approach the one side, at another time the other, according as he was treating a matter which harmonised more with one side than with the other.'[33] In any case not all the assertions of the philosophers were proved by them by necessary reasons; but 'frequently they had only some probable persuasions (some probable and persuasive arguments) or the general opinion of preceding philosophers.'[34] The authority of Aristotle is, therefore, no certain argument for the soul's immortality.

As to the arguments adduced by St. Thomas and other Christian philosophers, these are not absolutely conclusive. In the *Summa Theologica*[35] St. Thomas argues that the human soul cannot be corrupted *per accidens*, in virtue of the corruption of the body, since it is a subsistent form, nor can it be corrupted *per se*, since *esse* belongs to a subsistent form in such a way that the natural corruption of the form would mean the separation of the form from itself. To this Scotus answers that St. Thomas is begging the question, since he presupposes that the soul of man is a *forma per se subsistens*, which is the very point which has to be proved. The proposition that the human soul is a form of this kind is accepted as an object of belief, but it is not known by natural reason.[36] If it be objected that this criticism is unfair, in view of the fact that St. Thomas has previously devoted an article (2) to showing that the human soul is an incorporeal and subsistent principle, Scotus retorts that though it can be shown that the rational soul in its intellectual activity does not use a corporeal organ and that its intellectual activity transcends the power of sense, it does not necessarily follow that the rational soul does not depend, as regards its being, on the whole *compositum*, which is certainly corruptible.[87] In other words, the fact that the human soul does not employ a corporeal organ in its purely intellectual activity does not necessarily prove that it is not naturally dependent for its existence on the continued existence of the *compositum*. It would have to be demonstrated that a form which transcends matter in a certain operation is necessarily independent in regard to existence, and this, according to Scotus, has not been conclusively proved.[88]

In regard to the argument drawn from the desire of beatitude, which involves immortality, Scotus observes that if by desire is meant a natural desire in the strict sense, one which is simply the inclination of nature to some thing, then it is clear that a natural desire for a thing cannot be proved, unless the latter's natural possibility has first been proved: to assert the existence of a natural inclination towards a state, the possibility of which is still unknown, is to be guilty of a *petitio principii*. If, however, by natural desire is meant a natural desire in a wider sense, that is, an elicited desire which is in accordance with a natural inclination, it cannot be shown that the elicited desire is natural in this sense until it has been proved that there is a natural desire in the strict sense. It may be said that an object which becomes the object of an elicited desire immediately it is apprehended must be the object of a natural desire or inclination; but in this case one might as well argue that because a vicious man is immediately inclined to desire the object of his vice when he apprehends it, he has a natural inclination or a natural desire for it, whereas in point of fact nature is not of itself vicious, and certainly not in everybody. It is no good saying that an object which, directly it is apprehended, is the object of an elicited desire according to right reason is the object of a natural desire, since the whole question is to discover whether the desire for immortality is or is not in accordance with right reason: this cannot legitimately be taken for granted. Furthermore, if it is said that man has a natural desire for immortality because he naturally flees from death, and that therefore immortality is at least a possibility, one might equally well argue that a brute has a natural desire for immortality and that it can and does survive.[39]

It may be as well to recall the fact that Scotus is not saying that the arguments for immortality are not probable or persuasive, still less that they are worthless: he is saying that they are not, in his opinion, demonstrative. The argument from desire does not conclude, because if one is speaking of the biological inclination to avoid death or what leads to death, brutes also possess this inclination, while if one is speaking of an elicited, conscious desire, one cannot legitimately argue from the desire of immortality to the fact of immortality unless one has first shown that immortality is a possibility, that the human soul can survive the disintegration of the *compositum*. It is all very well to say that the sufferings of this life demand a counterpoise in another life; but it remains true that man is exposed to suffering in this life, just as he is capable of pleasure and joy in this life, by the very fact of his nature, so that exposure to suffering is natural, and we cannot argue without more ado that suffering must be counterbalanced by other-worldly happiness. As to the argument that there must be sanctions in an after life, and that an after life therefore exists, the argument is not valid until you have shown that God does actually reward and punish people in this way, and Scotus did not think that this can be proved purely philosophically.[40] The best argument for the immortality of the human soul may be that drawn from the intellect's independence of a corporeal organ, from its spiritual activity; but although Scotus thought that this proof constituted a highly probable argument, he did not consider that it was an absolutely conclusive argument, since it might be that the soul, which is created as part of the *compositum*, cannot exist except as part of the *compositum*.

Chapter Fifty

SCOTUS—VI: ETHICS

Morality of human acts—Indifferent acts—The moral law and the will of God—Political authority.

My aim in this chapter is not to propound all the ethical doctrines of Scotus, but rather to show that the accusation which has been brought against him of teaching the purely arbitrary character of the moral law, as though it depended simply and solely on the divine will, is, in the main, an unjust accusation.

1. An act is naturally good (*naturaliter bonus*) when it possesses all that is required for its *esse naturale*, just as a body is beautiful when it possesses all those characteristics of size, colour, shape, etc., which befit the body itself and harmonise with one another. An act is morally good when it possesses all that is required, not by the nature of the act taken merely in itself, but by right reason (*recta ratio*). To enter the moral order at all an act must be free, for 'an act is neither praiseworthy nor blameworthy unless it proceeds from the free will'; but obviously this is required for both morally good and morally bad acts; something more than freedom is required for a morally good act and that is conformity with right reason.[1] 'To attribute moral goodness is to attribute conformity to right reason.'[2] Every morally good act must be objectively good, in the sense of having an object conformable to right reason; but no act is good on this count alone, save the love of God, which can in no circumstances be morally evil, just as no act is morally evil on account of its object alone, save hatred of God, which cannot be morally good in any circumstances.[3] It is impossible, for instance, to

love God with a bad intention, since there would then be no love, just as it is impossible to hate God with a good intention. In other cases, however, 'the goodness of the will does not depend on the object alone, but on all the other circumstances, and chiefly on the end' (*a fine*), which holds the primary place among the 'circumstances' of the act.[4] But though the end holds the primary place among the circumstances of the act, an act is not morally good merely because the end is good: the end does not justify the means. 'It is necessary that all the (requisite) circumstances should occur together in any moral act, for it to be morally good; the defect of any one circumstance is sufficient in order that (the act) should be morally bad':[5] 'evil things must not be done in order that good (results) may eventuate.'[6] For an act to be morally good, then, it must be free, and it must be objectively good and be done with the right intention, in the right way, and so on. If it possesses these circumstances, it will be in accordance with right reason.

2. Every human act, that is, every free act, is good or evil in some way, not only in the sense that every act, considered purely ontologically, i.e. as a positive entity, is good, but also in the sense that every act has an object which is either in accordance with right reason or contrary to it. But inasmuch as goodness of all the circumstances is required for a completely good moral act, it is possible, if some circumstance is deficient in the goodness it should have, for an act to be 'indifferent'. For example, in order for almsgiving to be a completely good moral act, to have full moral value, it must be done with a moral intention. Now, to give alms with a bad intention would make the act bad; but it is possible to give alms simply from an immediate inclination, for example, and such an act, says Scotus, can be called morally indifferent: it is neither a bad act nor is it a fully moral act.[7] In the admission of indifferent elicited acts (and Scotus insisted that he was not speaking of reflex acts like brushing away a fly from one's face)[8] Scotus adopted an opinion opposed to that of St. Thomas Aquinas; but in order to understand his opinion, it is important to realise that for Scotus 'the first practical principle is: God ought to be loved'.[9] A man is not obliged always to refer his act to God either actually or virtually, because, says Scotus, God has not laid us under this obligation, but unless this is done, the act will not be completely good morally. On the other hand, since we are

not obliged so to refer every act, it does not follow that an act which is not so referred is an evil act. If it is incompatible with the love of God, it will be evil; but it can be compatible with the love of God without being referred to God either actually or virtually. In this case it is an indifferent act. Apparently Scotus thought that 'habitual' reference is not sufficient to give an act full moral value.

3. We have seen that a morally good act must be in accordance with right reason. What, then, is the norm of right reason and of the morality of our actions? According to Scotus, 'the divine will is the cause of good, and so by the fact that He wills something it is good . . .'[10] This statement taken by itself naturally appears to imply that the moral law depends simply on the arbitrary will of God; but such was not Scotus's position, and he meant simply that what God wills is good because God of His very nature cannot will anything but what is good. Still, Scotus does make the moral law depend in one sense on the divine will, and his position must be made clear. Inasmuch as the divine intellect, considered as preceding an act of the divine will, perceives the acts which are in conformity with human nature, the eternal and immutable moral law is constituted in regard to its content; but it acquires obligatory force only through the free choice of the divine will. One can say, then, that it is not the content of the moral law which is due to the divine will, but the obligation of the moral law, its morally binding force. 'To command pertains only to the appetite or will.'[11] The intellect says that this is true or untrue, in the practical as in the speculative sphere, and though it inclines to action of a certain type, it does not dictate that one ought to act in that way. Scotus is not simply saying that obligation actually bears on human beings only because God has willed to create them, which would be obvious enough, since they could not be obliged if they did not exist; he is saying that the divine will is the fount of obligation. It seems to follow that if God had not chosen to impose obligation, morality would be a matter of self-perfection, in the sense that the intellect would perceive that a certain course of action is what befits human nature and would judge that it is reasonable and prudent to act in that way. One would have an ethic of the type represented by Aristotle's ethics. Actually, however, God has willed that course of action, and that will is reflected in

moral obligation: to transgress the law is thus not simply irrational, it is sin in the theological sense of the word.

That the content of the moral law is not due simply to the arbitrary caprice or choice of God is made abundantly clear by Scotus. Speaking of the sin of Adam,[12] he observes: 'A sin which is a sin only because it is forbidden, is less of a sin formally than that which is evil in itself and not because it is forbidden. Now to eat of that tree was not more a sin, as far as the act was concerned, than to eat of another tree, but only because it was forbidden. But all sins which concern the ten commandments are formally evil not merely because they are forbidden, but because they are evil; therefore they are forbidden, since by the law of nature the opposite of any commandment was evil, and by natural reason a man can see that any of those precepts is to be observed.' Here Scotus states clearly that the ten commandments are not simply arbitrary precepts and that a man can discern their validity through the natural use of reason, a statement which should involve the conclusion that God Himself could not change them, not because He is subject to them, as it were, but because they are ultimately founded on His nature.

The difficulty arises, however, that God seems to have dispensed in some of the secondary precepts of the decalogue (the precepts of the second table). For example, He told the Israelites to despoil the Egyptians, and He commissioned Abraham to sacrifice his son Isaac. Scotus, discussing this matter, asks first whether all the ten commandments belong to the law of nature, and he proceeds to make a distinction. Those moral laws which are self-evident or which follow necessarily from self-evident practical principles belong to the natural law in the strictest sense, and in the case of these principles and conclusions no dispensation is possible. God could not, for example, permit a man to have other gods than Himself or to take His name in vain, as such acts would be quite incompatible with man's end, the love of God as God, which necessarily involves exclusive worship and reverence. On the other hand, a moral law may belong to the law of nature, not as following necessarily from self-evident principles, but as being in accordance with the primary, necessary and self-evident practical principles; and of this type are the commandments of the second table. In the case of these moral commandments God can dispense.[13] Scotus proceeds to argue, or to suggest the argument,[14] that even if the love of the neighbour belongs to the natural law in the strict sense, so that I am necessarily bound to will that my neighbour should love God, it does not necessarily follow that I should will that he should have this or that particular good. This does not, however, prevent Scotus from going on to say[15] that the precepts of the decalogue are binding in every state and that before the giving of the written law all men were bound to observe them, 'because they were written interiorly in the heart, or perhaps by some external teaching given by God which parents learnt and handed on to their sons.' Moreover, he explains that the children of Israel did not really need any dispensation when they despoiled the Egyptians, since God, as supreme lord, transferred to the Israelites the goods of the Egyptians, so that the former did not take what was not their own. Nevertheless, Scotus's general position is that the first two commandments of the first table of the decalogue belong to the natural law in the strictest sense (about the third commandment, that concerning sabbath observance, he expresses doubt), whereas the precepts of the second table do not belong to the natural law in the strictest sense, though they do so belong in the wider sense. God can, then, dispense in the case of the precepts of the second table, though He cannot dispense in the case of commandments which belong strictly to the natural law. On this matter of dispensation Scotus's opinion is at variance with that of the Thomists, who do not allow that God can, properly speaking, dispense in the case of any of the precepts of the decalogue, since they all derive immediately or mediately from primary practical principles. The Thomists explain the apparent dispensations which troubled Scotus as instances of *mutatio materiae*, that is, in much the same way as Scotus himself explained the spoliation of the Egyptians by the Israelites.

There is no call to discuss such Scriptural passages here, as they do not enter into philosophy; but it should be observed that even if Scotus admits the possibility of dispensation in the case of some commandments, the fact that he refused to allow that possibility in regard to moral precepts which belong strictly to the natural law shows clearly that he did not regard the whole moral law as due simply to the arbitrary decision of the divine will. He may have thought that the inviolability of private property, and the consequent wrongness of stealing, were not so bound up with the natural law that no exceptions would be legitimate, even in 'hard cases'; but he certainly stated that if a moral precept belonged to the natural law in the strict sense, it was unalterable. It cannot be denied that Scotus makes remarks such as that the divine will is the first rule of rectitude and that 'whatever does not include a contradiction is not repugnant to the divine will absolutely speaking, so that whatever God does or may do will be right and just';[16] but he certainly did not think that God can, without contradiction, order or permit acts which are contrary to self-evident practical principles or principles necessarily following therefrom. Probably one should view in close connection Scotus's doctrine concerning moral obligation and that concerning the secondary precepts of the decalogue. The primary precepts are self-evident or are so intimately connected with self-evident principles that their obligatory character is obvious. The secondary precepts, however, are not immediately deducible from primary practical principles, even if their harmony with those principles and their immediate derivatives is evident. Their obligatory character is thus not self-evident or necessary, but depends on the divine will. Their content is not purely arbitrary, since their harmony and consonance with necessary principles is clear; but the connection is not so strict that God cannot make exceptions. If it is His will which so reinforces the natural harmony of the secondary precepts with necessary principles that the former become obligatory in the full moral sense, His will can also dispense.

It would seem, then, that Scotus occupies a position midway, if one may so put it, between St. Thomas and Ockham. He agrees with the former that there are moral principles which are unalterable and he does not teach that the entire moral law depends on the arbitrary decision of God's will. On the other hand he attributed a much greater degree of prominence to the divine will in the determination of the moral order than St. Thomas had done, and he appears to have held that obligation, at least in regard to certain commandments, depends on that will as distinct from the divine intellect. While, then, if we look at Scotus's philosophy by itself, we must allow that his moral doctrine is not that of arbitrary divine authoritarianism, we must also allow, if we look at the historical development of thought, that his moral doctrine helped to prepare the way for that of Ockham, in whose eyes the moral law, including the whole decalogue, is the arbitrary creation of the divine will.

4. As regards political authority, Scotus distinguishes it carefully from paternal authority,[17] and appears to suggest that it rests on free consent. 'Political authority . . . can be right by common consent and the choice of the community itself.'[18] Scotus speaks of people who see that they cannot get on without some authority and who agree together to commit the care of the community to one person or to a community of persons, and either to one man for himself alone, so that his successor would have to be elected, or to one man for himself and his posterity.[19] Elsewhere[20] he speaks of many independent peoples who, 'in order to attain a continual state of peace, were able by the mutual consent of all to elect from among them one prince . . .'

Legitimate authority is one of the factors which are required in the legislators, the other factor being 'prudence', the ability to legislate in accordance with right reason.[21] The legislator must not pass laws for his private advantage, but for the common good, which is the end of legislation.[22] Moreover, the positive human law must not be in conflict either with the natural moral law or with the divine positive law. No more than St. Thomas Aquinas would Scotus have had any sympathy with the idea of despotic government or with that of the State as the fount of morality.

Chapter Fifty-one

CONCLUDING REVIEW

Theology and philosophy—'Christian philosophy'—The Thomist synthesis—Various ways of regarding and interpreting mediaeval philosophy.

Any general review of mediaeval philosophy must obviously be left to the conclusion of the next volume; but it may be worth while to indicate here some general aspects of the course of philosophy treated of in the present book, even though the omission of Ockhamism, which will be considered in the third volume, restricts the scope of one's reflections.

1. One can regard the development of philosophy in the Christian world from the days of the Roman Empire up to the thirteenth-century syntheses from the point of view of its relation to theology. In the first centuries of the Christian era there was scarcely any philosophy in the modern sense, in the sense, that is, of an autonomous science distinct from theology. The Fathers were aware, of course, of the distinction between reason and faith, between scientific conclusions and the data of revelation; but to distinguish reason and faith is not necessarily the same as to make a clear distinction between philosophy and theology. Christian apologists and writers who were anxious to show the reasonable character of the Christian religion, employed reason to show that there is, for example, but one God, and to that extent they may be said to have developed philosophical themes; but their aim was apologetic, and not primarily philosophic. Even those writers who adopted a hostile attitude towards Greek philosophy had to employ reason for apologetic purposes and they gave their attention to themes which are considered to belong

to the province of philosophy; but though we can isolate those arguments and discussions which fall under the heading of philosophy, it would be idle to pretend that a Christian apologist of this kind was a professed philosopher; he may have borrowed from the philosophers to some extent, but he regarded 'philosophy' pretty well as a perverter of the truth and as a foe of Christianity. As to the Christian writers who adopted a predominantly favourable attitude to Greek philosophy, these tended to look on Greek philosophy as a preparation for Christian wisdom, the latter comprising not only the revealed mysteries of faith but all truth about the world and human life looked at through the eyes of a Christian. Inasmuch as the Fathers not only applied reason to the understanding, correct statement and defence of the data of revelation, but also treated of themes which had been considered by Greek philosophers, they helped not only to develop theology, but also to provide material for the construction of a philosophy which would be compatible with Christian theology; but they were theologians and exegetes, not philosophers in the strict sense, save occasionally and incidentally; and even when they did pursue philosophic themes, they were rounding out, as it were, the total Christian wisdom rather than constructing a distinct philosophy or branch of philosophy. This is true even of St. Augustine, for although one can reconstruct a philosophy from his writings, he was above all a theologian and was not concerned to build up a philosophical system as such.

Fathers of the Church, like St. Gregory of Nyssa and St. Augustine, who in their writings utilised elements borrowed from neo-Platonism, found in neo-Platonism material which helped them in their development of a 'philosophy' of the spiritual life, to which, as Christians and saints, they paid much attention. It was only natural that they should speak of the soul, of its relation to the body, and of its ascent to God, in terms strongly reminiscent of Platonism and neo-Platonism; but since they could not (and in any case would not wish to) consider the soul's ascent to God in abstraction from theology and revelation, their philosophy, which concentrated so much on the soul and its ascent to God, was inevitably intertwined with and integrated into their theology. To treat St. Augustine's doctrine of illumination, for example, as a purely philosophic doctrine is not easy; it really ought to be looked at in the light of his general doctrine concerning the soul's relation to God and its ascent to God.

The general attitude of the Fathers set the tone, so to speak, for what we call 'Augustinianism'. St. Anselm, for instance, was a theologian, but he saw that the existence of the God who revealed the mysteries of the Christian religion needs in some way to be proved, and so he developed a natural theology, or helped towards the development of natural theology, though it would be a mistake to picture him as sitting down to elaborate a system of philosophy as such. *Fides quaerens intellectum* may, to speak rather crudely, work forwards or backwards. Working forwards from the data of revelation and applying reasoning to theological dogmas, in order to understand them as far as is possible, it produces Scholastic theology; working backwards, in the sense of considering the presuppositions of revelation, it develops the proofs of God's existence. But the mind at work in either case is really the mind of the theologian, even though in the second case it works within the province and with the methods of philosophy.

If the spirit of Augustinianism, born of the writings of the Fathers, was that of *fides quaerens intellectum*, it might also be called a spirit of *homo quaerens Deum*. This aspect of Augustinianism is especially marked in St. Bonaventure, whose thought was steeped so deeply in the affective spirituality of Franciscanism. A man may contemplate creatures, the world without and the world within, and discern their natures; but his knowledge is of little worth unless he discerns in nature the *vestigium Dei* and in himself the *imago Dei*, unless he can detect the operation of God in his soul, an operation which is itself hidden but is rendered visible in its effects, in its power. A number of 'Augustinians' no doubt maintained the doctrine of illumination, for example, out of conservatism and a respect for tradition; but in the case of a man like St. Bonaventure the retention of the doctrine was something much more than traditionalism. It has been said that of two doctrines, of which one attributes more to God and the other less, the Augustinian chooses the one which attributes more to God and less to the creature; but this is true only in so far as the doctrine is felt to harmonise with and express spiritual experience and in so far as it harmonises with and can be integrated into the general theological outlook.

If one undertands the motto *fides quaerens intellectum* as expressing the spirit of Augustinianism and as indicating the place of philosophy in the mind of the Augustinian, it might be objected that such a description of Augustinianism is far too wide and that one might even have to class as Augustinians thinkers whom no one could reasonably call Augustinians. The passage from faith to 'understanding', to Scholastic theology on the one hand and to philosophy on the other hand, was ultimately the result of the fact that Christianity was given to the world as a revealed doctrine of salvation, not as a philosophy in the academic sense, nor even as a Scholastic philosophy. Christians believed first of all, and only afterwards, in the desire to defend, to explain and to understand what they believed, did they develop theology and, in subordination to theology, philosophy. In a sense this was the attitude not only of the early Christian writers and Fathers, but also of all those mediaeval thinkers who were primarily theologians. They believed first of all, and then they attempted to understand. This would be true of St. Thomas himself. But how could one call St. Thomas an Augustinian? Is it not better to confine the term 'Augustinian' to certain philosophical doctrines? Once one has done that, one has a means for distinguishing Augustinians from non-Augustinians: otherwise, one is involved in hopeless confusion.

There is a great deal of truth in this contention, and it must be admitted that in order to be able to discriminate between Augustinians and non-Augustinians in regard to the content of their philosophies, it is desirable to be clear first of all about what doctrines one is prepared to recognise as Augustinian and why; but I am speaking at present of the relation between theology and philosophy, and in regard to this point I maintain that, with an important qualification to be mentioned shortly, there is no essential difference in attitude between St. Augustine himself and the great theologian-philosophers of the thirteenth century. St. Thomas Aquinas certainly made a formal and methodological distinction between philosophy and theology, a distinction which was not clearly made by St. Gregory of Nyssa, St. Augustine, or St. Anselm; but the attitude of *fides quaerens intellectum* was none the less the attitude of St. Thomas. On this point, therefore, I should be willing to rank St. Thomas as an 'Augustinian'. In regard to doctrinal content one must adopt another criterion, it is true. St. Bonaventure too made a formal distinction between theology and philosophy, though he clung to and emphasised doctrines generally recognised as 'Augustinian', whereas St. Thomas rejected them, and in regard to these doctrines one can call the philosophy of Bonaventure 'Augustinian' and the philosophy of Thomas non-Augustinian. Again, St. Bonaventure, as we have seen, emphasised far more than St. Thomas the insufficiency of independent philosophy, so that it has even been said that the unity of Bonaventure's system must be sought on the theological and not on the philosophical level. All the same, St. Thomas himself did not believe that a purely independent philosophy would be, in actual fact and practice, completely satisfactory, and he, like St. Bonaventure, was primarily a theologian. There is a great deal to be said for M. Gilson's contention that for St. Thomas the sphere of philosophy is the sphere of *le révélable* (in the sense in which M. Gilson uses the term, and not, obviously enough, in every sense).

The 'important qualification' I mentioned above is this. Owing to the discovery of the complete Aristotle and his adoption by St. Thomas, so far as adoption was consistent with theological orthodoxy, St. Thomas provided the material for an independent philosophy. As I have suggested when treating of St. Thomas, the utilisation of the Aristotelian system helped philosophy to become self-conscious and to aspire after independence and autonomy. When philosophical material was comparatively scanty, as in the Patristic period and in the earlier centuries of the mediaeval era, there could be little question of an autonomous philosophy going its own way (it is not necessary to take the phenomenon of the *dialectici* very seriously); but once Aristotelianism, which appeared at least to be a complete philosophical system, elaborated independently of theology, had arrived on the scene and had won its right to be there, a parting of the ways was morally inevitable: philosophy had grown up, and would soon demand its birthright and wander out of the house. But this was by no means the intention of St. Thomas, who had meant to utilise Aristotelianism in the construction of a vast theologico-philosophical synthesis, in which theology should constitute the ultimate measuring-rod. Yet children, when they grow up, do not always behave exactly as their parents expected or wished. Bonaventure, Albert, Thomas utilised and incorporated an increasing amount of the new philosophical materials, and all the while they were rearing a child who would soon go his own way; but the three men, though differing from one another on many points of philosophical doctrine, were really at one in the ideal of a Christian synthesis. They belonged to the *Sancti*, not to the *philosophi*; and if one wishes to find a radical contrast between mediaeval thinkers in regard to their view of the relation between theology and philosophy, one should contrast not so much St. Anselm and St. Bonaventure on the one hand with St. Thomas on the other as St. Anselm, St. Bonaventure, St. Thomas and Scotus on the one hand with the Latin Averroists and, in the fourteenth century, the Ockhamist School on the other. The *philosophi* and radical Peripatetics stand over against the Fathers and theologians and *Sancti*.

2. What has already been said brings one to the question of 'Christian philosophy'. Can one speak of the 'Christian philosophy' of the Middle Ages, and if so, in what sense? If philosophy is a legitimate and autonomous province of human study and knowledge ('autonomous' in the sense that the philosopher has his own method and subject-matter), it would appear that it is not and cannot be 'Christian'. It would sound absurd to speak of 'Christian biology' or 'Christian mathematics': a biologist or a mathematician can be a Christian, but not his biology or his mathematics. Similarly, it might be said, a philosopher can be a Christian, but not his philosophy. His philosophy may be true and compatible with Christianity; but one does not call a scientific statement Christian simply because it is true and compatible with Christianity. Just as mathematics can be neither pagan nor Moslem nor Christian, though mathematicians can be pagans or Moslems or Christians, so philosophy can be neither pagan nor Moslem nor Christian, though philosophers can be pagans or Moslems or Christians. The relevant question about a scientific hypothesis is whether it is true or false, confirmed by observation and experiment or refuted, not whether it is proposed by a Christian or a Hindoo or an atheist; and the relevant question about a philosophic doctrine is whether it is true or false, more or less adequate as an explanation of the facts it is supposed to explain, not whether it is expounded by a believer in Zeus, a follower of Mahomet or a Christian theologian. The most that the phrase 'Christian philosophy' can legitimately mean is a philosophy compatible with Christianity; if it means more than that, one is speaking of a phi-

losophy which is not simply philosophy, but which is, partly at least, theology.

This is a reasonable and understandable point of view, and it certainly represents one aspect of St. Thomas's attitude towards philosophy, an aspect expressed in his formal distinction between theology and philosophy. The philosopher starts with creatures, the theologian with God; the philosopher's principles are those discerned by the natural light of reason, the theologian's are revealed; the philosopher treats of the natural order, the theologian primarily of the supernatural order. But if one adheres closely to this aspect of Thomism, one is placed in a somewhat difficult position. St. Bonaventure did not think that any satisfactory metaphysic can be achieved save in the light of the Faith. The philosophic doctrine of exemplary ideas, for example, is closely linked up with the theological doctrine of the Word. Is one to say, then, that St. Bonaventure had no philosophy properly speaking, or is one to sort out the theological elements from the philosophical elements? And if so, does not one run the risk of constructing a 'Bonaventurian philosophy' which St. Bonaventure himself would hardly have recognised as an adequate expression of his thought and intentions? Is it not perhaps simpler to allow that St. Bonaventure's idea of philosophy *was* that of a Christian philosophy, in the sense of a general Christian synthesis such as earlier Christian writers endeavoured to achieve? An historian is entitled to adopt this point of view. If one speaks simply as a philosopher who is convinced that philosophy either stands on its own feet or is not philosophy at all, one will not admit the existence of a 'Christian philosophy'; or, in other words, if one speaks simply as a 'Thomist', one will be forced to criticise any other and different conception of philosophy. But if one speaks as an historian, looking on from outside, as it were, one will recognise that there were two conceptions of philosophy, the one that of St. Bonaventure, the conception of a Christian philosophy, the other that of St. Thomas and Scotus, the conception of a philosophy which could not properly be called Christian, save in the sense that it was compatible with theology. From this point of view one can say that St. Bonaventure, even though he made a formal distinction between theology and philosophy, continued the tradition of the Fathers, whereas with St. Thomas philosophy received a charter. In this sense Thomism was 'modern' and looked forward to the future. As a system of self-sufficient philosophy Thomism can enter into competition and discussion with other philosophies, because it can prescind from dogmatic theology altogether, whereas a Christian philosophy of the Bonaventurian type can hardly do so. The true Bonaventurian could, of course, argue with modern philosophers on particular points, the proofs of God's existence, for example; but the total system could hardly enter the philosophical arena on equal terms, precisely because it is not simply a philosophical system but a Christian synthesis.

Yet is there not a sense in which the philosophies of St. Augustine and St. Bonaventure and St. Albert and St. Thomas can all be called Christian? The problems which they discussed were in large measure set by theology, or by the necessity of defending Christian truth. When Aristotle argued to the existence of an unmoved mover, he was answering a problem set by metaphysics (and by physics); but when St. Anselm and St. Bonaventure and St. Thomas proved God's existence, they were showing the rational foundation for the acceptance of a revelation in which they already believed. St. Bonaventure was concerned also to show God's immanent activity within the soul; and even though St. Thomas employed Aristotle's own argument, he was not answering simply an abstract problem nor was he interested simply in showing that there is an unmoved mover, an ultimate cause of motion; he was interested in proving the existence of God, a Being who meant a great deal more to St. Thomas than an unmoved mover. His arguments can naturally be considered in themselves and, from the philosophic standpoint, they must be so considered; but he approached the question from the viewpoint of a theologian, looking on the proof of God's existence as a *praeambulum fidei*. Moreover, although St. Thomas certainly spoke of philosophy or metaphysics as the science of being as being, and though his declaration that the rational knowledge of God is the highest part of philosophy, that to which other parts lead, can certainly be regarded as suggested by Aristotle's words, in his *Summae* (which are of the greatest importance from the philosophical, as well as from the theological standpoint) he follows the order suggested by theology, and his philosophy fits closely into his theology, making a synthesis. St. Thomas did not approach philosophical problems in the spirit of a professor of the Parisian faculty of arts; he approached them in the spirit of a Christian theologian. Moreover, in spite of his Aristotelianism and in spite of his repetition of Aristotelian statements, I think it can be maintained that for St. Thomas philosophy is not so much a study of being in general as a study of God, God's activity and God's effects, so far as the natural reason will take us; so that God is the centre of his philosophy as of his theology, the same God, though attained in different ways. I have suggested earlier on that St. Thomas's formal charter to philosophy meant that philosophy would in the end go her own way, and I think that this is true; but that is not to say that St. Thomas envisaged or desired the 'separation' of philosophy from theology. On the contrary, he attempted a great synthesis, and he attempted it as a Christian theologian who was also a philosopher; he would doubtless have considered that what would have appeared to him as the vagaries and errors of philosophers in later centuries were largely due to those very causes in view of which he declared revelation to be morally necessary.

3. More chapters have been devoted to the philosophy of St. Thomas Aquinas than to any other philosopher, and rightly so, since Thomism is unquestionably the most imposing and comprehensive synthesis considered in this book. I may have emphasised those aspects of Thomism which are of non-Aristotelian origin, and one should, I think, bear these aspects in mind, lest one forget that Thomism is a synthesis and not simply a literal adoption of Aristotelianism; but none the less Thomism *can*, of course, be regarded as the culminating process of a movement in the Christian West towards the adoption and utilisation of Greek philosophy as represented by Aristotle. Owing to the fact that philosophy in the time of the Fathers meant, to all intents and purposes, neo-Platonism, to utilise Greek philosophy meant, for the Fathers, to utilise neo-Platonism: St. Augustine, for instance, did not know much of the historic system of Aristotle, as distinct from neo-Platonism. Moreover, the spiritual character of neo-Platonism appealed to the mind of the Fathers. That the categories of neo-Platonism should continue to dominate Christian thought in the early Middle Ages was only natural, in view of the fact that the Fathers had utilised them and that they were consecrated through the prestige attaching to the writings of the Pseudo-Dionysius, believed to be St. Paul's convert. Furthermore, even when the *corpus* of Aristotle's writings had become available in Latin transla-

tions from the Greek and the Arabic, the differences between Aristotelianism proper and neo-Platonism proper were by no means clearly recognised: they could not be clearly recognised so long as the *Liber de causis* and the *Elementatio theologica* were ascribed to Aristotle, especially when the great Moslem commentators had themselves drawn copiously on neo-Platonism. That Aristotle had criticised Plato was, of course, perfectly clear from the *Metaphysics*; but the precise nature and scope of the criticism was not so clear. The adoption and utilisation of Aristotle did not mean, therefore, the negation and rejection of all neo-Platonism, and though St. Thomas recognised that the *Liber de causis* was not the work of Aristotle, one can regard his interpretation of Aristotle in a manner consonant with Christianity, not merely as an interpretation *in meliorem partem* (which it was, from the viewpoint of anyone who is both a Christian and an historian), but also as following from the general conception of Aristotle in his time. St. Bonaventure certainly thought that Aristotle's criticism of Plato involved a rejection of exemplarism (and in my opinion St. Bonaventure was quite right); but St. Thomas did not think so, and he interpreted Aristotle accordingly. One might be tempted to think that St. Thomas was simply whitewashing Aristotle; but one should not forget that 'Aristotle' for St. Thomas meant rather more than Aristotle means to the modern historian of Greek philosophy; he was, to a certain extent at least, an Aristotle seen through the eyes of commentators and philosophers who were themselves not pure Aristotelians. Even the radical Aristotelians by intention, the Latin Averroists, were not pure Aristotelians in the strict sense. If one adopts this point of view, one will find it easier to understand how Aristotle could appear to St. Thomas as 'the Philosopher', and one will realise that when St. Thomas baptised Aristotelianism he was not simply substituting Aristotelianism for neo-Platonism, but that he was completing that process of absorbing Greek philosophy which had begun in the early days of the Christian era. In a sense we can say that neo-Platonism, Augustinianism, Aristotelianism and the Moslem and Jewish philosophies came together and were fused in Thomism, not in the sense that selected elements were juxtaposed mechanically, but in the sense that a true fusion and synthesis was achieved under the regulating guidance of certain basic ideas. Thomism, in the fullest sense, is thus a synthesis of

Christian theology and Greek philosophy (Aristotelianism, united with other elements, or Aristotelianism, interpreted in the light of later philosophy) in which philosophy is regarded in the light of theology and theology itself is expressed, to a considerable extent, in categories borrowed from Greek philosophy, particularly from Aristotle.

I have asserted that Thomism is a synthesis of Christian theology and Greek philosophy, which might seem to imply that Thomism in the narrower sense, that is, as denoting simply the Thomist philosophy, is a synthesis of Greek philosophy and that it is nothing else but Greek philosophy. In the first place, it seems preferable to speak of Greek philosophy rather than of Aristotelianism, for the simple reason that St. Thomas's philosophy was a synthesis of Platonism (using the term in a wide sense, to include neo-Platonism) and of Aristotelianism, though one should not forget that the Moslem and Jewish philosophers were also important influences in the formation of his thought. In the first volume of my history I have argued that Plato and Aristotle should be regarded as complementary thinkers, in some respects at least, and that a synthesis is needed. St. Thomas Aquinas achieved this synthesis. We cannot speak of his philosophy, therefore, as simply Aristotelianism; it is rather a synthesis of Greek philosophy, harmonised with Christian theology. In the second place, Thomism is a real synthesis and is not a mere juxtaposition of heterogeneous elements. For example, St. Thomas did not take over the Platonic-Plotinian-Augustinian tradition of exemplary ideas and merely juxtapose it with the Aristotelian doctrine of substantial form: he gave each element its ontological status, making the substantial form subordinate to the exemplary idea, and explaining in what sense one is entitled to speak of 'ideas' in God. Again, if he adopted the (originally) Platonic notion of participation, he did not employ it in a manner which would conflict with the Aristotelian elements of his metaphysic. St. Thomas went beyond the Aristotelian hylomorphism and discerned in the real distinction between essence and existence a profounder application of the principle of potentiality and act. This distinction enabled him to use the Platonic notion of participation to explain finite being, while at the same time his view of God as *ipsum esse subsistens* rather than as mere unmoved mover enabled him to use the idea of participation in such a way as to throw into relief the idea of creation, which was to be found neither in Plato nor in Aristotle. Needless to say, St. Thomas did not take participation, in the full sense, as a premiss; the complete idea of participation could not be obtained until God's existence had been proved, but the material for the elaboration of that idea was provided by the real distinction between essence and existence.

4. Some of the viewpoints adopted in this book may appear to be somewhat inconsistent; but one must remember that it is possible to adopt different viewpoints in regard to the history of mediaeval philosophy, or indeed in regard to the history of philosophy in any epoch. Apart from the fact that one will naturally adopt a different viewpoint and interpret the development of philosophy in a different light according as one is a Thomist, a Scotist, a Kantian, an Hegelian, a Marxist or a Logical Positivist, it is possible even for the same man to discern different principles or modes of interpretation, none of which he would be willing to reject as totally illegitimate and yet for none of which he would be prepared to claim complete truth and adequacy.

Thus it is possible, and from certain viewpoints perfectly legitimate, to adopt the linear or progressive mode of interpretation. It is possible to view the absorption and utilisation of Greek philosophy by Christian thinkers as starting practically from zero in the early years of the Christian era, as increasing through the thought of the Fathers up to the Scholasticism of the early Middle Ages, as being suddenly, comparatively speaking, enriched through the translations from the Arabic and the Greek, and as developing through the thought of William of Auvergne, Alexander of Hales, St. Bonaventure and St. Albert the Great, until it reached its culmination in the Thomist synthesis. According to this line of interpretation it would be necessary to regard the philosophy of St. Bonaventure as a stage in the development of Thomism, and not as a parallel and heterogeneous philosophy. One would regard the achievement of St. Thomas, not so much as an adoption of Aristotle in place of Augustine or of neo-Platonic Platonism, but rather as a confluence and synthesis of the various currents of Greek philosophy, and of Islamic and Jewish philosophy, as well as of the original ideas contributed by Christian thinkers. Mediaeval philosophy before St. Thomas one would regard, not as 'Augustinianism' as opposed to Aristotelianism, but as pre-Thomist Scholasticism or as the Scholasticism of the earlier Middle Ages. This line of interpretation seems to me to be perfectly legitimate, and it has the very great advantage of not leading to a distorted idea of Thomism as pure Aristotelianism. It would even be possible and legitimate to look on Thomism as an Aristotelianised Platonism rather than as a Platonised Aristotelianism. What has been said of the 'synthetic' character of Thomism and of its relation to Greek, and Islamic, philosophy in general rather than to Aristotelianism in particular supports this line of interpretation, which was also suggested by what was said in the first volume of this history concerning the complementary character of the Platonic and Aristotelian philosophies.

On the other hand, if one follows this line of interpretation exclusively, one runs the risk of missing altogether the rich variety of mediaeval philosophy and the individuality of the different philosophers. The spirit of St. Bonaventure was not the same as that of Roger Bacon nor the same as that of St. Thomas, and French historians like M. Gilson have done us a great service in drawing attention to and throwing into relief the peculiar genius of individual thinkers. This 'individualisation' of mediaeval philosophers is all the more to be welcomed in view of the fact that the Christian thinkers shared a common theological background, so that their philosophical differences were expressed within a comparatively restricted field, with the result that mediaeval philosophy might seem to consist of a series of repetitions on salient points and a series of differences on relatively insignificant points. If one said simply that St. Bonaventure postulated a special illumination and that St. Thomas rejected it, the difference between them would not present so much interest as it does if St. Bonaventure's theory of illumination is linked up with his total thought and if St. Thomas's denial of any special illumination is seen against the background of his system in general. But one cannot depict the total thought of Bonaventure or the general system of Thomas without setting in relief the peculiar spirit of each thinker. It may very well be true that M. Gilson, as I suggested earlier in this book, has exaggerated the differences between St. Bonaventure and St. Thomas, and that it is possible to look on St. Bonaventure's philosophy as a stage in the evolution of Thomism rather than as a parallel and different philosophy; but it is also possible for different men to have different conceptions of what philosophy is, and if a man does not accept the

Thomist point of view, he will probably be no more inclined to look on Bonaventure as an incomplete Thomas than a Platonist would be inclined to look on Plato as an incomplete Aristotle. It is, I think, a mistake to insist so much on the linear type of interpretation that one rules out as illegitimate the type of interpretation represented by M. Gilson or, conversely, so to insist upon the individual characteristics and spirits of different thinkers as to lose sight of the general evolution of thought towards a complete synthesis. Narrowness of vision can hardly produce adequate understanding.

Again, while it is possible to view the development of mediaeval philosophy as a development towards the Thomist synthesis and to regard pre-Thomist philosophies as stages in that development, and while it is possible to concentrate more on the peculiarities of different philosophies and the individual geniuses of different thinkers, it is also possible to see and to throw into relief different general lines of development. Thus it is possible to distinguish different types of 'Augustinianism' instead of being content with one portmanteau word; to distinguish, for example, the typically Franciscan Augustinianism of St. Bonaventure from the Aristotelianised Augustinianism of Richard of Middleton or the Avicennian Augustinianism of Henry of Ghent and, in a certain measure, of Duns Scotus. It is possible to trace the respective influences on mediaeval thought of Avicenna, Averroes and Avicebron, and to attempt a corresponding classification. Hence phrases such as *augustinisme avicennisant*, *augustinisme avicebronisant*, *avicennisme latin*, of which French historians have made use. An investigation of such influences is certainly of value; but the classification produced by such an investigation cannot be regarded as a *complete* and entirely adequate classification of mediaeval philosophies, since insistence on the influence of the past tends to obscure original contributions, while it depends largely on what points of his philosophy one happens to have in mind whether one classes a philosopher as falling under the influence of Avicenna or Averroes or Avicebron.

Again, one can regard the development of mediaeval philosophy in regard to the relation of Christian thought to 'humanism', to Greek thought and culture and science in general. Thus if St. Peter Damian was a representative of the negative attitude towards humanism, St. Albert the Great and Roger Bacon represented a positive attitude, while

from the political point of view Thomism represents a har-
monisation of the natural and humanistic with the supernatural which is absent in the characteristic political theory
of Giles of Rome. St. Thomas, again, through the greater
part he attributes to human activity in knowledge and action
compared with some of his predecessors and contemporaries,
may be said to represent a humanistic tendency.

In fine, mediaeval philosophy can be considered under
several aspects, each of which has its own justification, and
it ought to be so considered if one is to attain anything like
an adequate view of it; but any more extensive treatment of
mediaeval philosophy in general must be reserved until the
conclusion of the next volume, when the philosophy of the
fourteenth century has been discussed. In the present volume
the great synthesis of St. Thomas naturally and rightly occupies the central position, though, as we have seen, mediaeval
philosophy and the philosophy of St. Thomas are not syn-
onymous. The thirteenth century was the century of speculative thought, and the century was exceptionally rich in speculative thinkers. It was the century of original thinkers, whose
thought had not yet become hardened into the dogmatic traditions of philosophical Schools. But though the great thinkers
of the thirteenth century differed from one another in their
philosophical doctrines and criticised one another, they did
so against a background of commonly accepted metaphysical
principles. One must distinguish criticism concerning the
application of accepted metaphysical principles from criticism
of the very foundations of metaphysical systems. The former
was practised by all the great speculative thinkers of the
Middle Ages; but the latter did not appear until the fourteenth century. I have concluded this volume with a consideration of Duns Scotus, who, from the chronological point
of view, stands at the juncture of the thirteenth and fourteenth centuries; but even if one can discern in his philosophy the faint beginnings of the more radical spirit of criticism
which was to characterise the Ockhamist movement of the
fourteenth century, his criticism of his contemporaries and
predecessors did not involve a denial of the metaphysical
principles commonly accepted in the thirteenth century.
Looking back on the Middle Ages, we may tend to see in the
system of Scotus a bridge between the two centuries, between
the age of St. Thomas and the age of Ockham; but Ockham
himself certainly did not see in Scotus a kindred spirit, and

I think that even if Scotus's philosophy did prepare the way for a more radical criticism his system must be regarded as the last of the great mediaeval speculative syntheses. It can hardly be denied, I think, that certain of Scotus's opinions in rational psychology, in natural theology and in ethics look forward, as it were, to the Ockhamist critique of metaphysics and the peculiar Ockhamist view of the nature of the moral law; but if one considers Scotus's philosophy in itself, without reference to a future which we know but he did not, we are forced to realise that it was just as much a metaphysical system as any of the great systems of the thirteenth century. It seemed to me, then, that Scotus's place was in this volume rather than in the next. In the next volume I hope to treat of fourteenth-century philosophy, of the philosophies of the Renaissance and of the revival of Scholasticism in the fifteenth and sixteenth centuries.

APPENDIX I

Honorific titles applied in the Middle Ages to philosophers treated of in this volume.

RHABANUS MAURUS:	Praeceptor Germaniae.
ABELARD:	Peripateticus Palatinus.
ALAN OF LILLE:	Doctor universalis.
AVERROES:	Commentator.
ALEXANDER OF HALES:	Doctor irrefragibilis.
ST. BONAVENTURE:	Doctor seraphicus.
ST. ALBERT THE GREAT:	Doctor universalis.
ST. THOMAS AQUINAS:	Doctor angelicus and Doctor communis.
ROGER BACON:	Doctor mirabilis.
RICHARD OF MIDDLETON:	Doctor solidus.
RAYMOND LULL:	Doctor illuminatus.
GILES OF ROME:	Doctor fundatissimus.
HENRY OF GHENT:	Doctor solemnis.
DUNS SCOTUS:	Doctor subtilis.

APPENDIX II

A SHORT BIBLIOGRAPHY

General Works on Mediaeval Philosophy

BRÉHIER, E. Histoire de la philosophie: tome 1, l'antiquité et le moyen âge. Paris, 1943.

CARLYLE, R. W. & A. J. A History of Mediaeval Political Theory in the West. 4 vols. London, 1903–22.

DEMPF, A. Die Ethik des Mittelalters. Munich, 1930.
  Metaphysik des Mittelalters. Munich, 1930.

DE WULF, M. Histoire de la philosophie médiévale. 3 vols. Louvain, 1934–47 (6th edition). English translation of first two vols. by E. C. Messenger, London, 1935–8 (3rd edition).

GEYER, B. Die patristische und scholastische Philosophie. Berlin, 1928. (This is the second volume of the revised edition of Ueberweg.)

GILSON, E. La philosophie au moyen âge. Paris, 1944 (2nd edition, revised and augmented). English translation, 1936.
  L'esprit de la philosophie médiévale. 2 vols. Paris, 1944 (2nd edition).
  Études de philosophie médiévale. Strasbourg, 1921.
  The Unity of Philosophical Experience. London, 1938.
  Reason and Revelation in the Middle Ages. New York, 1939.

GRABMANN, M. Die Philosophie des Mittelalters. Berlin, 1921.
  Mittelalterliches Geistesleben. 2 vols. Munich, 1926 and 1936.

GRUNWALD, G. Geschichte der Gottesbeweise im Mittelalter bis zum Ausgang der Hochscholastik. Münster, 1907.

(Beiträge zur Geschichte der Philosophie und Theologie des Mittelalters, 6, 3.)

HAURÉAU, B. Histoire de la philosophie scolastique. 3 vols. Paris, 1872–80.

HAWKINS, D. J. B. A Sketch of Mediaeval Philosophy. London, 1946.

LOTTIN, O. Psychologie et morale aux XIIe et XIIIe siècles. Tome 1: Problèmes de Psychologie. Louvain, 1942. Tome 2: Problèmes de Morale. 1948.
Le droit naturel chez S. Thomas d'Aquin et ses prédécesseurs. Bruges, 1931 (2nd edition).

PICAVET, F. Esquisse d'une histoire générale et comparée des philosophies médiévales. Paris, 1907 (2nd edition).
Essais sur l'histoire générale et comparée des théologies et des philosophies médiévales. Paris, 1913.

ROMEYER, B. La philosophie chrétienne jusqu'à Descartes. 3 vols. Paris, 1935–7.

RUGGIERO, G. DE. La filosofia del cristianesimo. 3 vols. Bari.

STÖCKL, A. Geschichte der Philosophie des Mittelalters. 3 vols. Mainz, 1864–6.

VIGNAUX, P. La pensée au moyen âge. Paris, 1938.

Chapter XXX: St. Albert the Great

Texts

Opera Omnia. A. Borgnet. 38 vols. Paris, 1890–9. (See also G. Meersseman. Introductio in opera omnia beati Alberti Magni, O.P. Bruges, 1931.)

De vegetalibus. C. Jessen. Berlin, 1867.

De animalibus. H. Stradler. Münster, 1916 (Beiträge, 15–16).

Studies

ARENDT, W. Die Staats- und Gesellschaftslehre Alberts des Grossen nach den Quellen daargestellt. Jena, 1929.

BALES, H. Albertus Magnus als Zoologe. Munich, 1928.

FRONOBER, H. Die Lehre von der Materie und Form nach Albert dem Grossen. Breslau, 1909.

GRABMANN, M. Der Einfluss Alberts des Grossen auf das mittelalterliche Geistesleben, in Mittelalterliches Geistesleben, vol. 2. Munich, 1936.

LIERTZ, R. Der selige Albert der Grosse als Naturforscher und Lehrer. Munich, 1931.

REILLY, G. C. Psychology of St. Albert the Great compared with that of St. Thomas. Washington, 1934.

SCHEEBEN, H. C. Albertus Magnus. Bonn, 1932.

SCHMIEDER, K. Alberts des Grossen Lehre von natürlichem Gotteswissen. Freiburg im/B., 1932.

SCHNEIDER, A. Die Psychologie Alberts des Grossen, Münster, 1903–6 (Beiträge, 4, 5–6).

Chapters XXXI–XLI: St. Thomas Aquinas

Texts

Opera omnia (Leonine edition). Rome, 1882. So far 15 vols. have been published.

Opera omnia (Parma edition). 25 vols. Parma, 1852–73. Reprint, New York, 1948.

Opera omnia (Vivès edition). 34 vols. Paris, 1872–80.

The English Dominican Fathers have published translations of the *Summa Theologica*, the *Summa contra Gentiles*, and the *Quaestiones disputatae*. London (B.O.W.) There is a volume of selections (in English) in the Everyman Library, London.

Basic Writings of St. Thomas Aquinas, edit. A. Pegis. 2 vols. New York, 1948.

Bibliography

BOURKE, V. J. Thomistic Bibliography, 1920–40. St. Louis, Mo., U.S.A., 1945.

GRABMANN, M. Die echten Schriften des heiligen Thomas von Aquin. Münster, 1920.

(2nd edition) Die Werke des heiligen Thomas von Aquin. Münster, 1931.

MANDONNET, P. Des écrits authentiques de St. Thomas. Fribourg (Switzerland), 1910 (2nd edition).

MANDONNET, P. and DESTREZ, J. Bibliographie thomiste. Paris, 1921.

Life

CHESTERTON, G. K. St. Thomas Aquinas. London, 1933, 1947.

DE BRUYNE, E. St. Thomas d'Aquin, Le milieu, l'homme, la vision du monde. Brussels, 1928.

GRABMANN, M. Das Seelenleben des heiligen Thomas von Aquin. Munich, 1924.

General Studies

D'ARCY, M. C. Thomas Aquinas. London, 1931.

DE BRUYNE, E. See above.

GILSON, E. Le Thomisme. Paris, 1944 (5th edition).
English translation, *The Philosophy of St. Thomas Aquinas*. Cambridge, 1924, 1930, 1937.

LATTEY, C. (editor). St. Thomas Aquinas. London, 1924. (Cambridge Summer School Papers.)

MANSER, G. M. Das Wesen des Thomismus. Fribourg (Switzerland), 1931.

MARITAIN, J. St. Thomas Aquinas. London, 1946 (3rd edition).

OLIGIATI, F. A Key to the Study of St. Thomas. Translated by J. S. Zybura. St. Louis (U.S.A.), 1925.

PEILLAUBE, E. Initiation à la philosophie de S. Thomas. Paris, 1926.

RIMAUD, J. Thomisme et méthode. Paris, 1925.

SERTILLANGES, A. D. Foundations of Thomistic philosophy. Translated by G. Anstruther. London, 1931.
S. Thomas d'Aquin. 2 vols. Paris, 1925. (4th edition).

VANN, G. Saint Thomas Aquinas. London, 1940.

Metaphysics

FINANCE, J. DE. Être et agir dans la philosophie de S. Thomas. Bibliothèque des Archives de philosophie. Paris, 1945.

FOREST, A. La structure métaphysique du concret selon S. Thomas d'Aquin. Paris, 1931.

GILSON, E. L'Être et l'essence. Paris, 1948.

GRABMANN, M. Doctrina S. Thomae de distinctione reali inter essentiam et esse ex documentis ineditis saeculi XIII illustrata. Rome, 1924. (Acta hebdomadae thomisticae.)

HABBEL, J. Die Analogie zwischen Gott und Welt nach Thomas von Aquin und Suarez. Fribourg (Switzerland), 1929.

MARC, A. L'idée de l'être chez S. Thomas et dans la scolastique postérieure. Paris, 1931. (Archives de philosophie, 10, 1.)

PIEPER, J. Die Wirklichkeit und das Gute nach Thomas von Aquin. Münster, 1934.

Régnon, T. de. La métaphysique des causes d'après S. Thomas et Albert le Grand. Paris, 1906.

Roland-Gosselin, M. D. Le 'De ente et essentia' de S. Thomas d'Aquin. Paris, 1926. (Bibliothèque thomiste, 8.)

Schulemann, G. Das Kausalprinzip in der Philosophie des heiligen Thomas von Aquin. Münster, 1915 (Beiträge, 13, 5).

Wébert, J. Essai de métaphysique thomiste. Paris, 1926.
And see General Studies.

Natural Theology

Garrigou-Lagrange, R. God: His Existence and His Nature. 2 vols. Translated by B. Rose. London, 1934–6.

Patterson, R. L. The Concept of God in the Philosophy of Aquinas. London, 1933.

Rolfes, E. Die Gottesbeweise bei Thomas von Aquin und Aristoteles. Limburg a.d. Lahn, 1927 (2nd edition).
And see General Studies.

Cosmology

Beemelmanns, F. Zeit und Ewigkeit nach Thomas von Aquin. Münster, 1914 (Beiträge, 17, 1).

Choisnard, P. Saint Thomas d'Aquin et l'influence des astres. Paris, 1926.

Cornoldi, G. M. The Physical System of St. Thomas. Translated by E. H. Dering. London, 1895.

Marling, J. M. The Order of Nature in the Philosophy of St. Thomas Aquinas. Washington, 1934.
And see General Studies.

Psychology

Lottin, O. Psychologie et morale aux XIIe et XIIIe siècles. Tome 1: Problèmes de Psychologie. Louvain, 1942.

Monahan, W. B. The Psychology of St. Thomas Aquinas. London, no date.

O'Mahony, L. E. The Desire of God in the Philosophy of St. Thomas Aquinas. London, 1929.

Pegis, A. C. St. Thomas and the Problem of the Soul in the Thirteenth Century. Toronto, 1934.
And see General Studies.

Knowledge

GRABMANN, M. Der göttliche Grund menschlicher Wahr-
heitserkenntnis nach Augustinus und Thomas von
Aquin. Cologne, 1924.

HUFNAGEL, A. Intuition und Erkenntnis nach Thomas von
Aquin. Cologne, 1924.

MARÉCHAL, J. Le point de départ de la métaphysique.
Cahier 5; Le thomisme devant la philosophie critique.
Louvain, 1926.

MEYER, H. Die Wissenschaftslehre des Thomas von Aquin.
Fulda, 1934.

NOEL, L. Notes d'épistémologie thomiste. Louvain, 1925.

PÉCHAIRE, J. Intellectus et Ratio selon S. Thomas d'Aquin.
Paris, 1936.

RAHNER, K. Geist in Welt. Zur Metaphysik der endlichen
Erkenntnis bei Thomas von Aquin. Innsbruck, 1939.

ROMEYER, B. S. Thomas et notre connaissance de l'esprit
humain. Paris, 1928 (Archives de philosophie, 6, 2).

ROUSSELOT, P. The Intellectualism of St. Thomas. Translated by Fr. James, O.S.F.C. London, 1935.

TONQUÉDEC, J. DE. Les principes de la philosophie thomiste. La critique de la connaissance. Paris, 1929 (Bibliothèque des Archives de philosophie).

VAN RIET, G. L'épistémologie thomiste. Louvain, 1946.

WILPERT, P. Das Problem der Wahrheitssicherung bei
Thomas von Aquin. Münster, 1931 (Beiträge, 30, 3).

Moral Theory

GILSON, E. S. Thomas d'Aquin. (Les moralistes chrétiens.)
Paris, 1941 (6th edition).

LEHU, L. La raison règle de la moralité d'après St. Thomas
d'Aquin. Paris, 1930.

LOTTIN, O. Le droit naturel chez S. Thomas et ses prédécesseurs. Bruges, 1926.

PIEPER, J. Die ontische Grundlage des Sittlichen nach
Thomas von Aquin. Münster, 1929.

ROUSSELOT, P. Pour l'histoire du problème de l'amour au
moyen âge. Münster, 1908 (Beiträge, 6, 6).

SERTILLANGES, A. D. La Philosophie Morale de S. Thomas
d'Aquin. Paris, 1942 (new edition).

Political Theory

DEMONGEOT, M. Le meilleur régime politique selon S. Thomas. Paris, 1928.

GRABMANN, M. Die Kulturphilosophie des heiligen Thomas von Aquin. Augsburg, 1925.

KURZ, E. Individuum und Gemeinschaft beim heiligen Thomas von Aquin. Freiburg im/B., 1932.

MICHEL, G. La notion thomiste du bien commun. Paris, 1932.

ROCCA, G. DELLA. La politica di S. Tommaso. Naples, 1934.

ROLAND-GOSSELIN, B. La doctrine politique de S. Thomas d'Aquin. Paris, 1928.

Aesthetic Theory

DE WULF, M. Études historiques sur l'esthétique de S. Thomas d'Aquin. Louvain, 1896.

DYROFF, A. Über die Entwicklung und den Wert der Aesthetik des Thomas von Aquino. Berlin, 1929 (Festgabe Ludwig Stern).

MARITAIN, J. Art and Scholasticism. London, 1930.

Controversies

EHRLE, F. Der Kampf um die Lehre des heiligen Thomas von Aquin in den ersten fünfzig Jahren nach seinem Tode. In *Zeitschrift für katholische Theologie*, 1913.

Chapter XLII: Latin Averroism: Siger of Brabant

Texts

BAEUMKER, C. Die Impossibilia des Siger von Brabant. Münster, 1898 (Beiträge, 2, 6).

BARSOTTI, R. Sigeri de Brabant. De aeternitate mundi. Münster, 1933 (Opuscula et Textus, 13).

DWYER, W. J. L'Opuscule de Siger de Brabant 'De Aeternitate Mundi'. Louvain, 1937.

GRABMANN, M. Die Opuscula De summo bono sive de vita philosophi und De sompniis des Boetius von Dacien. In *Mittelalterliches Geistesleben*, vol. 2. 1936.

Neuaufgefundene Werke des Siger von Brabant und Boetius von Dacien. (Proceedings of the Academy of Munich, Philosophy.) 1924.

MANDONNET, P. Siger de Brabant et l'averroïsme latin. (Les Philosophes Belges, 6.) Louvain, 1908, 1911.

STEGMÜLLER, F. Neugefundene Quaestionen des Sigers von Brabant. In *Recherches de théologie ancienne et médiévale*, 1931.

VAN STEENBERGHEN, F. Siger de Brabant d'après ses œuvres inédits. (Les Philosophes Belges, 12.) Louvain, 1931.

Studies

BAEUMKER, C. Zur Beurteilung Sigers von Brabant. In *Philosophisches Jahrbuch*, 1911.

MANDONNET, P. See above (Les Philosophes Belges, 6–7).

OTTAVIANO, C. S. Tommaso d'Aquino, Saggio contro la dottrina avveroistica dell'unita dell'intelletto. Lanciano, 1930.

SASSEN, F. Siger de Brabant et la double vérité. *Revue néoscolastique*, 1931.

VAN STEENBERGHEN, F. Les œuvres et la doctrine de Siger de Brabant. Brussels, 1938.

See above (Les Philosophes Belges, 12–13).

Aristote en Occident. Louvain, 1946.

Chapter XLIII: *Franciscan Thinkers*

1. *Bacon: Texts*

BREWER, J. S. Fratris Rogeri Baconi opera quaedam hactenus inedita. London, 1859.

BRIDGES, J. H. The Opus Maius of Roger Bacon, 2 vols. Oxford, 1897.

Supplementary volume. Oxford, 1900.

BURKE, R. B. The Opus Maius of Roger Bacon. 2 vols. (English). Philadelphia, 1928.

RASHDALL, H. Fratris Rogeri Baconi Compendium studii theologiae. Aberdeen, 1911.

STEELE, R. Opera hactenus inedita Rogeri Baconi. 16 fascicules so far published. Oxford, 1905–40.

Studies

BAEUMKER, C. Roger Bacons Naturphilosophie. Münster, 1916.

CARTON, R. La synthèse doctrinale de Roger Bacon. Paris, 1929.

L'expérience mystique de l'illumination intérieure chez Roger Bacon. Paris, 1924.

L'expérience physique chez Roger Bacon, contribution à l'étude de la méthode et de la science expérimentale au XIIIe siècle. Paris, 1924.

CHARLES, E. Roger Bacon, sa vie, ses ouvrages, ses doctrines. Paris, 1861.

LITTLE, A. G. Roger Bacon, Essays contributed by various writers. Oxford, 1914.

2. Matthew of Aquasparta: Texts

Quaestiones disputatae de fide et de cognitione. Quaracchi, 1903.

A. Daniels (Beiträge, 8, 1–2; Münster, 1909) gives extracts from the Commentary on the Sentences.

Studies

LONGPRÉ, E. Matthieu d'Aquasparte. Dictionnaire de théologie catholique, vol. 10. 1928.

3. Peter John Olivi: Texts

B. Jansen. Petri Johannis Olivi Quaestiones in 2 librum Sententiarum. 3 vols. Quaracchi, 1922–6.

Petri Joannis Provencalis Quodlibeta. Venice, 1509.

Studies

CALLAEY, F. Olieu ou Olivi. Dictionnaire de théologie catholique, vol. 11. 1931.

JANSEN, B. Die Erkenntnislehre Olivis. Berlin, 1931.

Die Unsterblichkeitsbeweise bei Olivi und ihre philosophiegeschichtliche Bedeutung. In Franziskanische Studien. 1922.

Quonam spectet definitio Concilii Viennensis de anima. In Gregorianum, 1920.

4. Roger Marston: Texts

Fratris Rogeri Marston, O.F.M., Quaestiones disputatae. Quaracchi, 1932.

Studies

BELMOND, S. La théorie de la connaissance d'après Roger Marston. In France franciscaine, 1934.

GILSON, E. Roger Marston, un cas d'augustinisme avicennisant. In *Archives d'histoire doctrinale et littéraire du
moyen âge*, 1932.

JARRAUX, L. Pierre Jean Olivi, sa vie, sa doctrine. In *Études
franciscaines*, 1933.

PELSTER, F. Roger Marston, ein englischer Vertreter des
Augustinismus. In *Scholastik*, 1928.

5. *Richard of Middleton: Texts*

Quodlibeta. Venice, 1509; Brescia, 1591.
Supra quatuor libros Sententiarum. 4 vols. Brescia, 1591.

Study

HOCEDEZ, E. Richard de Middleton, sa vie, ses œuvres, sa
doctrine. Paris, 1925.

6. *Raymond Lull: Texts*

Opera omnia, I. Salzinger. 8 vols. Mainz, 1721–42.
Obras de Ramón Lull. Palma, 1745.
O. Keicher (see below) has published the *Declaratio
Raymundi* in the Beiträge series.

Studies

BLANES, F. SUREDA. El beato Ramón Lull, su época, su
vida, sus obras, sus empresas. Madrid, 1934.

CARRERAS Y ARTAU, T. & J. Historia de la Filosofia Es-
pañola. Filosofia Christiana de los Siglos XIII al XIV.
Vols. 1 and 2. Madrid, 1939–43.

KEICHER, O. Raymundus Lullus und seine Stellung zur
arabischen Philosophie. Münster, 1909 (Beiträge, 7,
4–5).

LONGPRÉ, E. Lulle. In *Dictionnaire de théologie catholique*, vol. 9.

OTTAVIANO, C. L'ars compendiosa de Raymond Lulle.
Paris, 1930.

PEERS, E. A. Fool of Love; the Life of Ramon Lull. London, 1946.

PROBST, J. H. Caractère et origine des idées du bienheureux
Raymond Lulle. Toulouse, 1912.

La mystique de Raymond Lull et l'Art de Contemplation. Münster, 1914 (Beiträge, 13, 2–3).

Chapter XLIV: Giles of Rome and Henry of Ghent

1. Giles of Rome: Texts

Ancient editions. See Ueberweg-Geyer, Die patristische und scholastische Philosophie, pp. 532–3.

HOCEDEZ, E. Aegidii Romani Theoremata de esse et essentia, texte précedé d'une introduction historique et critique. Louvain, 1930.

KOCH, J. Giles of Rome; Errores Philosophorum. Critical Text with Notes and Introduction. Translated by J. O. Riedl. Milwaukee, 1944.

SCHOLZ, R. Aegidius Romanus, de ecclesiastica potestate. Weimar, 1929.

Studies

BRUNI, G. Egidio Romano e la sua polemica antitomista. In *Rivista di filosofia neoscolastica*, 1934.

HOCEDEZ, E. Gilles de Rome et saint Thomas, In *Mélanges Mandonnet*. Paris, 1930.

Gilles de Rome et Henri de Gand. In *Gregorianum*, 1927.

2. Henry of Ghent: Texts

Summa theologica. 2 vols. Paris, 1520; 3 vols. Ferrara, 1646.
Quodlibeta, 2 vols. Paris, 1518; Venice, 1608.

Studies

HOCEDEZ, E. Gilles de Rome et Henri de Gand. In *Gregorianum*, 1927.

PAULUS, J. Henri de Gand. Essai sur les tendances de sa métaphysique. Paris, 1938.

Chapters XLV–L: John Duns Scotus

Texts

WADDING, L. Opera Omnia. Lyons, 1639. 12 vols.

Opera Omnia (2nd edition). Paris (Vivès), 1891–5. 26 vols.

B. J. D. Scoti Commentaria Oxoniensia (on the first and second books of the *Sentences*). Quaracchi, 1912–14. 2 vols.

Tractatus de Primo Principio. Quaracchi, 1910.

MULLER, P. M., O.F.M. Tractatus de Primo Principio. Editionem curavit Marianius. Freiburg im/B., 1941.

The critical edition of Scotus's works is yet to come.
Cf. *Ratio criticae editionis operum omnium J. Duns Scoti Relatio a Commissione Scotistica exhibita Capitulo Generali Fratrum Minorum Assisii A.D.* 1939 *celebrato.* Rome, 1939.

For a summary of recent controversy and articles on the works of Scotus, as on his doctrine, cf.:

BETTONI, E., O.F.M. Vent'anni di Studi Scotisti (1920–40). Milan, 1943.

Studies

BELMOND, S., O.F.M. Essai de synthèse philosophique du Scotisme. Paris, Bureau de 'la France Franciscaine'. 1933.

Dieu. Existence et Cognoscibilité. Paris, 1913.

BETTONI, E., O.F.M. L'ascesa a Dio in Duns Scoto. Milan, 1943.

DE BASLY, D., O.F.M. Scotus Docens ou Duns Scot enseignant la philosophie, la théologie, la mystique. Paris, 'La France Franciscaine'. 1934.

GILSON, E. Avicenne et le point de départ de Duns Scot. Archives d'histoire doctrinale et littéraire du moyen âge, vol. 1, 1927.

Les seize premiers Theoremata et la pensée de Duns Scot. Archives d'histoire doctrinale et littéraire du moyen âge. 1937–8.

GRAJEWSKI, M. J., O.F.M. The Formal Distinction of Duns Scotus. Washington, 1944.

HARRIS, C. Duns Scotus. Oxford, 1927. 2 vols. (Makes copious use of the unauthentic De Rerum Principio.)

HEIDEGGER, M. Die Kategorien—und Bedeutungslehre des Duns Scotus. Tübingen, 1916.

KRAUS, J. Die Lehre des J. Duns Skotus von der Natura Communis. Fribourg (Switzerland), 1927.

LANDRY, B. Duns Scot. Paris, 1922.

LONGPRÉ, E., O.F.M. La philosophie du B. Duns Scot. Paris, 1924. (Contains a reply to Landry's work.)

MESSNER, R., O.F.M. Schauendes und begriffliches Erkennen nach Duns Skotus. Freiburg im/B., 1942.

MINGES, P., O.F.M. Der angeblich exzessive Realismus des Duns Skotus. 1908 (Beiträge, 8, 1).

J. Duns Scoti Doctrina Philosophica et Theologica quoad res praecipuas proposita et exposita. Quaracchi. 1930. 2 vols.

(Cites spurious writings; but a very useful work.)

PELSTER, F. Handschriftliches zu Skotus mit neuen Angaben über sein Leben. Franzisk. Studien, 1923.

ROHMER, J. La finalité morale chez les théologiens dès saint Augustin à Duns Scot. Paris, 1939.

NOTES

Chapter Thirty

1. *Liber 6, de Veget. et Plantis*, Tract. 1, c. 1.
2. Cf. *De Natura Locorum*, Tract. 1, cc. 6, 7, 8, 12.
3. *Liber 3, Meteorum*, Tract. 4, c. 11.
4. 1 *Summa Theol.*, 1, 4, *ad* 2 *et* 3.
5. *Comm. in Epist.* 9 *B. Dion. Areop.*, 7, 2.
6. *Lib.* 1, *de causis et proc. universitatis*, 1, 7.   7. *Ibid.*, 1, 8.
8. *Ibid.*, 3, 6.   9. *Comm. in Epist.* 9 *B. Dion. Areop.*, 1.
10. *Lib.* 1, *de causis et proc. universitatis*, 4, 1.
11. *In Phys.*, 8, 1, 13.
12. *Liber de natura et origine animae*, 2, 6; cf. also *De Anima*, 3.
13. C. 3.   14. C. 7.   15. *Summa de bono*, 4, 3, 9.

Chapter Thirty-one

1. The supplement to the Commentary on the *Meteorologica* seems to have been completed by an anonymous writer, drawing on Peter of Auvergne.
2. Recent research, however, tends to show that there was more development in St. Thomas's thought than is sometimes supposed.
3. *Le Thomisme*, 5th edition, Paris, 1944.
4. *Contra Gent.*, 3, 25.   5. *Ibid.*, 1, 5.

Chapter Thirty-two

1. *S.T.*, Ia, 1, 1, *ad* 2.   2. *Contra Gent.*, 1, 4.
3. Cf. *S.T.*, Ia, 1, 1; *Contra Gent.*, 1, 4.   4. 14, 9.
5. *S.T.*, Ia, 2, 2, *ad* 1; *De Verit.*, 14, 9, *ad* 9.
6. *S.T.*, Ia, 2, 2, *ad* 1.   7. *Contra Gent.*, 1, 4.   8. 14, 3.
9. Cf. *In Boethium de Trinitate*, 6, 4, 5; *In* 1 *Sent.*, prol., 1, 1; *De Veritate*, 14, 2; *S.T.*, Ia, IIae, 5, 5.   10. 3, 27 ff.
11. *In* 2 *Sent.*, 29, 1, 2; *ibid.*, 29, 2, 3; *S.T.*, Ia, 95, 1, 4; *Quodlibet*, 1, 8.   12. *De Gratia, Prolegom.*, 4, c. 1, n. 2.
13. *In* 4 *Sent.*, 49, 2, 1; p. 903, 1613 edit.
14. *In Summam Sancti Thomae*, Ia, 1, 1, t. 1, pp. 17–19, 1869 edit.

15. *Contra Gent.*, 1, 4.   16. *Ibid.*
17. *S.T.*, Ia, 1, 1, *in corpore.*

Chapter Thirty-three

1. *In 7 Metaph., lectio* 2.   2. *S.T.*, Ia, 66, 1, *in corpore.*
3. *In 2 Sent.*, 18, 1, 2.
4. St. Thomas certainly employed the name, *rationes seminales*, but he meant thereby primarily the active forces of concrete objects, e.g. the active power which controls the generation of living things and restricts it to the same species, not the doctrine that there are inchoate forms in prime matter. This last theory he either rejected or said that it did not fit in with the teaching of St. Augustine (cf. *loc. cit., S.T.*, Ia, 115, 2; *De Veritate*, 5, 9, *ad* 8 and *ad* 9).   5. Cf. *In* 1 *Sent.*, 8, 5, 2; 2 *Sent.*, 3, 1, 1.
6. 4, 81.   7. *Quodlibet*, 11, 5, 5, *in corpore.*
8. Cf. *De spirit. creat.*, 1, 5.
9. *S.T.*, Ia, 50, 2; *De spirit. creat.*, 1, 1.
10. *De spirit. creat.*, 1, 1; *S.T.*, Ia, 50, 2, *ad* 3; *Contra Gent.*, 2, 30; *Quodlibet*, 9, 4, 1.   11. *Contra Gent.*, 2, 54.   12. *Ibid.*
13. *Ibid.*, 1, 22.   14. Cf. *S.T.*, Ia, 3, 4; *Contra Gent.*, 1, 22.
15. *De Potentia*, 7, 2, *ad* 9.   16. *C.* 4.
17. *De Potentia*, 7, 2, *ad* 9.

Chapter Thirty-four

1. Ia, 2, 1.   2. 1, 10–11.   3. *De fide orthodoxa*, 1, 3.
4. It may appear that St. Thomas's attitude in regard to 'innate' knowledge of God does not differ substantially from that of St. Bonaventure. In a sense this is true, since neither of them admitted an explicit innate idea of God; but St. Bonaventure thought that there is a kind of initial implicit awareness of God, or at least that the idea of God can be rendered explicit by interior reflection alone, whereas the proofs actually given by St. Thomas all proceed by way of the external world. Even if we press the 'Aristotelian' aspect of Bonaventure's epistemology, it remains true that there is a difference of emphasis and approach in the natural theology of the two philosophers.
5. See Ch. XXXVIII.   6. See Ch. XXXV.
7. *Metaph.*, Bk. 12; *Physics*, Bk. 8.   8. *S.T.*, Ia, 2, 3, *in corpore.*
9. *Ibid.*   10. 1, 13.   11. *C.* 2.   12. 2, 1; 4, 4.
13. Ch. 13.   14. Ch. 1.

Chapter Thirty-five

1. 1, 14.   2. *Contra Gent.*, 1, 14.
3. *S.T.*, Ia, 12, 12, *in corpore.*   4. *Ibid.*

5. S.T., Ia, 13, 2, in corpore.   6. Contra Gent., 1, 30.
7. S.T., Ia, 13, 2.   8. Contra Gent., 1, 34; S.T., Ia, 13, 5.
9. 2, 11, in corpore.   10. In 4 Sent., 49, 2, 1, ad 6.
11. Cf. S.T., Ia, 13, 5, in corpore.   12. Cf. ibid., Ia, 14, 13.
13. Cf. Ch. XXXVIII, sect. 4.   14. S.T., Ia, 15, 1.
15. Cf. ibid., Ia, 15, 1–3; Contra Gent., 1, 53–4.
16. Contra Gent., 1, 31.
17. Cf. S.T., Ia, 13, 12, in corpore and ad 3.
18. S.T., Ia, 13, 11; Contra Gent., 1, 22.   19. Exodus 3. 14.

Chapter Thirty-six

1. On the sense of creatio ex nihilo, cf. De Potentia, 3, 1, ad 7; S.T., Ia, 45, 1, ad 3.
2. Contra Gent., 2, 11–13; S.T., Ia, 45, 3; De Potentia, 3, 3.
3. Cf. De Potentia, 3, 4.   4. S.T., Ia, 44, 4.
5. Cf. ibid., Ia, 65, 2.   6. Vol. II, Pt. I, pp. 292–3.
7. De Potentia, 3, 17.
8. On this subject see Contra Gent., 2, 31–7; S.T., Ia, 46, 1; De Potentia, 3, 17; De aeternitate mundi contra murmurantes.
9. 2, 10.   10. Ia, 7, 4; 1, 46, ad 8.
11. Cf. S.T., Ia, 25, 3–4; De Potentia, 1, 7.
12. Cf. Contra Gent., 1, 84.
13. Cf. S.T., Ia, 19, 3; 1, 25, 5; Contra Gent., 2, 26–7; De Potentia, 1, 5.   14. S.T., Ia, 25, 6.   15. Cf. ibid., Ia, 48, 1–3.
16. On the subject of evil and its relation to God see, for example, S.T., Ia, 19, 9; Ia, 48–9; Contra Gent., 3, 4–5; De Malo, questions 1–3; De Potentia, 1, 6.

Chapter Thirty-seven

1. Ch. XXXIII.   2. Cf. In 1 Sent., 8, 5, 2; In 2 Sent., 3, 1, 1.
3. S.T., Ia, 76, 1.   4. Ibid., Ia, 76, 4.
5. Cf. ibid., Ia, 76, 5; Ia, 89, 1.
6. Ibid., Ia, 77, 1–3; De Anima, 1, lectio 2.   7. S.T., Ia, 78, 4.
8. Ibid., Ia, 83, 1.   9. Ibid., Ia, IIae, 13, 6.
10. De Veritate, 24, 4 and 6.   11. Ibid., 24, 6.
12. De Veritate, 22, 11; cf. S.T., Ia, 82, 3.
13. S.T., Ia, 75, 6; Contra Gent., 2, 79.   14. S.T., Ia, 75, 2.
15. Contra Gent., 2, 49.   16. S.T., Ia, 75, 6.
17. Contra Gent., 2, 79.   18. Opus Oxon., 4, 43, 2, nos. 29 ff.
19. S.T., Ia, 89, 1 ff.   20. Ibid., Ia, 76, 2.   21. 2, 76.
22. Ia, 79, 4–5.   23. 3, 5; 430 a. 17 ff.
24. On Aristotle, see Summa contra Gentiles, 2, 78, and the Commentary on the De Anima, 3, lectio 10.   25. 2, 73–5.

Chapter Thirty-eight

1. *S.T.*, Ia, 5, 2.   2. *Ibid.*, Ia, 86, 1.   3. *Ibid.*, Ia, 85, 1.
4. *Ibid.*, Ia, 86, 1, *ad* 3.   5. *Ibid.*, Ia, 87, 1.
6. *Ibid.*, Ia, 84, 7.   7. *Ibid.*   8. *Ibid.*, Ia, 88, 1.
9. *Ibid.*, Ia, 84, 7, *ad* 3.   10. *Ibid.*, Ia, 79, 7.
11. *Ibid.*, Ia, 5, 2.   12. *Ibid.*, Ia, 84, 7 *ad* 3.
13. *Ibid.*, Ia, 84, 6, *in corpore* and *ad* 3.
14. Cf. *ibid.*, Ia, 84, 7, *in corpore* and *ad* 3.

Chapter Thirty-nine

1. For a fuller treatment of the Aristotelian ethic, see the first volume of this history, Vol. I, Pt. II, pp. 51–2.
2. On the foregoing, see particularly *S.T.*, Ia, IIae, questions 1–3.
3. See *S.T.*, Ia, IIae, 4.
4. This is true of St. Thomas's moral teaching in the *Summae*. I do not mean to imply that St. Thomas rejected the possibility of a purely philosophical ethic.   5. *S.T.*, Ia, IIae, 3, 8.
6. *Ibid.*, 4, 4.   7. *Ibid.*, 3, 8.   8. *Ibid.*, Ia, IIae, 5, 4.
9. *Ibid.*   10. 3, 25.   11. 3, 18.   12. 3, 39.
13. 3, 40.   14. 3, 51.   15. 3, 52.   16. 3, 52–4.
17. 3, 51.   18. 3, 47–8.   19. 3, 52.   20. 27, 2.
21. Cf. *De Veritate, loc. cit.*, and cf. also *De Malo*, 5, 1, 15.
22. On the question of the 'natural desire' for the vision of God, cf. the summary and discussion of the opinions by A. Motte in the *Bulletin Thomiste*, 1931 (nos. 651–76) and 1934 (nos. 573–90).
23. *S.T.*, Ia, IIae, 18, 9.   24. *Ibid.*, Ia, IIae, 55 ff.
25. *Ibid.*, Ia, IIae, 58, 4–5.   26. *Ibid.*, Ia, IIae, 64, 1.
27. *Ibid.*, Ia, IIae, 90, 1.   28. *Ibid.*, Ia, IIae, 94, 2.
29. Cf. *ibid.*, IIa, IIae, 152, 2.   30. *Ibid.*, Ia, IIae, 94, 5.
31. *Ibid.*, Ia, IIae, 95, 6; 99, 2, *ad* 2.
32. *Ibid.*, Ia, IIae, 9, 1; 93, 1 ff.   33. *Ibid.*, Ia, IIae, 91, 4.
34. On the virtue of religion, cf. *S.T.*, IIa, IIae, 81, 1–8.
35. *S.T.*, Ia, IIae, 80, *articulus unicus*.

Chapter Forty

1. This at least was the view which Aristotle took over and which he can hardly be said to have repudiated expressly, though it is true that the individualistic ideal of theoretic contemplation tended to break through the ideal of the City-state's self-sufficiency.   2. 1, 1.   3. *S.T.*, Ia, 96, 4.
4. Cf. *ibid.*, Ia, IIae, 90, 2.   5. Cf. *De regimine principum*, 1, 15.
6. Dante was actually more concerned to uphold the authority of the Emperor against that of the Pope and was somewhat behind the times in his imperial dreams; but he carefully adhered to the two spheres theory.   7. 1, 14.   8. Romans 6. 23.

9. *De regimine principum*, 1, 15.
10. St. Thomas is, of course, addressing a Christian prince.
11. Ia, IIae, 90, 2. 12. *S.T.*, IIa, IIae, 65, 1.
13. 3 *Ethic.*, *lect.* 4.
14. *S.T.*, IIa, IIae, 47, 10, *in corpore* and *ad* 2.
15. *Ibid.*, Ia, IIae, 91, 5. 16. *Ibid.*, 3. 17. *Ibid.*, 95, 1.
18. *Ibid.*, Ia, IIae, 95, 2. 19. Cf. *ibid.*, Ia, IIae, 96, 4.
20. Cf. *ibid.*, Ia, IIae, 90, 3.
21. Though apparently referring to elected government.
22. *S.T.*, Ia, IIae, 97, 3, *ad* 3. 23. *De regimine principum*, 1, 6.
24. *S.T.*, Ia, IIae, 105, 1. 25. *De regimine principum*, 1, 2.
26. *S.T.*, Ia, IIae, 90, 4. 27. *Ibid.*, IIa, IIae, 58, 6.
28. *Ibid.*, Ia, 5, 4, *ad* 1. 29. *Ibid.* 30. *Ibid.*, Ia, 39, 8.

Chapter Forty-one

1. The answer can only be that it is *conveniens*, but not a strict debt, since it cannot be realised by natural means. We would then seem to be faced by the dilemma, that either the soul after death would, apart from God's intervention, remain in an 'unnatural' condition or that the doctrine of the soul's union with the body must be revised. 2. *In 12 Metaph.*, *lect.* 11.
3. Cf. the first volume of this history, Vol. I, Pt. II, pp. 56–7.
4. *S.T.*, IIIa, 50, 5.

Chapter Forty-two

1. Cf. P. Mandonnet: *Siger de Brabant*, second edit., 1911; B. Nardi: *Sigieri di Brabante nella Divina Commedia* and *le fonti della filosofia di Dante*, 1912; F. Van Steenberghen: *Les œuvres et la doctrine de Siger de Brabant*, 1938; E. Gilson: *Dante et la philosophie*, 1939 (English translation, 1948).

Chapter Forty-three

1. I refer, of course, to experimental science.
2. *Roger Bacon: The Philosophy of Science in the Middle Ages*, p. 7.
3. J. H. Bridges: Introduction to *Opus Maius*, pp. xci–xcii.
4. *Opus Tertium*, c. 25.
5. *Opus Minus*, edit. J. S. Brewer, p. 326. 6. *Ibid.*, p. 322 ff.
7. *Compendium philosophiae*, p. 469.
8. Peter's name of *Peregrinus* seems to be due to the fact that he went on a crusade. 9. *Opus Tertium*, c. 13.
10. Obviously this doctrine is not Averroistic. The latter's monopsychism Bacon condemned as error and heresy.
11. *Q. Disp. de cognitione*, p. 291 and p. 280. 12. *Ibid.*, p. 254.

13. p. 307.   14. *De cognitione*, p. 311.   15. *Ibid.*, p. 328.
16. *Ibid.*, p. 329.   17. *Ibid.*
18. The doctrines of the soul's intuition of itself and of the intel-
    lectual knowledge of the singular thing appear also in the teach-
    ing of the Franciscan *Vital du Four* (d. 1327).
19. In support of Olivi's thesis the reason was given that if the in-
    tellectual form informed the body directly, it would either give
    its own immortality to the body or lose its own immortality
    through informing the body.   20. *De Anima*, p. 259.
21. *Ibid.*, p. 263.   22. *Ibid.*, p. 262.   23. *Ibid.*, p. 273.
24. *Ibid.*, p. 256.   25. *In 2 Sent.*, 12, 1, 10.
26. *Ibid.*, 12, 1, 1.   27. *In 2 Sent.*, 3, 1, 1; *Quodlibet*, 1, 8.
28. Paris, 1925.   29. *Compendium artis demonstrativae*, prol.
30. *Beiträge*, 7, 4–5, p. 19.
31. Ueberweg-Geyer, *Die patristische und scholastische Philosophie*,
    p. 460.
32. Cf. Article, 'Lulle' by Père E. Longpré in *Dictionnaire de théologie
    catholique*, Vol. 9.

Chapter Forty-four

1. *De gradibus formarum*, f. 211 v.   2. 1, 12, 16.
3. Prop. 47, f. 36 v.   4. 1, 11.
5. On the question of the dating and authenticity of the *Errores
   Philosophorum* see the edition by J. Koch, listed in the bibliography.
6. It might appear that on Giles's theory the soul (i.e. the form)
   in a state of separation from the body would not be individual;
   but it must be remembered that for him, as for St. Thomas, it
   was individuated by union with matter and retained its individuality.
7. I do not mean to imply that Augustine rejected the pre-eminence
   of the Roman See; but it would be absurd to say that he maintained the doctrine of Papal jurisdiction in temporal affairs.
8. 1, 5.   9. Cf. 1, 8–9.   10. 2, 4.
11. *Summa*, 3, 3, 4; 3, 4, 4.   12. *Ibid.*, 1, 2, 11 and 13.
13. *Ibid.*, 1, 2, 26.
14. Avicenna, *Metaphysics*, 1, 2, 1; Henry, *Summa*, 1, 12, 9; 3, 1, 7.
15. Cf. *Summa*, 1, 11, 6; 1, 5, 5.   16. Cf. *ibid.*, 1, 11, 18.
17. For the qualification which makes this statement not strictly
    true, see section 10.   18. *Quodlibet*, 4, 4, 143.
19. *Ibid.*, 7, 1, 389.   20. Cf. *ibid.*, 3, 2, 80.
21. Scotus attacked this theory of Henry of Ghent.
22. Cf. *Quodlibet*, 2, 1, 46.   23. *Ibid.*, 8, 57 f.
24. For Henry's doctrine of the double negation, cf. *Quodlibet*, 5, 8,
    245 ff.   25. Cf. *Quodlibet*, 3, 9, 100; *Summa*, 21, 4, 10.
26. Cf. *Summa*, 21, 4, 7 ff.; 27, 1, 25; 28, 4, 7.

27. *Quodlibet*, 10, 7, 153.   28. *Summa*, 21, 4, 10.
29. Cf. *ibid.*, 24, 6, 7; 22, 4; 22, 5.   30. *Ibid.*, 22, 3; 25, 2–3.
31. *Ibid.*, 24, 8, 6; 7, 7.   32. Cf. *ibid.*, 21, 2, 14.
33. Cf. *ibid.*, 21, 2, 6 and 8.   34. Cf. *ibid.*, 21, 2, 17; 21, 2, *ad* 3.

Chapter Forty-five

1. Scotus is said to have taught at Cambridge also, either before or after his teaching at Oxford.
2. P. Glorieux: *La littérature quodlibétique*, t. 2 (Bibliothèque thomiste, 21), Paris, 1935.   3. *Ox.*, Prol., 4, no. 32.
4. *Ibid.*, 1, 3, 1; *Rep.*, 1, 3, 1; *Rep.*, Prol., 3, nos. 1 and 4.
5. *Rep.*, Prol., 3, 1.
6. Minges, accepting the *Theoremata*, tries to show that in that work Scotus understands demonstration in the strictest Aristotelian sense, as *demonstratio ex causis*. If that could be proved, there would, of course, be no contradiction between the *Theoremata* and the certainly authentic works of Scotus. Longpré, however, argues against this interpretation of the author's meaning. Cf. Minges, Vol. 2, pp. 29–30; Longpré, p. 109 (cf. Bibliography).

Chapter Forty-six

1. *Ox.*, Prol., q. 1.   2. *Ibid.*, 1, 3, 3, no. 24.
3. *Ox.*, 3, 2, 16, cf. *Quodlibet* 14: *Utrum anima suae naturali perfectioni relicta possit cognoscere Trinitatem personarum in Divinis.*
4. *S.T.*, Ia, 12, 4.   5. Cf. *ibid.*, Ia, 85, 1.
6. *Ox.*, 1, 3, 3, nos. 1 ff.   7. *Ibid.*
8. *Ibid.*, 1, 3, 3, no. 3.   9. *De Anima*, 13.
10. Cf. *Ox.*, 1, 3, 3, no. 24; 2, 3, 8, no. 13.
11. As in *S.T.*, Ia, 5, 2, for instance.   12. *S.T.*, Ia, 89, 1.
13. Cf. *ibid.*, Ia, 87, 1.   14. *Ox.*, 2, 3, 8, no. 13.
15. *S.T.*, Ia, 86, 1.   16. *Ox.*, 4, 45, 3, no. 17.
17. J. *Duns Scoti Doctrina Philosophica et Theologica*, p. 247.
18. *Ox.*, 2, 3, 6, no. 16.   19. *Ibid.*, 2, 3, 9, no. 9.
20. 13, 8–10.   21. 22.   22. *De Anima*, 22, 3.
23. *Ox.*, Prol., 3, no. 28.   24. *Ibid.*, Prol., 2 lat., no. 4.
25. *Ibid.*, Prol., 3, no. 28.   26. *Ibid.*, Prol., 3, no. 29.
27. *Ibid.*, Prol. 4.   28. *S.T.*, Ia, 1, 4.   29. *Ibid.*, Ia, 1, 2.
30. *Ibid.*, Ia, 1, 2.   31. *Ibid.*, Ia, 1, 4.   32. 2, 1, no. 2.
33. 2, 23, no. 3.   34. *Ox.*, 1, 3, 4, nos. 2–4.
35. *Ibid.*, 1, 3, 4, no. 5.   36. *Ibid.*, 4, 45, 2.
37. 4, 50, 1, 1; and cf. *S.T.*, Ia, 89, 1–4.
38. *Ox.*, 1, 2, 7, no. 42; 2, 9, 2, no. 29.   39. *Ibid.*, 3, 14, 3, no. 6.
40. *Ibid.*, 2, 3, 9, no. 6.   41. *Quodlibet*, 7, no. 8.

42. *Ox.*, 2, 9, 2, no. 29.   43. *Ibid.*, 4, 14, 3, no. 6.
44. *Ibid.*, 1, 3, 4, no. 9.

Chapter Forty-seven

1. *Quodlibet*, 7, no. 14; 1, 39, no. 13.   2. *Ox.*, 1, 3, 2, no. 24.
3. *Quodlibet*, 3, no. 2.   4. *Ox.*, 2, 1, 4, no. 26.
5. *Ibid.*, 1, 3, 3, no. 7; 2, 16, no. 17.   6. *Ibid.*, 1, 8, 3, no. 19.
7. *Ibid.*, 1, 39, no. 13.
8. *Ibid.*, 1, 8, 3, nos. 4 ff. This represents Scotus's interpretation of
   Henry's doctrine.   9. 1, 3, 2, no. 5.
10. *Ox.*, 1, 8, 3, no. 18.   11. *Ibid.*, 1, 8, 3, no. 19.   12. *Ibid.*
13. *Ibid.*, 1, 3, 2, no. 10.   14. *Ibid.*
15. Cf. *ibid.*, 1, 3, 2, no. 6.   16. *Ibid.*, 1, 8, 3, no. 16.
17. *Ibid.*, 1, 8, 3, no. 11.   18. *Ibid.*, 1, 8, 3, no. 12.
19. 21, no. 14.   20. *Ox.*, 1, 8, 3, no. 12.
21. *Rep.*, 1, 3, 1, no. 7.   22. *Ox.*, 1, 3, 2; 1, 8, 3, no. 9.
23. *De Anima*, 21, no. 14.   24. 2, 12, 2, no. 2.
25. *Ox.*, 2, 12, 2, no. 8.   26. *Ibid.*, 2, 3, 1, no. 7.
27. For Scotus 'equivocal' means, of distinct or different meanings.
   The scientist, for instance, considers actual bodies, which differ,
   but one can form a common concept of body in general.
28. *Ox.*, 2, 16, *quaestio unica*, no. 17.
29. It must be admitted that Scotus confines himself to denying the
   real distinction and does not explicitly apply the formal objective
   distinction to the relation of essence and existence in the creature; but the doctrine of Scotists on this point seems to me to
   be a reasonable interpretation of Scotus's meaning.
30. *Ox.*, 4, 13, 1, no. 38.   31. *Ibid.*, 2, 16, no. 10.
32. *De ente et essentia*, 5.   33. *Ox.*, 1, 36, no. 3.
34. *Ibid.*, 1, 30, 2, no. 15.
35. *Disputationes Metaphysicae*, 6, 1, no. 2.
36. *Rep.*, 2, 12, 5, no. 12.   37. *Ibid.*, 2, 12, 5, no. 13.
38. In *Metaphysics*, 5, 1.   39. *Ibid.*, 5, 11.
40. *De Anima*, 1, 8.   41. *Rep.*, 2, 12, 5, no. 13.
42. *Die Lehre des J. Duns Skotus von der natura communis*, Fribourg,
   1927.   43. *Loc. cit.*   44. Cf. *Ox.*, 2, 12, 1.
45. p. 46.   46. 15, no. 3 ff.   47. *Ox.*, 2, 12, 1, no. 10.
48. Cf. *ibid.*, 2, 12, 2; *Rep.* 2, 12, 2.   49. *Ox.*, *loc. cit.*, no. 3.
50. *Rep.*, 2, 12, 2, no. 5.
51. *Ox.*, 2, 12, 2, no. 7. The distinction of prime matter into *materia
   primo prima*, *materia secundo prima* and *materia tertio prima* is
   found only in the unauthentic *De rerum principio*.
52. *Rep.*, 2, 18, 1.   53. *Ox.*, 4, 11, 3, nos. 54 ff.
54. *Ibid.*, 2, 16, no. 17.   55. *Ibid.*, 2, 3, 5, no. 1.
56. *Ibid.*, 2, 3, 6, no. 15.   57. *Ibid.*, 2, 3, 6, no. 15.

58. 2, 12, 5, nos. 1, 8, 13, 14.   59. 7, 13, nos. 9 and 26.
60. *Quaestiones in libros Metaph.*, 7, 13, no. 7.

Chapter Forty-eight

1. *Rep.*, Prol., 3, no. 1.   2. *Ibid.*, Prol., 3, no. 6.
3. *Ox.*, 1, 1, 2, no. 2.   4. *Ox.*, Prol., 4, no. 32.
5. *Ibid.*, Prol., 4, no. 20.   6. E.g. 4, nos. 36, 37.
7. *Quodlibet*, 7, no. 8.   8. *Ox.*, 1, 3, 2, nos. 1 and 30.
9. *Ibid.*, Prol., 1, no. 17.   10. *Rep.*, Prol., 3, 2, no. 4.
11. *Ox.*, 1, 3, 2, no. 18.   12. *Ibid.*
13. Prol., 2 lateralis, no. 21.   14. 3, 7.
15. 2, 25, *quaestio unica*, no. 12.   16. 3.
17. *De primo principio*, 3, 3.   18. *Ibid.*, 3, 4.
19. *Ibid.*, 3, no. 5.   20. *Ibid.*, 3, no. 6.
21. *Ibid.*, 3, nos. 6–7.   22. *Ibid.*, 3, no. 9.
23. *Ibid.*, nos. 9–10.   24. *Ibid.*, nos. 11–14.
25. *Ox.*, 2, 2, nos. 10 ff.   26. *Ibid.*, 2, 2, no. 11.
27. *Ibid.*, nos. 14–15.   28. *Ibid.*, no. 17.   29. *Ibid.*, no. 18.
30. *Ibid.*   31. *De primo principio*, 4, nos. 1–4.
32. *Ibid.*, 4, no. 14.   33. *Ox.*, 1, 2, 3, no. 17.
34. *Ibid.*, 4, 3, 1, no. 32.   35. *Ibid.*, 4, 13, 1, no. 32.
36. 2, 2, nos. 25 ff.   37. 4, nos. 15 ff.
38. Cf. *Ox.*, 1, 2, 2, nos. 25–9.
39. *Ox.*, 1, 2, 2, no. 30; cf. *De primo principio*, 15 ff.
40. *Ox.*, 1, 2, 2, no. 31.   41. 1, 2, 2, nos. 31–2.
42. 4, no. 21.   43. *Ox.*, 1, 2, 3; *De primo principio*, 4, nos. 38–40.
44. *Ox.*, 1, 2, 2, no. 32.   45. *Rep.*, 1, 2, 3, no. 8.
46. 4, no. 37.   47. *Ox.*, 1, 42, *quaestio unica*, no. 2.
48. Cf. *Rep.* 1, 42, 2, no. 4; *Quodlibet*, 7, nos. 4 and 18.
49. *S.T.*, Ia, 8, 1, *ad* 3.   50. *Rep.*, 1, 37, 2, nos. 6 ff.
51. Cf. *De primo principio*, 4, nos. 36 ff; *Ox.*, Prol., 2, no. 10; 3, 23, no. 5; 3, 24, no. 22.
52. Cf. *ibid.*, 4, 17, no. 7; *Rep.*, 4, 17, no. 7.
53. Cf. *Ox.*, 4, 43, 2, no. 27.   54. *Ibid.*, 1, 8, 4, no. 17.
55. *Ibid.*, 1, 8, 4, no. 18.   56. *Ibid.*, nos. 19 ff.
57. *Ibid.*, 1, 36, no. 4, cf. no. 6.   58. *Rep.*, 1, 36, 2, no. 33.
59. *Ox.*, 1, 3, 4, no. 20.   60. *Ibid.*, 2, 1, 2, no. 6.
61. *Rep.*, 1, 36, 3, no. 27.   62. *Collationes*, 31, no. 5.
63. *Ox.*, 1, 35, no. 8.   64. *Ibid.*, 1, 38, no. 5.
65. *Rep.*, 1, 45, 2, no. 7.   66. *Ox.*, 1, 17, 3, no. 18.
67. *Ibid.*, 1, 39, no. 21, cf. *ibid.*, 2, 1, 2, no. 7.
68. *Ibid.*, 3, 32, no. 6.   69. *Ibid.*, 2, 1, 2, no. 65.
70. *Ibid.*, 1, 8, 5, nos. 23 f.; cf. *Quodlibet*, 16.
71. *Rep.*, 1, 10, 3, no. 4.   72. *Quodlibet*, 16, no. 8.
73. *Ibid.*, 16, no. 9; cf. *Rep.*, 1, 10, 3, nos. 3 ff.

74. *Rep.*, 2, 1, 3, nos. 9–11; cf. *Ox.*, 2, 1, 2; *Collationes*, 13, no. 4.
75. *Ox.*, 4, 1, 1, nos. 27 ff.   76. *Ibid.*, 2, 1, 3, no. 19.

Chapter Forty-nine

1. *Ox.*, 4, 43, 2, nos. 4–5.   2. *Ibid.*, 4, 43, 2, no. 5.
3. *Ibid.*, 4, 43, 2, no. 6.   4. *Ibid.*, 4, 43, 2, nos. 6–11.
5. *Ibid.*, 4, 43, 2, no. 12.   6. *Ibid.*, 2, 16, no. 6.
7. *Ibid.*, 2, 1, 4, no. 25.   8. *Ibid.*, 4, 12, 1, no. 19.
9. *Quodlibet*, 9, no. 7, and 19, no. 19.   10. *Ibid.*, 2, 3 ff.
11. *Ox.*, 4, 43, 1, nos. 2–6.   12. *S.T.*, Ia, 89, 1.
13. Cf. *ibid.*, Ia, 84, 7.   14. *Ox.*, 4, 45, 2, no. 14.
15. *Ibid.*, 2, 6, 2, no. 11.   16. *Ibid.*, 1, 17, 3, no. 5; 2, 25, no. 16.
17. *Ibid.*, 2, 23, nos. 8 and 7.   18. *Ibid.*, 3, 15, no. 37.
19. Cf. *ibid.*, 4, 49, 10, no. 3; 2, 23, no. 8; 1, 1, 4, no. 16; *Collationes*, 16, no. 3.   20. Cf. *Ox.*, 4, 49, 10, nos. 8 f.
21. *Ox.*, 1, 1, 4, nos. 13 ff.   22. *Ibid.*, 4, 49, 6, no. 9.
23. Cf. *Collatio*, 15.   24. *Rep.*, 2, 42, 4, no. 7.
25. *Collationes*, 2, no. 7.   26. *Rep.*, 1, 35, 1, no. 27.
27. *Ox.*, 4, 49, *quaestio ex latere*, nos. 16 and 18.
28. *Ibid.*, no. 17.   29. *Ibid.*, no. 21.
30. *Rep.*, 4, 49, 3, no. 7; *Ox.*, 4, 49, 3, nos. 5 ff.
31. *Ox.*, 4, 43, 2, no. 26.   32. Cf. *Rep.*, 4, 43, 2, nos. 15 ff.
33. *Ox.*, 4, 43, 2, no. 16.   34. *Ibid.*   35. Ia, 75, 6.
36. *Ox.*, 4, 43, 2, no. 23.   37. *Ibid.*, 4, 43, 2, no. 18.
38. Cf. also *Rep.*, 4, 43, 2, no. 18.   39. *Ox.*, 4, 43, 2, nos. 29–31.
40. *Ibid.*, 4, 43, 2, no. 27.

Chapter Fifty

1. *Ox.*, 2, 40, *quaestio unica*, nos. 2–3.   2. *Ibid.*, 1, 17, 3, no. 14.
3. *Rep.*, 4, 28, no. 6.   4. *Ox.*, 1, *distinctio ultima*, nos. 1 and 2.
5. *Ibid.*   6. *Ibid.*, 4, 5, 2, no. 7.
7. *Rep.*, 2, 41, no. 2.   8. Cf. *Ox.*, 2, 41, no. 4.
9. *Ibid.*, 4, 46, 1, no. 10.   10. *Rep.*, 1, 48, *quaestio unica*.
11. *Ox.*, 4, 14, 2, no. 5.   12. *Rep.*, 2, 22, *quaestio unica*, no. 3.
13. *Ox.*, 3, 37, *quaestio unica*, nos. 5–8.
14. *Ibid.*, 3, 37, *quaestio unica*, no. 11.
15. *Ibid.*, 3, 37, *quaestio unica*, nos. 13–15.
16. *Rep.*, 4, 46, 4, no. 8.   17. *Ibid.*, 4, 15, 4, nos. 10–11.
18. *Ox.*, 4, 15, 2, no. 7.   19. *Ibid.*, 4, 15, 2, no. 7.
20. *Rep.*, 4, 15, 4, no. 11.   21. *Ox.*, 4, 15, 2, no. 6.
22. *Ibid.*, 4, 14, 2, no. 7.

INDEX OF NAMES

(References followed by an asterisk refer to the Appendices)

INDEX OF SUBJECTS

OTHER IMAGE BOOKS

OTHER IMAGE BOOKS

OTHER IMAGE BOOKS

OTHER IMAGE BOOKS